Your First Computer

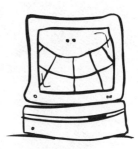

Your First Computer

Second Edition

• •

Alan Simpson

SYBEX®

San Francisco • Paris • Düsseldorf • Soest

Acquisitions Editor: Dianne King
Developmental Editor: Richard Mills
Editors: Abby Azrael and Kathleen Lattinville
Technical Editor: Maurie Duggan
Production Editor: Carolina Montilla
Book Designer: Alissa Feinberg
Production Artist: Suzanne Albertson
Screen Graphics: Cuong Le and Aldo Bermudez
Typesetter: Deborah Maizels
Proofreader/Production Assistant: Sarah Lemas
Indexer: Nancy Guenther
Cover Designer: Ingalls + Associates
Cover Illustrator: Harumi Kubo

Screen reproductions produced with Collage Plus.

Collage Plus is a trademark of Inner Media Inc.

SYBEX is a registered trademark of SYBEX Inc.

TRADEMARKS: SYBEX has attempted throughout this book to distinguish proprietary trademarks from descriptive terms by following the capitalization style used by the manufacturer.

SYBEX is not affiliated with any manufacturer.

Every effort has been made to supply complete and accurate information. However, SYBEX assumes no responsibility for its use, nor for any infringement of the intellectual property rights of third parties which would result from such use.

Library of Congress Card Number: 93-86584
ISBN: 0-7821-1418-0

Manufactured in the United States of America
10 9 8 7 6 5 4 3

To Susan, Ashley, and Alec

Acknowledgments

• •

In order to present a well-rounded and authoritative view of the computer industry, I called upon the knowledge, skills, and talents of many people to help create this book.

On the authorial side of things, talented writers Sharon Crawford, Sheldon Dunn, Elizabeth Olson, and Bill Sanders all contributed their knowledge and writing skills to many passages throughout the book.

Martha Mellor managed the entire project from the practical end—from coordinating the various experts' efforts to finding the photos used throughout the book.

Waterside Productions handled all the contractual matters (as they do for all my books).

On the publication side of things, Richard Mills served as the developmental editor, Abby Azrael and Kathleen Lattinville handled all the copy editing, Maurie Duggan did an excellent technical review, Carolina Montilla served as production editor, Alissa Feinberg designed the book, Deborah Maizels did the desktop publishing, Suzanne Albertson was the production artist, and Sarah Lemas did the proofreading.

Contents at a Glance

Table of Contents

Part One
Making Computers Work for You

One
Getting Started

Two
Hardware and Software

Part Two

Finding the Right Tools

Three

Operating Systems

Four
Word Processing

Five
Desktop Publishing

Six
Graphics

Seven
Spreadsheets

Eight

Database Management Systems

Nine

Telecommunications

Ten

Application-Specific Software

Part Three

Getting the Right Equipment

Eleven

Inside Computers

Twelve

Computer Systems

Thirteen
Interacting with Your Computer

Fourteen
Storing Your Work

Fifteen

Multimedia: Just Bells and Whistles?

Sixteen

Printing Your Results

Appendix

Your First Day with Your New Computer

Glossary

Definition of Terms

Introduction

♦ · ♦ · ♦ · ♦ · ♦ · ♦ · ♦ · ♦ · ♦ · ♦ · ♦ · ♦ · ♦ · ♦ · ♦

Let's face it—the tremendous influx of personal and small business computers into the workplace has created a whole new class distinction of "haves" and "have nots," the "haves" being those who are computer literate and the "have nots" being those who know little or nothing about computers.

If you work in a field that has been even slightly affected by the computer revolution, and have ever had to compete for a job, you've undoubtedly seen that the "haves" enjoy a definite advantage over the "have nots," particularly when it comes to getting the good jobs.

That's the bad news for the "have nots." The good news is that becoming computer literate is not nearly as difficult as you might think it is. Once you understand a bit of the language, and move beyond the misconceptions about computers popularized in the movies, you will be pleasantly surprised at how simple and uncomplicated most computer concepts really are.

Who This Book Is For

My experience as an author and teacher has been that most people give up on computers before even trying. They consider themselves techno-klutzes. (As in "I can't even figure out how to get my VCR to record a TV show while I'm away—so how would *I* ever learn to use a computer?") After a few weeks of working with a computer, these same people say "I never realized it would be that easy."

This book is for anyone who wants to make the transition from computer-bewildered to computer-confident. If any of the following descriptions are of you, you're sure to find this book useful:

- You want to learn about computers, but don't know where to start.

- You've already begun your venture into the world of computers (whether through desire or necessity), but you're being driven nuts by the seemingly endless techno-jargon.

- You're already using your computer, but you feel as though you're just scraping by and would like to become more efficient and productive in your computer use.

- You are seriously considering buying a computer system, but you want to have a clue before you go into the computer store and before you start spending any money.

Keep in mind that this book is not designed just for the person who will be sitting at the keyboard and personally using the computer. If your job involves selling or buying computer equipment, or you need to manage or interact with colleagues who use computers, you'll also find lots of useful information in this book.

How This Book Is Organized

Although the goal of this book is to *teach* computer literacy, it's not necessary to read it from cover to cover. Instead, we've tried to organize the book so you can identify and find the information you need—when you need it. To meet this goal, we've divided the book into three main parts, plus an appendix and a glossary, as described below.

 NOTE

When the term "IBM-compatible" is used, it is meant to include both IBM computers and their clones. These are also referred to as "personal computers" or "PCs."

Part One: Making Computers Work for You

The first part of this book deals with that all-important question: *What can the computer do for me?* Chapter 1 provides an overview of the various capabilities of computers. This will help you find the information most relevant to your needs in later chapters.

The second chapter introduces and defines basic buzzwords like *hardware, software, memory, megabyte,* and others. Once you understand the plain-English definitions of these various terms, you'll be well on your way to understanding the tools available to you and the type of equipment you'll need to use those tools.

Part Two: Finding the Right Tools

Part Two focuses on the various types of programs (software) that are available. The goals in Chapters 3 through 10 are threefold:

- to give you a general idea of how a particular type of program works
- to provide you with some ideas about which features to look for when purchasing a program
- to discuss specific products in each category to give you an idea of equipment requirements and general pricing

You'll also learn about the terminology used with various types of programs. This knowledge will give you a head start when the time arrives to really learn how to use a particular program.

Part Three: Getting the Right Equipment

Part Three (Chapters 11 through 16) focuses on hardware. In these chapters you'll learn about all of the pieces that make up a computer system—the monitor, keyboard, mouse, disk storage, memory, printers, and multimedia extras.

Here again, I'll be sure to translate the countless buzzwords and acronyms into plain English, so that when you see a classified ad that looks like this:

    486—33MHz w/ 4MB RAM, 120MB HD, SVGA, mouse, and
      8ppm laser printer. $3,500.00

you'll actually understand what the seller is offering!

Appendix

In this section you'll learn what precautions to take before you bring your new system home and how to set it up once it's there.

Glossary

The glossary at the back of the book provides a quick reference section for finding the plain-English definitions of various terms and acronyms used throughout the computer industry and in this book. There's also a useful cross-referencing feature provided in the glossary.

Products, Prices, and Manufacturers

In some cases, we display brief descriptions and/or photographs of particular products. These are provided *only* as examples. They're certainly not intended to be an exhaustive survey. There are enough products on the market to fill a book *triple* the size of this one. Nor are these descriptions intended to be endorsements of the products.

Be aware that prices change constantly in the computer business. (Fortunately, they usually go down!) So *all* of our pricing examples are just ballpark estimates to give you a sense of what prices are like.

Also, because the computer industry is still in its infancy, the big companies tend to buy up the smaller ones. So a product that is manufactured by "ABC Company" today might become a product manufactured by "XYZ Corporation" tomorrow.

Your best bet for getting up-to-the-minute information on products, prices, and manufacturers would be to go to your local computer store, browse around, and chat with a salesperson. Or, pick up a current computer magazine and check out the ads and product reviews.

Of course, this is not to say that *all* the information in this book is likely to become outdated as you read. On the contrary, the basic concepts, terminology, and types of programs and equipment available remain pretty stable. So when you go to the computer store to have that chat, you'll still know what you're talking about. Or, when you leaf through a magazine, you'll know what you're reading about. That's what makes computer literacy so much fun.

Part One

Making Computers Work for You

• •

One

Getting Started

• •

f you're just getting started in computers, you may have already been bowled over by the sheer number of books and magazines on the subject. And then when you try to read the books and magazine articles, none of them seems to be written in English!

Chances are you're not looking for technical details about individual products. Maybe you haven't even figured out yet what kinds of products you might be interested in, because you don't even know what all these countless products *do*. Probably, you're just trying to get an answer to a much simpler but all-important question: "*What can it do for me?*"

Whether you're just beginning to think about learning to use computers or you're considering buying one, or even if you have one on your desk that you're expected to start using today, finding out what the computer can *do for you* is an important first step; and that's what this book is all about.

We'll start out by covering some of the basics. First, we'll go through some of the (seemingly endless) jargon, and then we'll shed some light on some of the mysteries and misconceptions that surround this machine that has insinuated itself into everyone's life in one way or another.

What Is a Computer?

In a nutshell, a computer is a general-purpose electronic machine designed to help people get a job done. Almost every job begins as an idea —something that "needs to get done." The idea may take only a few seconds to concoct, but getting the job done takes time. Using a computer reduces the time span between the idea and the finished product.

Computers don't come up with original ideas, but they're especially good at the stuff that makes the human brain go numb: calculating, record-keeping, trial-and-error experimenting, communicating, information-gathering, and myriad other managerial tasks involved in translating an idea into reality.

The reason the computer can do these things quickly is simply that it *is* an electronic device. And, as we all know from the simple experience of turning on a light switch, electricity is pretty fast. Just as light instantly fills a room when you flip the switch, it takes very little time for the computer to do just about any task you ask of it.

What Can Computers Do?

Aside from physical labor, there are few jobs that a computer *can't* do. And if your job requires any paperwork, record-keeping, math, or information-gathering, the computer can lighten your load and make your work day more productive.

Just as a compact disc player is a general-purpose machine in that it can play any type of music, be it classical, jazz, or heavy metal, a computer can "play" various types of *programs* (also called *software*). When you buy a compact disc player, you'll probably also buy some CDs of whatever kind of music you like. When you buy a computer, you'll also want to buy some programs to do the kind of work you need to do. Here's a quick summary of the kinds of programs you can get:

 **NOTE**

The various programs available to you are described in more detail in Part Two.

Word Processing: Replaces the typewriter as a tool for writing and typing any type of document—be it letters, memos, legal documents, contracts, reports, articles, books, form letters—whatever.

Graphics and Desktop Publishing: Replaces the pen and X-ACTO knife to simplify creating everything from corporate logos to business graphics, newsletters to books, ads to catalogs.

Database Management: Replaces the Rolodex, card file, and file cabinet, making it much easier to manage large collections of data (information) such as customer lists, mailing lists, accounts payable and receivable, invoices, appointments, inventories, and more.

Spreadsheets: Replaces the calculator and ledger sheet to speed any type of math calculations, from financial analyses to scientific data analyses.

Communications: Replaces the library card file and book stacks, providing instant access to massive volumes of information stored on computers around the world, all from your own desktop.

Education: Complements classroom materials providing activities in geography, math, science, logic, and other subjects.

Entertainment: If you like gadgets and electronic entertainment, you can even use your computer to relax with a wide variety of computer games. (Unlike the other categories of programs, however, entertainment programs will not be discussed in this book.)

Keep in mind that this is just a list of the general types of programs that are available. As you'll learn in this book, chances are you can find a program to help you with any kind of task in any field, from astrology to zoology.

How Much Time Do I Need to Invest?

"Learning to use computers" is one of those things that many of us put on the to-do list, but never quite get around to doing until something (or someone) forces us to grapple with it. And for many people, the big question is "How long will it take?" The answer is a resounding "It depends."

Going back to our other more familiar electronic gadget, the CD player, how much time you spend learning to use it is largely a matter of what you want to do with it. If all you want is to hook it up, use the basic functions , and start listening to music, most likely your learning time will be pretty brief.

If, on the other hand, you want to be able to fix it yourself if it breaks, or to build your own CD player from parts, then you're in for the long haul, and had best plan on spending a few years in college becoming an electrical engineer.

Similarly, if you want to be a computer programmer, you can count on spending some long hours in classes or with programming books. But if you're like most people, you just want to *use* the computer to get some work done. And, in that case, you'll probably be surprised at how quickly you can start putting the computer to work for you. Unlike the intimidating and baffling programs of just a few years ago, modern programs are designed for ease of use, quick comprehension, and prompt productivity.

Of course, your learning time will also be shorter if you can focus on the things you *need* to know to do your work, rather than wasting time on irrelevant topics. This book will help you get the kind of focus you'll need to minimize your learning time.

If, on the other hand, you want to make a career of computers, you can spend years learning about them. A quick glance at the huge numbers of computer books in any bookstore will verify that. (And in a bookstore, you're only seeing the tip of the iceberg of material that's available.)

But again, it's not necessary to spend your life learning about computers. In fact, most people who use computers just use them to be more productive in their regular work—from the practice of law or medicine to trading pork-belly futures. Once you've figured out what you want the computer to do for you, you can learn the necessary skills in a matter of days, or perhaps even a few hours, with a little instruction and guidance.

How Much Money Do I Need to Invest?

If you're thinking about buying a computer, time is not the only investment that concerns you. You can spend anywhere from $500 to $50,000 on a personal or small business computer, although the vast majority of computers sold are at the lower end of that scale. Regardless of how much or little you spend, the important point is to spend it wisely and get the most bang for your buck.

This book will also help you to make the buying decisions that are right for you by explaining what's available and most useful and by decoding and translating the many buzzwords you'll encounter from sales people and advertisements. Granted, any knowledgeable computer person can advise you to get "an 8-meg 486 with a 200-meg hard drive and Super VGA." But if you're like most people, you would probably like to know what that means before you spend your hard-earned money on it. We'll cover those topics in Part Three of this book.

What about Computer Phobia?

For some people, just the thought of sitting down with a computer and trying to run it is a frightening prospect. But like many fears, computer phobia is rooted in superstition and incorrect information. Let's take a moment to replace a few common myths with these simple truths:

Computers don't know anything: In the early days of computers, science-fiction writers had a ball imagining computers that were so smart, they outwitted their human counterparts (remember HAL in the movie *2001*?). Fortunately, all that fiction is still just that—make believe. The old term "electronic brain" to describe computers was not particularly accurate. A more precise term is "electronic file cabinet with built-in calculator." Just as you can store information in a file cabinet, you can store information in a computer. And just as a new file cabinet is empty when you first buy it, a new computer is also "empty." The only information in a personal or small business computer is the information that you put into it—there are no secrets lurking within its parts.

Computers don't think: When you fill a file cabinet with information, the file cabinet does not get "smarter," nor does it think about the information that's in its drawers. Ditto for computers. About the only difference between a file cabinet and a computer is that the information in a file cabinet is usually on paper, and the information in a computer is stored magnetically, like music on a cassette tape. But one thing is for sure, the computer is no "smarter" than your file cabinet. In fact, a computer is no smarter than a screwdriver, drill press, or toaster. It's a mindless, inanimate machine.

Computer's don't "just do" things: Like all machines, from cars to blow dryers to washing machines, computers are designed to be used by people—not to do things on their own. True, a computer can perform calculations, transmit information across phone lines, and erase vast amounts of information. However, it does these things only *if,* and *when,* you tell it to.

There is no "wrong key": Perhaps the most common and down-to-earth computer fear centers around that oft-asked and seldom-answered question—"What if I press the wrong key?" If this thought has been nagging you, you'll be delighted to know that there is no "wrong key" to even worry about. Just as car designers have avoided putting a "right steering wheel" and a "wrong steering wheel" into cars, computer designers have avoided putting a devastating "wrong key" onto the computer keyboard.

In fact, short of throwing it out the second-story window, or going at it with a sledgehammer, there's virtually nothing you can do to break a computer. Even if you sat at the keyboard and pounded the keys for hours, *trying* to do some damage, the chances are you wouldn't do the least bit of harm.

Granted, we all make mistakes, and from time to time you'll press some key other than the one you mean to. And here's what will probably happen when you do—nothing. You can just press the Backspace or Escape key and then press the key you originally meant to press. And that's that—no big deal.

Sure, you can delete the information inside the computer, and people occasionally do so by accident. But it's not easy to delete information, and doing so takes quite a bit more effort than pressing a key. So it's quite unlikely that you'll ever "accidentally" erase some useful information.

Furthermore, there are programs available to perform "backup and recovery" techniques and procedures, so that even if you do inadvertently delete something you wanted to keep (or intentionally delete something and then change your mind), usually you can just as easily "undelete" it.

Now I'm not saying that you should run around and *try* to wreak computer havoc—because it can be done. I'm just saying that your chances of wreaking havoc by mistake are practically nil. Certainly just pressing the wrong key from time to time is absolutely harmless. (I know that for a fact, because I'm a terrible typist—I press the wrong key hundreds of times a day, and have been doing so for a decade and a half, and I have yet to damage a single computer!)

Where Do I Start?

The first thing you need to do is to learn a little terminology, and become familiar with the basic components of the machine. So without any further ado, let's move onto Chapter 2 and learn a little about the marvelous machine of our time—the computer.

Hardware and Software

· ·

When you talk about computers, there are always two sides to the issue: the *hardware* and the *software*. The hardware consists of the things you can see and touch. The software consists of the less tangible instructions that tell the hardware what to do, and when to do it.

In this chapter, we'll discuss both hardware and software and introduce the terminology used to describe each. This will help to pave the way for the more detailed discussions in the chapters that follow.

Computer Hardware

NOTE
Chapter 12 covers specific brands of computers in more detail.

As previously mentioned, computer hardware is the stuff you can see and touch. A full *computer system* is made up of several pieces of hardware. Figure 2.1 shows a sort of "generic" microcomputer system with the various components labeled.

The Monitor

The monitor, also called the CRT (for Cathode Ray Tube), is the main tool the computer uses to communicate with *you*. You look at the screen to see what the computer is doing, you get the information that you're looking for on-screen, and you read the messages that the computer sends to you on-screen.

The Keyboard

The keyboard (and the mouse, below) is the tool you use to communicate with the computer. You use the keyboard to type in the information that you want to store in the computer, and also to type in *commands* to run programs. What you type generally appears on the monitor.

Figure 2.1
A sample computer system shown with labeled components.

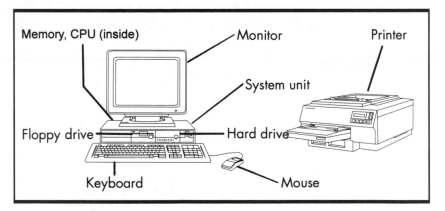

The computer keyboard is laid out in pretty much the same way as a standard typewriter keyboard, with some extra keys that are unique to computers. We'll talk about these extra keys in Chapter 13.

The Mouse

The mouse offers an alternative means of interacting with the computer. All programs written in the past few years support the use of a mouse, so when you're purchasing a computer, you'll definitely want to include a mouse as part of your system.

A mouse is very easy to operate. As you roll the mouse around on your desktop, a small arrow called a *mouse pointer* moves on the screen in the same direction in which you roll the mouse. When the mouse pointer is resting on an option that you want to access, you click one of the buttons on the mouse to select that option.

An alternative to a mouse is a trackball—sort of an upside-down mouse. There's more on mice and trackballs in Chapter 13.

The System Unit

The system unit is the computer proper. That's the box that everything else plugs into. The keyboard, mouse, monitor, and printer are called *peripherals*, and they generally plug into the back of the system unit. The system unit houses the disk drives, central processing unit (CPU), and memory. We'll discuss the role that each of these plays later in this chapter.

The Printer

The printer, although optional, is an important part of most computer systems. While the monitor gives you a small screen for interacting with the computer, the printer provides you with printed "hardcopy." Obviously, if you need to print letters, reports, graphics—whatever—a printer is essential.

Differences among Systems

Now that you can identify the various components that make up a complete computer system, we can discuss some of the features of modern microcomputers that make some systems "better" (and more expensive) than others. This will also help us to define a lot of buzzwords used to describe various components and systems, and that should help you to get a better feel for what to look for when purchasing a system.

Disk Storage Capacity

One of the main reasons to use a computer is to store and retrieve information. That information, be it text, numbers, or graphics, is stored on disks. Obviously, the more disk storage capacity a computer has, the more information you can store in it.

The amount of information a computer can store is measured in *bytes*. One byte is roughly equivalent to a single character. Hence, it takes three bytes to store the word "cat," and six bytes to store the word "banana."

A *kilobyte*, often abbreviated as K or KB, is about 1,000 bytes. You can get about 3,000 characters on a single-spaced $8^{1}/_{2}$- by-11-inch sheet of paper. Therefore, it takes about 3 kilobytes, or 3K, to store the amount of text on a page that size.

A *megabyte*, abbreviated MB, and often pronounced *meg*, is about one million bytes. A single megabyte (1MB) can store about 333 pages of single-spaced typed text. A *gigabyte* is about a billion bytes, or 333,333 pages of text. Table 2.1 summarizes the storage capacities.

All modern computers use a *hard disk* to store information. The storage capacity of a hard disk is measured in megabytes. Typical storage capacities range from a minimum of about 40MB to about 540MB; although it's possible to get hard drives in the gigabyte range, they are very expensive and are not necessary for the average computer user.

Measurement	Abbreviation	Stores*
Byte		1 character
Kilobyte	K or KB	about 1/3 page
Megabyte	M or MB	about 333 pages
Gigabyte	G or GB	about 333,333 pages

*These numbers refer to single-spaced text.

Table 2.1
Storage Terms and Typed-Page Equivalents

In most cases, the hard disk stays in the computer; you don't ever remove it. In fact, you never even see the hard disk, because it's permanently housed in the main system unit. You will, however, see a small red light on the computer box that glows when the computer is reading information from, or writing information to, the hard disk.

Most computers also have one or two *floppy disk drives*. These are the slots in the front of the computer box where you insert and remove floppy disks. In modern microcomputers, the floppy disks are used to copy information to or from the hard disk. For example, when you buy a new program, it's stored on one or more floppy disks. *Installing* a program so that you can use it on your computer is just a matter of moving it from the floppy disks onto your hard disk—a task that generally involves simply inserting the floppy disk into a floppy drive and then typing the command INSTALL.

Floppy disks, which are also called *diskettes*, come in two sizes, 5¼-inch and 3½-inch, as shown in Figure 2.2. Actually, the figure shows the casing that houses the round magnetic disk. But you never remove the actual disk from inside this casing.

The amount of information that you can store on a floppy disk is determined by how densely the information is packed on the disk. In general,

Figure 2.2

This is what a 5¼-inch and a 3½-inch floppy disk look like.

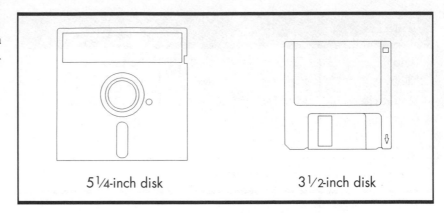

5¼-inch disk   3½-inch disk

 NOTE

There's also a 3½-inch diskette known as quad density. It holds 2.88MB of information but it's not widely available.

there are two densities—low density and high density. The storage capacities of the various disk sizes and densities are shown in Table 2.2.

The more modern 3½-inch disks are enclosed in hard plastic shells (they're not so "floppy"), and have a small sliding door that covers the magnetic surface of the disk. The 3½-inch disks generally are more reliable and durable than the 5¼-inch disks, which have only a cardboard shell over the magnetic recording part of the disk (they are quite floppy), and leave a small portion of the disk exposed at all times through an oblong hole. The 3½-inch disks also have the advantage of holding more information than their 5¼-inch counterparts.

New computers have floppy drives designed for high-density disks. These drives can read and write both high-density and low-density floppies. When purchasing a computer, the most sensible thing to do is to buy a computer that has both a 5¼-inch and 3½-inch high-density drive. That way, you will be able to handle either size disk.

We'll discuss disk drives and other means of storing information in detail in Chapter 14. Now let's look at another important feature of computers worthy of careful consideration when purchasing a computer—memory.

Table 2.2

Storage Capacities of Commonly Used Floppy Disks

Size	Density	Storage Capacity
5¼-inch	Low density	360KB
5¼-inch	High density	1.2MB
3½-inch	Low density	720KB
3½-inch	High density	1.4MB

Memory Storage Capacity

In addition to disks, all computers have a secondary means of storing information, called *random access memory*, (RAM), and also called simply *memory*. For many new users, one of the more perplexing aspects about computers is the difference between RAM and disk storage, and why two different types of storage are needed in the first place. Well, here are the differences:

- Information stored only in RAM is lost forever when you turn off the computer. That's because RAM stores information electronically, which requires a constant source of electric current.

- Information stored on disk stays there even after you turn off the computer. Like a cassette tape, the computer disk stores information as magnetic patterns, which remain unchanged until you erase them or replace them with new information.

You're getting sleepy... sleeepy....

- RAM operates at very fast speeds, because there are no moving parts. RAM simply consists of tiny electrical "switches" that can be either positive or negative, on or off (although they're all "off" when the computer is turned off).

- Disks require moving parts. The disk drive spins the disk around, and a moving head, that works something like the needle on a phonograph turntable, reads and writes information to and from the disk. When compared to the nearly instantaneous electronic means of storing information that RAM uses, this "mechanical" process of reading and writing information is quite slow.

So, if a computer had only RAM, its usefulness would be severely limited because every time you turned the computer off, you'd lose all your day's work, not to mention all the programs you'd purchased! On the other hand, if a computer had only disks, it would take much longer to get any work done, because the disks are so slow in contrast to RAM. Having both types of memory gives you the best of both worlds—the ability to store information indefinitely, and the speed to get the job done quickly.

From a functional standpoint, disk drives act as a sort of file cabinet, a storage unit for holding large amounts of information for long periods of time. RAM acts more like your desktop, the place where you store whatever it is you're working on at the moment.

Just as there's no need to remove all the files from a file cabinet and pile them up on your desk just to use one file, there's no need to pull all the information from the disk into RAM just to use one program or a single file. That's why RAM storage capacities are generally much smaller than disk storage capacities. Most modern computers come equipped with anywhere from 640KB to 16MB of RAM, with 2MB to 8MB being about average.

Deciding how much RAM you need is a matter of knowing what kind of work you want to do, and what kind of program(s) you'll be using. We'll go into those issues in more detail in the software chapters that follow. But as a general rule, buy as much memory as you can afford, for several reasons:

First, as programs become bigger, better, and easier to use, their need for memory increases. Therefore, the more memory a system has, the more likely you'll be able to keep up with advances in software.

Second, as your computer skills increase, you may find that you want to use two or more programs at the same time. A program is "active" only while it's stored in memory. So if you want to run two or more programs at the same time, you will need enough memory to store those programs simultaneously.

Third, in some ways, more memory means more speed. Not because larger amounts of memory operate faster than smaller amounts, but because the more information that is stored in RAM, the faster that information can be processed.

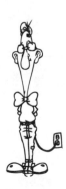

For example, suppose you have two dump trucks, each of which travels at exactly the same speed—60 miles per hour. However, one dump truck can hold two tons of dirt, and the other dump truck can hold only one ton of dirt. Now, let's say you have to move two tons of dirt to a construction site. Even though the two dump trucks run at exactly the same speed, the larger dump truck will get the job done faster, because it can do the whole job in one trip. The smaller dump truck has to make three trips: one there, one back, and another back to the destination, as Figure 2.3 illustrates.

We'll talk more about memory and the different types of memory available to you in Chapter 11.

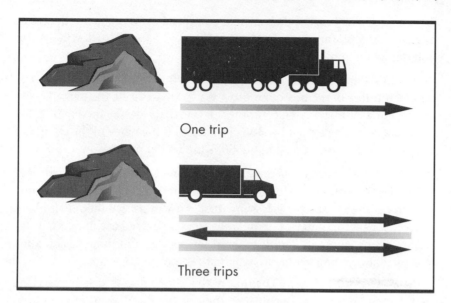

One trip

Three trips

Central Processing Unit

So far we've discussed how information is stored in computers, but we haven't actually talked about how the work gets done. That is, when you use the computer to add a bunch of numbers, or draw a graph, or move sentences and paragraphs around in a typed document, what actually does the work?

The answer to that question is the *central processing unit*,(CPU), also called the *microprocessor* or sometimes just the *processor*. The processor is also called a microchip, or *chip*. The processor is the brains of the computer, the part that does the actual work.

The main factor that makes one processor better than (and more expensive than) another is its speed. Generally, the higher the model number, the faster the processor. That is, an 80486 chip is faster, and thus more powerful, than an 80386 chip.

Earlier in this chapter I said that the amount of memory in a computer determines, in part, how fast it gets a job done, and that's true, as our dump truck analogy showed. But now we're talking about sheer speed, not storage capacity. Given two dump trucks with a two-ton storage capacity, and a two-ton pile of dirt to move, either truck can get the job done

NOTE
The speed of the processor affects the overall speed of the computer much more than the amount of memory does.

in one trip. But if one of those trucks can travel at 60 mph, and the other can go 120 mph (and there's no speed limit), the faster truck will get the job done more quickly than the smaller one.

In the IBM family of computers, particularly the compatible "clones," the model number of the processor often is used to describe the overall computer. For example, a "386 computer" is one that uses the Intel 80386 microprocessor or a compatible 386 chip. (Intel is the name of the company that makes the processor, and 80386 is the model number.)

The Macintosh family of computers uses processors that are manufactured by an entirely different company, Motorola. Apple, the manufacturer of the Macintosh, is less inclined to use processor model numbers to describe its computers, but different Macs do indeed use different processors. Some commonly used modern processors, and the types of computers that they're used in, are summarized below.

8086 and 8088 (Intel): The first of the Intel microprocessors used in microcomputers, these chips are the heart of the IBM PC and IBM XT computers. Computers based on these chips are of very limited usefulness. If someone gives you one to learn on, take it, but don't buy one.

80286 (Intel): The 286 chip is the heart of the IBM AT (Advanced Technology) family of computers, as well as some of the low-end IBM PS/2 models. A used 80286 will cost around $500.

80386 (Intel): Considered to be the "minimum" processor with capabilities for modern small business computers, the 80386 is in all the IBM and compatible 386 machines, and the IBM PS/2 Model 80. A 386 (or 386SX computer) can cost anywhere in the range of $800 to $3000.

80486 (Intel): Now the standard for new personal and business computers, 486 machines run at extremely fast speeds. These machines make all their predecessors look like slow pokes. They now cost a minimum of about $1250 going up to $4000.

Pentium (Intel): The newest super-duper chip. Machines based on these chips are priced from $3000 to outta-sight. These systems are designed for processor-intensive applications such as AutoCAD and high-end graphics. They're also used by engineers and other scientists.

68000 (Motorola): The M 68000 is the heart of the Mac Classic and Mac Portable (the M standing for "Motorola"). You can pick up a 68000-based Mac for anywhere in the range of $1000 to $1500.

NOTE

In the past, Intel processor model numbers started with 80, so the last three numbers are used to describe the chip. That is, the 80386 processor is frequently called just the 386. Now, however, the newest chip has been christened the Pentium. This chip is, in fact, an 80586 but Intel wanted to be able to trademark the name. Hence, the Pentium.

68020 (Motorola): The Mac LC uses this chip, and the basic machine will run you about $1400 to $2000.

68030 (Motorola): Many of the latest Macintosh computers are based on this chip. Check with your dealer for the most up-to-date prices.

68040 (Motorola): The Motorola 68040 chip is the high-end chip of the Motorola line. The Macintosh Quadra and the Centris line are based on this chip.

I should mention that even though we refer to the 8086–80486 chips as being manufactured by Intel, other manufacturers produce "clones" of these chips with the same or similar model numbers. These clone chips are virtually identical in speed and capability to the corresponding Intel chips. For example, the "386" chip manufactured by Advanced Micro Devices works identically to the Intel 80386. The Pentium is Intel's alone—at least for now. However, I'm sure it won't be long before someone clones the Pentium chip under a new name.

As mentioned above, the model number of a computer's central processing unit is a pretty good indication of its speed: the higher the model number the faster the computer (and the higher its price tag). But there's also a second number that describes the internal speed of the processor. This number is in MegaHertz (MHz)—that's how many million operations per second the computer can perform. So a chip described as a 386/25 is an 80386 processor with an internal speed of 25 MegaHertz. This means it does 25 million operations every single second! Don't think about this number for too long or your brain will explode.

You can purchase a 386/20, which is a computer with a 386 chip running at 20MHz. Or, you can purchase a 386/40, which is a computer with a 386 chip running at 40MHz. The latter is faster (though not necessarily *twice* as fast) and it will cost more.

But there's really no need to go into this level of detail right now. For now, it's sufficient for you to know that different computers are based on different processor models. And the higher the model number of the processor, the faster, and more expensive, the machine will be.

Display Quality

Monitors come in two basic flavors, monochrome and color. A monochrome monitor is generally black and white, or black and a single color such as amber. Color monitors, of course, display a wide range of colors, as does a color TV.

The other basic distinction is between purely text monitors, which are incapable of showing any sort of graphics, and graphics monitors, which are capable of displaying both text and graphics.

Within the IBM family of computers, there's a wide range of monitor display qualities, generally having to do with how many colors the monitor can display (from 16 to several hundred), and also *resolution*. Basically, resolution determines how "crisply" or finely detailed the monitor can display text and graphics. The different monitor display types and qualities are discussed in more detail in Chapter 13.

Print Quality

Printers vary tremendously in price and performance. A low-cost *dot-matrix* printer can be purchased for as little as $100. They're slow and noisy, and their output ranges from lousy to near letter-quality. However, if you just want printouts for your own records, a low cost dot-matrix printer may suit your needs.

NOTE
Chapter 15 describes the various types of printers and print qualities in more detail.

Laser printers range in price from as little as $700 to tens of thousands of dollars. The low-end models are slow, but produce high-quality text and graphics. The high-end models rival modern typesetting equipment, can produce publication-quality output at pretty high speeds, and can include color.

Ease of Use

Almost everyone who purchases a first computer wants to buy one that's easy to use. And nearly everyone agrees that computers from the Mac family are easier to use than those from the IBM family. But the truth of the matter is that all computers are fairly similar in terms of ease of use, because they all consist of the same basic components that we've just described: mouse, monitor, keyboard, and so forth.

In the end, it's not the computer hardware that makes one computer easier to use than another. Rather, it's the computer software. Specifically, it's the *operating system* that determines how you'll interact with your computer and with all the programs you'll use.

The Mac is generally thought to be easier to use than an IBM because its built-in operating system, the Finder, is graphical, and designed to be intuitive and user-friendly. The main operating system used on IBM computers, DOS (short for Disk Operating System), is text-based, and not so intuitive. In fact, DOS has been described as clunky, awkward, difficult to learn and use, and by other, more impolite terms.

But that has all changed. The 1990s have brought us new operating systems for the IBM, namely Windows and OS/2, which are indeed graphical and much more user-friendly. In fact, the term most often used to describe these newer operating systems is "Mac-like."

So, before you start searching for a computer that's easy to use, you would be better advised to learn a bit more about operating systems, and what modern graphical interfaces are all about, as described in Chapter 3.

Compatibility and "Clones"

NOTE
There really are no "clones" of Macs or other computer types for reasons that are discussed in Chapter 12.

Bear in mind that when discussing IBM computers or the IBM family, we're talking about all the computers that are IBM-compatible. These computers are still referred to as "clones" even though they usually have some brand name attached to them and there are lots more "clones" on the market than "original" IBM machines.

The feature that makes a computer compatible with the IBM family is the fact that it can run the same software as the IBM. That is, a program that's designed for IBM equipment will run just as well on any IBM-compatible computer.

Chapter 12 describes various computer brands in greater detail. For the time being, however, keep in mind that any program for IBM computers described in this book will work on any IBM-compatible computer, regardless of the company that actually manufactured the computer.

So What System Do I Buy?

Now that you know that computers vary in the amount of information they can store in memory and on disk, and that some computers run faster than others, how do you decide what to buy?

There's no simple answer to that question, until you know what you want to *do* with your computer. Before you can determine what is the best buy for your computer dollar, you should be able to answer the following four questions:

- What kind of work do I want to do with a computer?
- What software (programs) will best allow me to do the kind of work that I want to do?
- What hardware (computer system) will best run the program(s) I want to use?
- What hardware and software combination will be the easiest for me to learn and use?

As usual, a little knowledge will take you a long way in the right direction, while ignorance can carry you just as far the wrong way. Now that you know a bit about computer hardware, let's look at the other side of the equation—the software.

Computer Software

Software is to computers what music is to CD players. You don't buy a CD player to display it on a shelf as a piece of art; you buy it to listen to music. Similarly, you don't buy a computer to use as a paperweight; you buy it to run software. Many people are alarmed and annoyed to find that after carefully figuring out the exact computer system to buy and the exact amount of money to spend, they neglected to add a few hundred (or a few thousand) dollars for the other side of the equation—the software.

For this reason, we will focus on software for the next few chapters. But before we begin, let's talk about just what software is.

What Is Software?

Basically, a computer is designed to do one thing, and one thing only: to read and obey instructions. A computer without instructions is like a car without an engine; it goes nowhere. Software consists of the instructions that tell a computer what to do. Or, perhaps more importantly, software tells the computer how to help *you* get a job done quickly, productively, and efficiently.

You may be wondering how one goes about getting software, and what it looks like. The actual software doesn't "look like" anything, because it's stored magnetically on a disk. When you purchase it, you get a copy of that software in the form of a program stored on disk. Accompanying the disk(s) there's a user's guide and maybe some other documentation. Figure 2.4 is an example of a typical software package.

NOTE

Although there's a lot of very cheap software available (called "shareware"), most high-powered programs range from $50 to thousands of dollars.

Purchasing Software

There are lots of ways to purchase software. You can go to a local computer store, you can mail order from companies all over the country, or you can order directly from the manufacturer.

Before you purchase a given software product, you need to know if it's compatible with your hardware. That is, you need to know if you can run that software on your computer. (You may, of course, pick out your software first and then buy the hardware that the software requires.)

Typically, you can find out what the "minimum" hardware required for a program is just by looking at the System Requirements listed on the package, or in the ad for the program. (Do this *before* you purchase the software.) The requirements description might look something like this:

IBM or compatible with 80286 or higher processor
At least 640K RAM
DOS 2.1 or higher
Hard disk with 5MB available
EGA, VGA, high-resolution CGA, or Hercules graphics adapter
Graphics printer recommended

Figure 2.4
A typical software package
includes program(s) stored on
disk and supporting written
documentation.

Translating this into English tells us that you'll need an IBM or IBM-compatible computer with an 80286, 80386, 80486 or Pentium microprocessor. Neither an 8086 processor, an 8088 processor, nor any of the Motorola processors will do for this particular product. In addition, the system must have at least 640K of memory (RAM).

NOTE

DOS and other operating systems are discussed in Chapter 3.

The *DOS 2.1 or higher* entry refers to the operating system—the "main" piece of software that determines how all of the other programs will operate, and what programs can and cannot be used. In this example, DOS is the name of the operating system, and 2.1 is the version number.

You'll also need a hard disk to use this program—floppies alone won't work. And there must be 5MB of available space on the hard disk. The term "available" is very important here. For example, if you have a 40MB hard disk, but 38MB are used by other programs and data, then you have only 2MB available, which is not enough for this program.

EGA, VGA, CGA, and Hercules Graphics all describe types of graphics display cards, which, in a nutshell, refer to the display quality of the monitor. Chapter 13 describes the various types of displays.

A printer is never *required* to use any program. But this package recommends a graphics printer because otherwise you're probably not going to be able to print anything this software produces.

Remember that the listed software requirements are just the *minimum* requirements, not the *exact* requirements. That is, your hardware may be too underpowered to run a particular software product, but it could never, ever, be too overpowered for a product. So, although the example System Requirements description says that you need a minimum of an 80286 processor, an 80386, 80486, or Pentium will work just fine. You need at least 640K, but any more than that is OK. You need at least DOS Version 2.1, but DOS Versions 3.xx, 4.xx, 5, or 6 will be fine too. You need at least 5MB of available hard disk storage, but any more than that will do as well.

An important lesson to remember is that not *all* software is compatible with *all* hardware. So make sure you buy a computer that will run the kind of software you want and need to use.

Software Version Numbers

One of the things that can drive a would-be computer enthusiast batty is the little number that follows the name of the program, like DOS 2.1 or WordPerfect 5.1. That number is the *release* or *version* number of the program. Typically, when a new software product is released to the public, it's given a low version number such as version 1.0 or release 1.0.

As with all products, the people who buy programs will write to the manufacturers to ask questions and suggest improvements, either directly, in the form of irate criticism, or just out of curiosity, as in "Why can't it do such-and-such?" The software business is a very competitive

TIP

Some new products are given higher version numbers when first released, just so it looks as if they've been around for a while.

one, and software manufacturers want to keep their customers happy, so most strive to improve their product by incorporating these suggestions in later versions. When they release a "new and improved" version of their product, they assign a new version number to it. Thus, WordPerfect 5.1 is the "new and improved" version of its predecessor, WordPerfect 5.0.

There is a logic to these numbers (though software manufacturers have been known to depart from the rules):

- Whole numbers mean major changes. For example, the jump from version 4 of a program to version 5 is a major deal.

- Changes of 1/10, such as the change from Version 5.0 to 5.1 usually mean an incremental improvement. If the improvement is in a feature that means a lot to you, you'll want to upgrade.

- Changes of 1/100, such as from version 1.0 to 1.01 generally mean no new features—but the ones that are there will now actually work.

In some cases, a new software release will be specifically designed to take advantage of newer, more powerful hardware. But the software manufacturers don't want to lose the customers who don't have the newer equipment, so rather than *replacing* the previous version with a new version, they keep both versions on the market.

For example, Lotus 1-2-3, a popular spreadsheet program for the IBM family of computers, is available in several versions. Version 2.4 is for just about any IBM or IBM-compatible, version 3.1 requires an 80286 or higher processor, and 1-2-3 for Windows 4.0 is designed to run under Windows. The latter two versions have a few more bells and whistles. But, if you don't have an 80286 with 1MB or more of RAM, or if you don't have Windows, you can still use version 2.4 of Lotus 1-2-3 on your computer. Therefore, the usual approach to purchasing software is to find the latest version of the program that will run on your equipment.

When you open the software package, you'll find a registration card, which you can fill out and send to the manufacturer to get on their mailing list. This will get you an amazing amount of junk mail. On the plus side, when a "new and improved" version is released, you'll be notified by the manufacturer through the mail. If you're interested in *upgrading* to the new release, you can send for an upgrade. Typically, purchasing the upgrade is considerably less expensive than buying the product for the first time. So there's no point in waiting for the "final" version of a software product to be released. In fact, chances are, the product will be upgraded as long as there are customers who will buy the product.

Warranties

Like most manufactured goods, virtually all reputable hardware and software products are warranted against defects. Of course, just disliking a product is not always a justification for returning the product and getting your money back. Therefore, it's smart to know something about what you are purchasing before you spend your money.

The chapters that follow will describe various products in more detail. This information will help you to narrow your choices and to focus on products that will be of interest to you.

Many computer dealers have computers on display with software products installed so that you can try them out before you buy. Also, local stores and adult education schools offer classes in using software. Typically, you can take the course and use the computers in the classroom to try out a product. If you like the product, you can purchase one for yourself. Ask your friends and colleagues what *they* use and what they like and dislike about various products.

But keep in mind that, like all companies, the manufacturers of hardware and software products want to keep their customers happy. The likelihood of being "ripped off" by a faulty product is pretty slim. Nonetheless, an informed purchase is always better than an uninformed one.

So How Do I Work It?

So, now you know that there are two sides to computers—the hardware, which consists of the stuff you see sitting on a desktop, and the software, which allows you to tell the hardware what to do.

Now the question no doubt looming in your mind is "How do I work it?" Once again, I have to answer with a resounding "It depends on what you want to do."

On the one hand, I could say that you basically plug it in, turn it on, and type your material at the keyboard, or use your mouse to tell the computer what to do. The computer, in turn, does whatever you tell it, and then waits for you to tell it what to do next. Basically, that's it. You tell it what to do, it does it, ad infinitum.

But that's a pretty general description, and I think what most people are really asking when they pose this question is "How do I make it do…"—whatever it is you want it to do. The answer to that question is, first you buy a program that does the kind of work that you want to do, then install that program on your computer, and then learn how to use that program.

In the chapters that follow, I'll try to give you an idea of how you work each of the different types of software available, such as operating systems, spreadsheets, word processors, and so forth. But remember, if you want to get some hands-on experience before you buy, your local computer dealer or an adult education school might be your best bet.

Part Two

Find the Right Tools

Three

Operating Systems

• •

The *operating system* is the most important piece of software on your computer. For one thing, it's what gets the whole computer system started, and it coordinates the activities of the central processing unit and the various peripheral devices, such as the disk drives, keyboard, monitor, and printer.

Furthermore, the operating system determines which programs you can (and can't) use. One of the software requirements for using the sample program from Chapter 2 was "DOS 2.1 or higher." If your computer had some operating system other than DOS, (or a version before 2.1) you couldn't use that program.

Finally, the operating system is the main *interface* for using your computer. In other words, it determines how you'll interact with your computer, which, in turn, affects how easy the computer is to learn and use.

NOTE
Operating System is often abbreviated as OS.

This chapter will discuss all of these facets of the operating system, including the two different types of interfaces: textual interface and graphical interface. Then I'll describe some of the operating systems available to you, and complete the discussion by talking about *utilities,* which are optional programs you can use to "round out" and/or simplify the use of the operating system.

What Does the Operating System Do?

When you first turn on your computer it looks for an operating system stored on disk. If the computer can't find an operating system, it will power up but won't function in any useful way.

For this reason, when you buy a computer, it usually comes with an operating system already installed. That way, when you turn on a new computer for the first time, it works!

The operating system delivered with most PCs is DOS. In the Macintosh world, the most common operating system on newish Macs is System 7.

NOTE
The acronym PC (for personal computer) is used to describe all IBM and IBM-compatible computers.

People don't usually think much about operating systems. After all, you don't go out to buy a computer because you're dying to get the new version of DOS! Eventually, however, everyone has to deal with the operating system in order to manage (i.e., create, copy, move, delete, rename) *files.* These operations are simple, but the computer can't do them all by itself. You need to tell the computer how and when to manage files, and to do that, you need to know something about operating systems. But first, we need to define some terms.

Drives, Directories, and Files

As mentioned in Chapter 2, a disk drive is where you store information (and programs) for use with the computer, sort of like a file cabinet. One of the things that makes a file cabinet useful is that you can *organize* the information in it, to make it easier to find that information later. In a large company, each department might have its own set of file cabinets. Each file cabinet, in turn, has its own set of drawers, and each drawer contains its own set of files.

NOTE

On Macintoshes, a directory or file group is called a **folder**.

The operating system helps you organize information stored on disk in a similar manner. Any hard disk (or floppy disk) can be divided into separate *directories* or *file groups*. Each directory or file group contains its own set of files, just as a single drawer in the file cabinet contains a set of files.

Each *file* on the disk is like a file in the file cabinet drawer. It holds some specific information or a particular program.

Just as each manila file folder in a file cabinet drawer will have its own label, each file in a directory or group has a name, called its *file name*. With a file cabinet, the way you find information is generally to go to the correct file cabinet, open the correct drawer, then open the appropriate file. On a computer you do basically the same thing.

1. Go to the correct drive.
2. Go to the correct directory.
3. Open the appropriate file.

The operating system organizes your information and programs into drives, directories, and files. It's also the tool for retrieving that information in the future.

NOTE

In the world of computers, "old" is a relative term. For example, a 5-year-old PC is a virtual antique.

The specifics depend on the particular operating system you're using. But in general, there are two basic interfaces for managing information: the text-based interface and the graphical interface. As more users move to high-end computers and operating systems become more sophisticated, text-based interfaces are giving way to graphical interfaces. However, if you're using an older PC, you're probably using a text-based interface, so in the next sections, I'll describe both types of interfaces and techniques for using them.

The Text-Based Interface

In a text-based operating system, you communicate with the operating system by typing out words that you will see on screen. Each operating system has certain words called *commands* that it understands as instructions you are giving to it. The system works with normal alphanumeric characters like A,B,C and 1,2,3.

For example, on PCs (IBM and compatible computers) using the DOS operating system, some frequently used commands include:

- PRINT (prints a copy of a file)
- COPY (makes a duplicate of a file)
- REN (renames a file)

Looks easy enough, right? Unfortunately, these commands used alone will not get your computer to do anything; you must also include some other information. You have to provide the name of the file you want to print, the name of the file you want to copy and where to put the new copy, or the name of the file you want to rename and what to rename it.

It's when you start adding this "extra" information that the potential for frustration rises. For example, if you have a file named MYSALES in the directory named SALEDATA on your hard disk named C:, and you want to copy the file to a floppy disk in drive A:, you need to type this command, and then press the key marked ↵:

    COPY C:\SALEDATA\MYSALES A:

If you add or leave out any spaces or letters, or type the wrong letter or character (e.g., if you type / instead of \), the command won't work. Instead, the screen will just display an error message telling you it doesn't "understand" the command. So the less-than-perfect typist will do quite a lot of retyping with a text-based system.

To run a program with a text-based operating system, typically you type the name of the program, or an abbreviation of it, and press ↵. For example, to run WordPerfect on a PC (assuming you own and have installed the WordPerfect program), you type

    WP

and press ↵.

Once again, it's up to you to memorize the command required to start each program that's installed on your computer and to type the program name correctly. Mistyping the program name is no tragedy, just annoying; the computer responds with a message such as "Bad command or file name." After muttering a few bad words of your own, you try again—this time typing in the correct command, and the program proceeds.

NOTE

If you have DOS 5 on your computer, help is available by typing /? after a DOS command. If you have DOS 6, type HELP, a space, and then the name of the command. Don't know what version of DOS you have? Type VER at the prompt and press the Enter key.

The thing about a text-based interface that people generally hate is that it doesn't offer much help. You get a message like "File not found" or "Invalid directory" and not a clue as to what to do next. You're pretty much on your own for finding your way around the system. For example, when you first start a computer that uses some of the earlier versions of DOS, all you see is C:\>, as shown in Figure 3.1. However, DOS 5 and 6 and many newer DOS applications include on-line and context-sensitive help to make the text-based interface "friendlier."

As you can see, this screen doesn't tell you much about the many drives, directories, files, and programs available on the computer. In fact, it doesn't tell you *anything*! Commands are available for finding out these things, but until you read the documentation for the operating system to learn what those commands are, you're pretty much stuck.

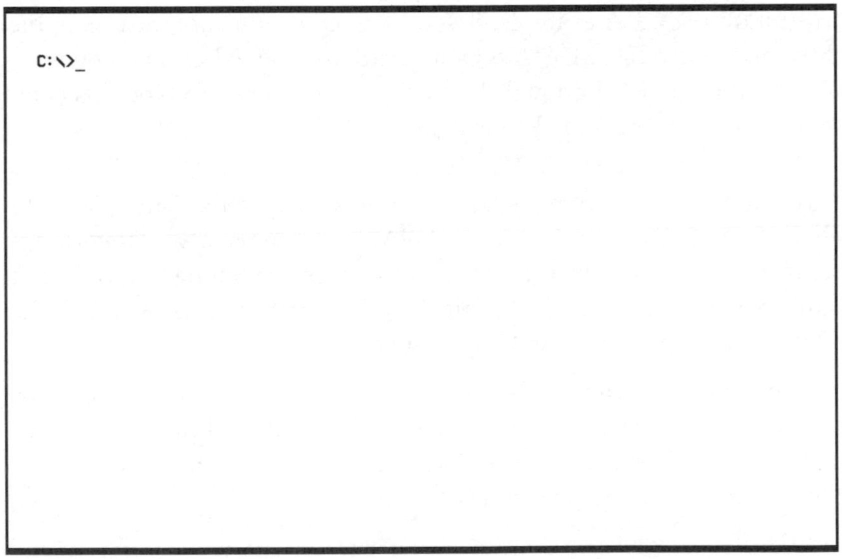

Figure 3.1

Starting a computer that offers only a text-based interface doesn't give you many clues about what's available, or how to get anything done.

```
c:\>_
```

Graphical Interface

A graphical interface is usually much easier to use than a text-based one. When you start a computer that has a graphical interface, you immediately get an overall picture of what's available on the system. For example, Figure 3.2 shows the screen you'll see when you start a computer with the DOS shell included with DOS 4.01 and above. Let's discuss just what the screen in Figure 3.2 is telling you.

Near the top of the screen, the icons (tiny pictures) labeled A, B, C, D, and so forth, through H, represent disk drives on the computer. To switch from one disk drive to another, you roll the mouse around until the mouse pointer (the hollow arrow) is on the drive that you want to switch to. Then you just click a mouse button.

Below the disk drive, in the box labeled Directory Tree, there's a list of the directories available on the current disk drive (drive C in this example).

NOTE

Early versions of DOS (pre-version 4) are all text. Versions 4 and above offer some graphical interface, as described in more detail later.

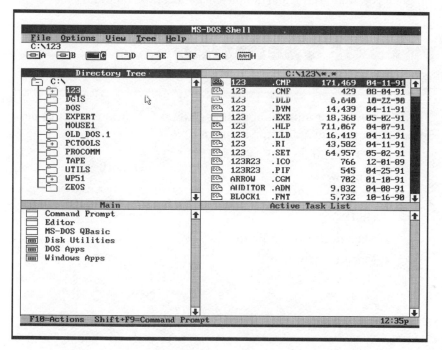

Figure 3.2

A graphical interface gives you much more information than a text-only interface.

If you switch to another drive, the Directory Tree automatically displays the directories on that particular drive.

To the right of the Directory Tree there's a list of the files in the current directory. You can switch to a different directory to see what files are in it by moving the mouse pointer to the directory you want to switch to and clicking the mouse button.

Now let's say you want to copy a file from one directory to another. To do so, you just move the mouse pointer to the name of the file you want to copy, hold down the mouse button and the Control (Ctrl) key, and drag the file name to the drive or directory that you want to copy the file to. This is much simpler (and less prone to error) than memorizing and typing in a long command such as **COPY C:\SALEDATA\MYSALES A:**. If you hold down the mouse button and drag the file without using the Ctrl key, you will *move* the file from one directory to another. The file at the previous location will be erased and the file will be moved to a new directory.

The Program List in the Main window lists programs available on the computer. To run a program, you just move the mouse pointer to the name of the program you want to run and double-click the mouse button.

Types of Operating Systems

NOTE
Individual computers and their backgrounds are discussed in Chapter 12, "Name Brand Shopping."

There are several prominent operating systems for various types of personal computers, including the following:

- DOS, including MS-DOS and PC-DOS
- Windows
- OS/2
- UNIX
- Macintosh System/Finder
- Macintosh System 7

DOS

When IBM entered the personal computer market at the beginning of the 1980s, the company chose to create a new operating system for its computers. But IBM wasn't terribly interested in developing this new operating system themselves, so they went shopping for a software company to develop it for them.

Initially, IBM went to a company named Digital Research, the same company that had created an earlier system called CP/M (Control Program for Microcomputers). As the story goes, the head of the company missed the meeting, and the IBM execs grew tired of waiting, so they went on to their next appointment.

The purpose of the next appointment was to find another group of people to do some programming language development for this new machine. The company they chose for this task was a tiny outfit called Microsoft.

During the meeting, the IBM execs mentioned that their previous meeting was fruitless, and as yet they did not have an operating system for their upcoming machine. The founder of Microsoft, Bill Gates, heard opportunity knocking. After all, every computer needs an operating system. And everyone who buys an IBM machine will need whatever operating system IBM picks. Gates jumped at the chance.

Microsoft ended up developing the operating system, now named DOS, and IBM has since sold several million computers. A copy of DOS is included with each one, and Microsoft gets a royalty for every copy sold. Microsoft is now the largest software company in the world and Mr. Gates is a multibillionaire.

DOS is now the most widely used operating system on modern microcomputers. Although it's commonly referred to simply as DOS, there are actually two flavors, PC-DOS and MS-DOS. PC-DOS is the version sold with true IBM computers, while MS-DOS is the version used on virtually every IBM-compatible computer. The two operating systems are essentially identical, but in version 6 they each come with a different set of add-on utilities.

DOS Versions

DOS has evolved through many versions, each taking advantage of improvements in the power and sophistication of PCs. Table 3.1 summarizes this evolution. (The .x after the version number stands for all the incremental versions within the main version, for example 3.0, 3.1, 3.2, and so forth.)

DOS has evolved from a text-based to a graphical interface. The text interface, which offered the nearly blank screen adorned only with the C:\> prompt, was the interface of DOS versions up through 3.x. DOS 4, 5, and 6 offer a graphical interface as an option, and indeed, the earlier discussion of graphical interfaces was based on DOS 6.

Table 3.1

The Evolution of DOS

Year	DOS Version	Features
1981	1.x	Only operating system for IBM computers
1983	2.x	First version capable of use with a hard disk
1984	3.x	Capable of taking advantage of the new, faster IBM AT class of computers, based on the 80286 processor
1988	4.x	First graphical interface for DOS
1991	5.x	Improved graphical interface, better use of advanced 80386 and 80486 processors
1993	6.x	Includes memory management and many disk utilities as part of the package

What You Need to Use DOS

One of the beauties of the DOS evolution is that you can still use the newer versions of DOS on older computers. For example, if you have an early IBM XT with as little as 256K RAM, you can still use the latest and greatest DOS 6 on that computer. Granted, it's not easy to get it to work on a computer with that few resources and a lot of the advanced features are unusable unless you have a 80386 or 80486 processor. You can, however, use many DOS features, including the graphical interface, with more modest computers.

Windows 3.x

In early 1990, Microsoft, the same company that developed DOS, released Windows 3.0. Version 3.1 followed in 1992. Windows is rapidly becoming the standard on newer PCs—it provides a truly graphical interface that includes icons, buttons that seem to depress when you click them, and gorgeous colors.

In fact, Windows is considered to be the first "true GUI" (graphical user interface) for PCs. What people generally mean by "truly" graphical is that the interface is much like the one that the Macintosh family of computers has had all along.

Figure 3.3 shows a sample screen from Windows. Notice the 3-D appearance of the crinkled paper in the background, and the plain English program names and icons. To run a program in Windows, you just roll the mouse pointer to the program name or icon and click a mouse button.

Multitasking with Windows

The dazzling graphical interface isn't the only thing that sets Windows apart from DOS. Windows also offers *multitasking,* which is the ability to

Figure 3.3

This is a sample screen from Windows, with sample icons.

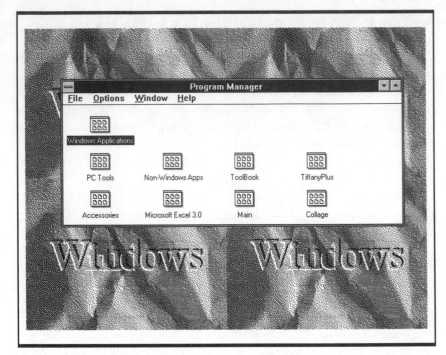

run more than one program at a time. In all versions of DOS, the program you're running takes over the entire screen, so you can interact with only one program at a time.

In Windows, however, you can have several programs loaded into memory and in use at the same time. Then you can divide the screen into separate *windows,* each of which displays a different actively running program. In Figure 3.4, three programs are running simultaneously: an appointment calendar, Paintbrush, a drawing program, and Excel, a popular spreadsheet program.

You can easily move, size, open, and close windows. Furthermore, you can easily copy and paste text and graphics between programs. For example, you might use your spreadsheet program to do some math or

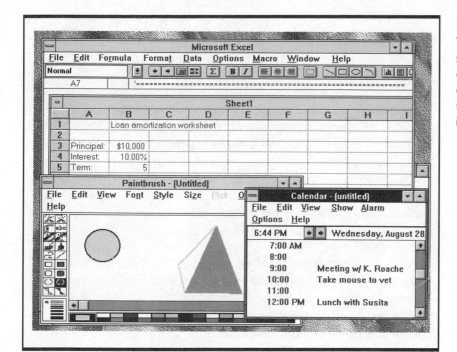

Figure 3.4

Three separate programs: a spreadsheet, an appointment calendar, and the Paintbrush drawing program, running at the same time and displayed in separate windows.

create a business graphic. You can then copy the numbers or the graph from the spreadsheet and *paste* them into a report you're writing with a word processor.

This between-program interaction was limited and difficult in DOS, but in Windows it's simple. In many cases you can even *link* programs so that when you change the numbers in the spreadsheet, the numbers are automatically changed in the word processing file to which it's linked.

Common User Access

Another advantage of Windows is that it's the first operating system to standardize how programs for it are designed. All programs that are specifically designed for Windows are called *Windows applications,* and they all follow the guidelines set forth in the Windows Common User Access (CUA).

In the microcomputer world, the same kind of disorderly confusion that you see in Figure 3.5 has periodically prevailed, with different software companies producing programs that follow only their own standards.

Modern operating systems and environments, such as Windows, OS/2, and the Macintosh's System 7, now set the standards needed to make different programs behave in similar ways. So even as computers are becoming more capable and powerful, it's likely that the programs we use on them will become increasingly easy to learn and more intuitive to use.

To appreciate the value of the Windows CUA, you need to realize that DOS programs generally do not follow any standardized guidelines for instructing people how to use a program. For example, a DOS word processing program may require one set of commands to access built-in help, move text around, save your work, and so forth, while a DOS spreadsheet

Figure 3.5
Before telephone technology was standardized, the telephone system was a mass of wires and confusion. (Photo courtesy of the Museum of the City of New York.)

program will require an entirely different set of commands to accomplish the same operations. This complicates the process of learning programs because, essentially, you start from scratch every time you want to learn a new program. Also, you probably will make a lot of mistakes because you will tend to use your old commands, out of habit, while learning a new program.

In Windows applications, however, you use the same set of commands to perform the same general activities in different programs. So once you learn one Windows program, you're a long way toward learning any other Windows program.

Windows Applications

Windows can run both programs that were designed for DOS and programs that were specifically designed for Windows. Only Windows applications, however, abide by the Windows CUA guidelines and take advantage of all the features that Windows offers.

Most popular programs originally designed for DOS are now available in Windows versions. For example, two flavors of WordPerfect, a popular word processing program for PCs, are now available: WordPerfect for DOS and WordPerfect for Windows. If you choose to use Windows as your operating system, you'll certainly want to buy the Windows version of whatever program tickles your fancy.

What You Need to Use Windows

About the only downside to Windows is that you need considerable hardware horsepower (which translates to *expense*) to use it. Technically speaking, you can run Windows with the following:

- An IBM-compatible computer with 80286 or higher processor
- At least 1MB RAM
- DOS 3.1 or later
- A hard disk with at least 6MB available disk space

But in reality, you can *start* Windows with the above system, but you'd be hard-pressed to get it to actually *do* anything.

A more realistic scenario for taking full advantage of Windows is an 80386 or higher processor with at least 4MB of RAM (preferably 8 to 16MB), a hard disk with at least 80MB storage (to store Windows and all your Windows applications), and a high-resolution monitor, preferably VGA or Super VGA (discussed in Chapter 13).

Now you may be wondering why, if Windows is an operating system, you also need DOS 3.1 or higher, since DOS is also an operating system.

In truth, Windows isn't really a true operating system at all. It's an operating environment, rather like a DOS *shell,* meaning a program that is added to DOS to make DOS easier to use. But for all intents and purposes, once Windows is up and running on your computer, you never really need to interact directly with DOS yourself; Windows takes care of that for you. Some functions, however, such as memory management, are completely turned over to Windows, allowing Windows to access more memory than DOS can alone.

● S/2

When IBM introduced its PS/2 line of computers in the mid-1980s, it wanted a new operating system to represent a complete break from its discontinued PC line. IBM hired Microsoft once again to create this new operating system for them. They wanted it to have all the bells and whistles of a great operating system: graphical user interface, multitasking, and the ability to run DOS programs as well as newer programs with a graphical user interface.

This new operating system was to be named OS/2, for Operating System 2. Initially, OS/2 was the great hope for people who were tired of the clumsy, limited interface represented by DOS.

Unfortunately, the dream did not materialize. OS/2 was plagued with problems. It required a minimum of 1.5MB of memory at a time when memory was very expensive and the vast majority of computers had less than half that amount, 640K. Also, it never seemed to run existing DOS programs quite right, and there were few programs designed to be used with OS/2. Many people who did switch to OS/2 eventually abandoned it because, even with all its grace and beauty, it just wasn't practical.

When memory prices finally began to drop, and people finally did start buying faster and better computers with lots of RAM, Windows 3 was right there, with most of the promises that OS/2 offered, and most of the problems resolved. Seemingly overnight, Windows became *the* graphic operating environment for IBM-compatible computers, and OS/2 fell even further into obscurity.

But OS/2 is making a comeback, and IBM is bundling it with many of its newer computers. OS/2 now promises complete connectivity among all types of computers, including large mainframe computers, minicomputers, and microcomputers—something that interests many large companies. In addition, OS/2 promises to "run DOS programs better than DOS, and Windows applications better than Windows." Maybe.

The latest version of OS/2 is 2.1, released in mid-1993. It's a much better system, but suffers from a lack of applications and IBM's inability to market it to the general public. Regardless of its merits, it may never be able to catch up to the head start that Windows has. In addition, Microsoft now has its own 32-bit operating system, Windows NT, introduced in mid-1993. Windows NT is a multitasking operating system that takes full advantage of the 32-bit data pathways that exist in all 386 and 486 microprocessors. In addition, it is portable to other microprocessor platforms, such as workstations based on RISC (Reduced Instruction Set Computing) microprocessor chips.

NIX

In case you're wondering, UNIX is short for UNiplexed Information and Computing System.

UNIX is a large, somewhat complicated operating system that has both multitasking (can run several different programs at the same time) and multiuser (several people, each with their own keyboard and monitor, can use the same computer at the same time) features. UNIX is used primarily on larger computers in corporations, but some versions of UNIX (and a somewhat scaled-down version, called XENIX) run on microcomputers.

The biggest drawback to UNIX is its text interface. As with DOS, you need to memorize and type commands to get the computer to do anything. That's slowly starting to change, however. Some new computers, including the NeXT machines and Amigas, are adopting UNIX as their main operating system, and adding graphical user interfaces to make the operating system more user-friendly—much like Windows makes DOS more user-friendly.

Graphical interfaces for UNIX and its various offshoots include X-Windows, Motif, and the NeXT user interface. But unfortunately, very few commercial programs are designed to run under UNIX. So UNIX, which has often been called the operating system of the future, remains in the future, while the less powerful and less dazzling DOS and Windows/DOS combination continue to dominate the IBM family of computers.

Macintosh System/Finder

The Macintosh, introduced in 1984, was the first personal computer to sport a graphical user interface. But unlike the PCs, which could support several operating systems, the Mac offered just one. In fact, you rarely even hear the term "operating system" discussed in relation to the Mac, since the one and only operating system is built in, and picking an operating system is not an issue.

But regardless of terminology, the Mac's graphical interface created much excitement in the industry when it was introduced. Instead of requiring users to type obscure commands to get the computer to do something, visionaries at Apple created *icons* (little pictures) that represented abstractions such as disk files and programs. These icons could easily be manipulated with a mouse. The invention of icons and some other graphical features of the Macintosh interface made lengthy and obscure typed commands unnecessary. With a Mac, instead of entering a command such as ERASE C:\DOS\OLDJUNK.TXT to delete a file, you just use your mouse to drag a file-folder icon of the file into a trashcan on the screen. (Notice in Figure 3.6 that the Trashcan even bulges when it's full.)

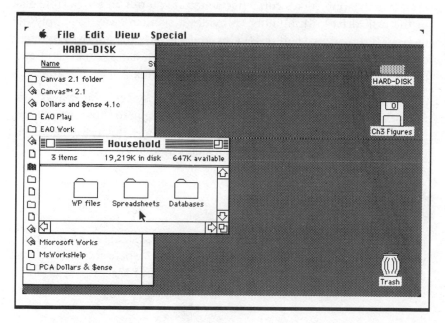

Figure 3.6

This is the graphical user interface of the Macintosh System 6 Finder.

NOTE

Despite this confusing terminology, most people refer to
the Mac operating system
just by its System version
number, as in System 7 or
System 6.0.x, where x is a
number.

The two core programs of the Macintosh operating system are the System and the Finder. They come as a matched set, and you need to use the right System with the right Finder. Even Apple doesn't make that simple, putting different version numbers after each of them. For example, System 6.0.4 goes with Finder 6.1.4— but since they arrive together in the same package it doesn't usually make for much of a problem.

The *Finder* is more visible to a Macintosh user than the finder. It's a special application used to organize and manage your documents and to start other applications. You use the Finder every time you start up your Mac, and whenever you switch from one application to another. The Finder names files (names can have up to 30 characters), creates folders to hold files or programs, and gets information to and from disks.

An expanded multitasking version of the Finder, called MultiFinder, lets you run multiple programs simultaneously and switch between them. It also lets you print files in the background, which means that you can continue to work with your computer at the same time that the printer is busy printing away.

NOTE

You'll need around 4MB of
memory to run MultiFinder.
In System 7, the MultiFinder
is built into the operating
system and is much easier
to use, although you'll still
need plenty of memory.

System is the portion of the Mac operating system that starts the computer and provides the services needed by all other programs. System consists of several packages, each doing a particular job. These packages include: Disk Initialization (takes corrective action if you put an unreadable disk in the disk drive), MiniFinder (provides a standard way to supply file names), International Utilities (helps conform to conventions of different countries for tasks such as formatting numbers, dates, times, and currency), and several additional utilities for mathematical calculations.

Although the traditional Macintosh operating system, known as System 6, served Mac users well for many years, it began to show signs of age, especially when Windows 3 made its appearance. But now Mac users have a newer operating system to consider: System 7.

Mac System 7

If Windows or the original Macintosh operating system seems appealing, you're sure to love the new Macintosh System 7 operating system. System 7 is the best enhancement you can add to your Macintosh, although like Windows, it requires serious hardware: a Mac Plus or better, at least

4MB of memory (RAM), and a hard disk, for starters. And if you want to take advantage of every new System 7 feature, you'll want a color Mac, preferably a powerful Mac LCIII, IIvx, or Quadra.

Stated simply, System 7 offers everything Windows does, but it's easier to use and more consistent than its PC rival. System 7 on a color Macintosh will astound you with its 3-D shading and rich, full-color windows and icons. And like its Windows competitor, System 7 offers multitasking, which means you can open any number of programs at once (as long as they fit into memory), and you can have other tasks, like printing, running unattended in the background. One of System 7's premier features is TrueType, which lets the computer display and print smooth text at any size: a real boon to desktop publishers and anyone else who yearns for a true what-you-see-is-what-you-get (WYSIWYG) environment.

The Finder offers a convenient way to organize folders and files (see Figure 3.7), a powerful Find feature that makes searching for files easier than ever before, a neat *alias* option that lets you organize your hard disk more conveniently, and a more predictable Trash can that empties only when

NOTE

Many System 6 applications run under System 7 with few if any problems. System 7 includes a Compatibility Checker that checks your existing applications for any potential compatibility problems. Your Apple dealer will also have information about compatibility.

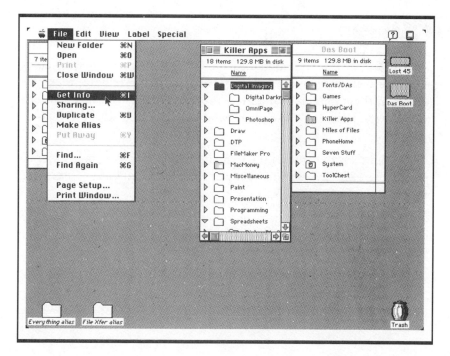

Figure 3.7

A sample screen display from the Macintosh System 7 operating system.

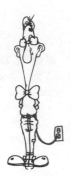

you ask it to do so. The icons in the upper-right corner of Figure 3.7 represent two more features: Balloon Help and the Application menu. When activated, Balloon Help displays cartoon-style word balloons containing useful information on various screen elements. As new application programs are written to take advantage of System 7, they too will include Balloon Help. The Application menu conveniently lists all your open applications, for easy switching from application to application.

Many of System 7's features are geared to more experienced users, especially those using Macintoshes on a network. For instance, there is interapplication communications (IAC). This term is a mouthful, but basically, IAC allows applications to exchange "live" information that is continually being updated. For example, if someone were to change the numbers in a spreadsheet, any word processor file using those numbers would be updated instantly and automatically. Additional features allow you to share files with other computers, open programs that are larger than the amount of memory available on your computer, link programs together to merge their capabilities, and copy data from large databases on other computers with one simple menu command.

Utilities

Older operating systems contained the bare essentials for getting along with your computer on a day-to-day basis. However, they were notably skimpy in the programs that add a bit of comfort to your life. This fact provided the basis for a fairly large industry that provides these *utility* programs.

Utilities fill the gap between the basic functions of the operating system and the more specific work done by application programs such as word processing and spreadsheets.

Hundreds of utilities have been written to perform almost every imaginable feat. Nevertheless, we can classify essential utilities into these basic categories:

- **Backup utilities**: Occasionally, hard disks do fail (this is called a *crash*), quite possibly causing you to lose all the files stored on them. For this reason, a smart user keeps backup copies of all files on floppy disks or magnetic tape. Several utility programs are available to make the process of backing up files relatively quick and painless.

- **Disaster recovery utilities**: Recovering an accidentally deleted file should be easy because deleted files are not actually erased. The operating system just makes the name of the file invisible and marks the space on the hard disk as "now available." So the file you erased is still there, at least until you create some new file to replace it. DOS 5 and 6 allow you to easily "undelete" a file you have inadvertently erased. Earlier versions of DOS didn't include this feature, which is why utilities were written to help you find and reinstate those accidentally deleted files that are still on the disk (although currently unavailable).

- **File and text search utilities**: A hard disk contains a lot of files and there can be a lot of places to go looking should you forget the name or location of a particular file. Where the operating system may offer only the ability to search for a particular file by name in one location (directory) at a time, file managers can search for files by their contents, creation date, and/or modification date. Most file managers can also simultaneously search multiple locations on the disk.

- **Hard disk optimizers**: As you create and delete files, the hard disk files can become *fragmented,* with bits and pieces of files scattered all over the disk in whatever space is available. The more fragmented a disk is, the slower it operates (and the more you can hear the drive head chattering away inside the disk drive). Hard disk optimizing programs (also called *defragmenting programs* or just *defraggers*) rearrange the broken up files into contiguous areas of the hard disk, which makes reading and writing them faster.

- **Desktop organizers**: With a computer and keyboard occupying most of the space on a desktop, often there's little space left for appointment books, calculators, Rolodexes, and such. If you want the equivalent of these organizers on your computer, you may want to acquire some desktop utility packages. If you're buying a Mac or are considering Windows as your PC operating platform, you needn't bother: These come

NOTE

System 7 on the Macintosh has many of these file and text search capabilities.

with several handy utilities, including the Cardfile, Calendar (appointment book), Calculator, and Notepad. Figure 3.8 shows some desktop utilities that come with Windows.

- **Screen savers**: If you walk away from your computer while a bright graphic image is displayed on the screen, that image can become permanently etched onto the screen. Screen saver programs can deliver your screen from this ugly fate, either by blanking the screen or by displaying ever-changing animated images when there's been no activity at the keyboard for a while (several minutes). As soon as you return and touch the keyboard or mouse, your original screen comes back into view.

- **Macro utilities**: If you're performing the same keystrokes over and over again, you might want to try a macro utility. Macro utilities let you record your keystrokes or mouse movements, and then play them back in the future with a single keystroke.

Figure 3.8

Desktop utilities perform the jobs of Rolodexes, appointment books, calculators, notepads, and more.

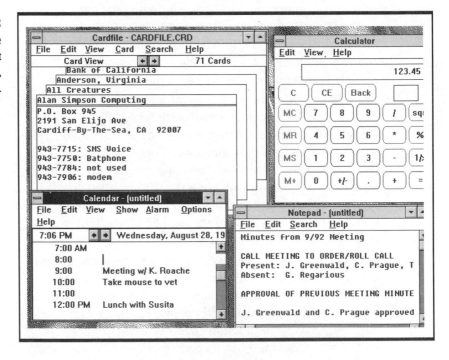

- **Virus protection utilities**: No, computers don't get sick. But occasionally high-tech vandals like to hide insidious programs, called *viruses,* inside innocent programs. Most viruses are designed just to shock the user with some bizarre message on the screen, but some can do real harm to your files. If you ever exchange disks with other users, an anti-viral utility will help prevent these nasty little varmints from infecting your computer.

NOTE

With the exception of a screen saver and a desktop organizer, DOS 6 comes with all of these utilities.

Finding Utilities

Before you go shopping for utilities, check to see which ones you already have. Most of the newer operating systems come with many, probably more, than you need. Then check your local computer store or the ads in any computer magazine to see which package or packages will suit your needs.

NOTE

See Chapter 9 for more information on bulletin boards.

To save money, you can find a lot of free shareware utilities on computer club bulletin boards (BBSs). Many computer magazines also give away handy utilities when you subscribe. And some computer books offer free utilities that you can create yourself or copy from a disk enclosed in the book.

Four

Word Processing

• •

The term "word processing" has its roots in the much earlier computer term "data processing." Originally, computers were designed to process data, i.e., to perform calculations on lots of numbers. Hence the term "data processing." However, not everyone works with numbers; in fact, far more people work with words.

Early in computer history, it became apparent that computers could help those people who work with words as well as those who work with data. As you'll see in this chapter, a word processor is to a typewriter as the car is to the horse. Cars have their problems and horses have their charm, but when you need to get downtown in a hurry, you don't saddle up old Dobbin! Word processing on a computer provides both speed and mastery as well as features unavailable on any kind of typewriter.

What Is Word Processing?

The act of writing is the continuous processing of words. Usually, we start with a rough draft. Then we change things: we move text around, insert new text, delete unnecessary text, and so forth, until we're pleased with the final document.

You're getting sleepy... sleeepy....

Doing all this with a typewriter requires the constant marking and retyping of drafts, mainly because you are typing directly onto paper and the only way to change what's on the paper is to start over again with a new piece of paper. But with word processing, you type your material into the computer's memory (and view your work on the screen). Because you're not typing directly onto paper, you can replace, move, copy, insert, delete, overwrite, or correct any words, sentences, paragraphs, pages—any amount of text—at any time, before your material becomes a document printed on paper.

You can make any editing changes, corrections, and refinements at any time without having to retype anything (except things you actually *want* to rewrite).

What Do I Need to Do Word Processing?

Just about any computer can be used as a word processor. Basically, all you need is the following:

- a computer system
- a word processing program that's compatible with your computer hardware and operating system
- a printer for printing your documents
- a mouse (desirable but not always essential)

The exact memory requirements and disk storage requirements are determined by the word processing program that you select. Just about any monitor will do. However, if you want to include graphics in your documents, you will need a high resolution graphics monitor.

The printer you choose will determine how professional your printout will look. If you want the output to look really good, you'll want a letter-quality dot matrix or, even better, a laser printer. If your documents contain graphics, a laser printer is really a must.

A mouse is also very handy because it simplifies cutting and pasting text and graphics within a document. If you want to learn more about the various monitors, printers, and such that are available, refer to the chapters referenced in Table 4.1.

Table 4.1
Hardware Reference Chart

To Learn More About...	Look Into...
Keyboard	"Getting the Data into the Computer" in Chapter 13
Mouse	"Getting the Data into the Computer" in Chapter 13
Monitor	"Getting the Data Out: Displays" in Chapter 13
Printer	Chapter 15

Incidentally, there are machines called "word processors" designed to do *just* word processing. These "dedicated" word processors are less expensive (but not all *that* much less) than a full computer system with a word processing program, but they can't do anything else besides produce simple documents. Buying one of these machines is like buying a phone that will only call your Mom. As much as you love Mom, sooner or later you're going to want to call someone else. And if you buy a dedicated "word processor," eventually you'll be sorry you limited your options so drastically.

Using a Word Processor

In many ways, word processing programs are the easiest of all programs to use, because they function so much like their predecessor, the typewriter. In both cases, you use a keyboard, but with a word processor, instead of typing on a blank piece of paper, you type on a screen.

Because you're typing on a screen rather than on paper, there are a few extra steps required to create a complete, printed document.

Typing a Document

There's nothing particularly special about typing on a screen as opposed to paper—you type as you normally would, using the backspace key to make small corrections as needed while you type. The first major difference between word processors and typewriters is that you don't have to press the carriage return (↵) at the end of each line. Instead, the word processor automatically *word wraps* text at the end of each line. This feature ensures that each line ends with a complete word rather than with part of a word. You need to press ↵ only at the end of each paragraph, or short line, or where you want to insert a blank line.

Figure 4.1 shows a sample letter typed on a screen— mistakes and all.

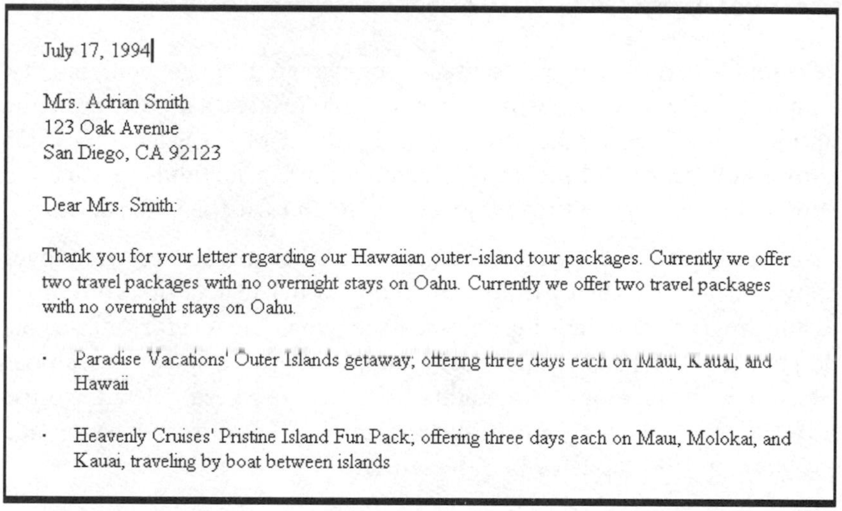

July 17, 1994

Mrs. Adrian Smith
123 Oak Avenue
San Diego, CA 92123

Dear Mrs. Smith:

Thank you for your letter regarding our Hawaiian outer-island tour packages. Currently we offer two travel packages with no overnight stays on Oahu. Currently we offer two travel packages with no overnight stays on Oahu.

· Paradise Vacations' Outer Islands getaway; offering three days each on Maui, Kauai, and Hawaii

· Heavenly Cruises' Pristine Island Fun Pack; offering three days each on Maui, Molokai, and Kauai, traveling by boat between islands

Figure 4.1
A sample document typed on a screen. Typing on a screen is virtually identical to typing with a typewriter.

Editing a Document

Since we never seem to type anything perfectly the first time, we must edit the document to make changes and corrections. This, of course, is where word processing programs really shine, because you can add, delete, move, and copy text right on the screen without having to retype anything. For example, notice how the repeated sentence in the first paragraph is selected (highlighted) in Figure 4.2.

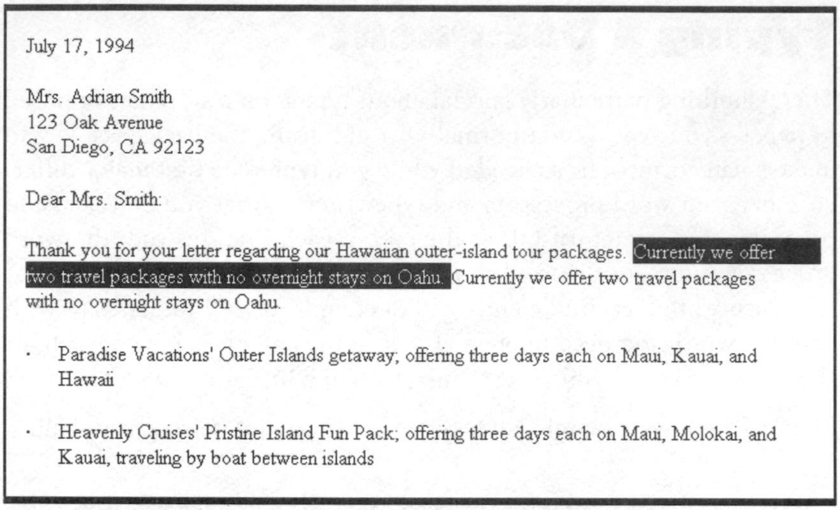

Figure 4.2

A sentence is selected in the document.

July 17, 1994

Mrs. Adrian Smith
123 Oak Avenue
San Diego, CA 92123

Dear Mrs. Smith:

Thank you for your letter regarding our Hawaiian outer-island tour packages. Currently we offer two travel packages with no overnight stays on Oahu. Currently we offer two travel packages with no overnight stays on Oahu.

- Paradise Vacations' Outer Islands getaway; offering three days each on Maui, Kauai, and Hawaii

- Heavenly Cruises' Pristine Island Fun Pack; offering three days each on Maui, Molokai, and Kauai, traveling by boat between islands

Selecting a particular word, sentence, or paragraph is generally a very simple thing to do with a word processor. You just use a mouse, or menu options (described in the next section, "About Menu Selections"). Of course, different word processors require different methods to select or "highlight" text, so we can't be specific here. But trust me, it's very easy.

Once you've selected a piece of text to work with, it is also easy to move, copy, or delete it. When you do move, copy, or delete text, the word processing program automatically *reformats* the remaining text for you, so you don't have to retype anything. For example, Figure 4.3 shows the sample letter after the previously highlighted sentence has been deleted. Notice how the program has automatically reformatted the entire first paragraph to "close up" the gap left when the sentence was deleted.

Formatting the Document

You can also easily change the format of the document without retyping. For example, you can change the margins, spacing, and tab stops with just a few keystrokes or menu selections. For example, Figure 4.4 shows the same sample letter after changing the format to double-spacing.

July 17, 1994

Mrs. Adrian Smith
123 Oak Avenue
San Diego, CA 92123

Dear Mrs. Smith:

Thank you for your letter regarding our Hawaiian outer-island tour packages. Currently we offer two travel packages with no overnight stays on Oahu.

· Paradise Vacations' Outer Islands getaway; offering three days each on Maui, Kauai, and Hawaii

· Heavenly Cruises' Pristine Island Fun Pack; offering three days each on Maui, Molokai, and Kauai, traveling by boat between islands

Figure 4.3

The sample letter after deleting the highlighted sentence. The program has automatically reformatted the paragraph and closed up the gap that otherwise would have been left after the deletion.

July 17, 1994

Mrs. Adrian Smith
123 Oak Avenue
San Diego, CA 92123

Dear Mrs. Smith:

Thank you for your letter regarding our Hawaiian outer-island tour packages. Currently we offer

two travel packages with no overnight stays on Oahu.

· Paradise Vacations' Outer Islands getaway; offering three days each on Maui, Kauai, and

Hawaii

Figure 4.4

You can also change the format of a document without retyping. Here we've changed the body of the letter from single- to double-spacing.

If you change your mind about formatting, you can "undo" the change as easily as you implemented it.

You might be wondering what happened to the rest of the letter after changing to double-spacing. Don't worry, it's still there. Because the screen is smaller than a sheet of paper, you can see only a portion of the letter now. To see the rest of it, you must *scroll* through the document, which (as you may have guessed) is also a simple procedure.

Printing and Saving a Document

The final step in creating a document is to print it. Figure 4.5 shows the completed, printed letter (after reverting back to single-spacing in the body of the letter). As you can see, it looks exactly like the screen version—the only difference is that (obviously) it's printed on paper.

Figure 4.5

The final printed document, looking exactly as it did on the screen (except, of course, that you can see the whole letter).

```
July 17, 1994

Mrs. Adrian Smith
123 Oak Avenue
San Diego, CA 92123

Dear Mrs. Smith:

Thank you for your letter regarding our Hawaiian outer-island
tour packages. Currently we offer two travel packages with no
overnight stays on Oahu.

  Paradise Vacations' Outer Islands getaway; offering three days
    each on Maui, Kauai, and Hawaii

  Heavenly Cruises' Pristine Island Fun Pack; offering three days
    each on Maui, Molokai, and Kauai, traveling by boat between
    islands

The enclosed brochures describe these tour packages in more
detail. If you have any questions, or wish to make a
reservation, please feel free to call me at (800) 555-1234
during regular business hours.

Best regards,


Olivia Newton
```

To keep a copy of the letter on disk for future reference, or to make additional changes and/or corrections later, you can save the document. Again, these simple jobs can be handled with a few easy keystrokes or menu selections.

About Menu Selections

We mentioned the term "menu selections" a few times in the preceding sections, so let's talk about what that means. Basically, a computer menu, like a restaurant menu, is a set of choices. To view a menu on the screen, typically, you press some special key or click a mouse button.

There are different styles of menus, the most common of which is the *pull-down* or drop-down menu, so named because it appears to "pull down" or "drop down" from the top of the screen. Note that when the menu appears, often it temporarily obscures the text in your document, as shown in Figure 4.6.

NOTE

Each option on a menu is referred to as a **command**, because when you choose an option, you are commanding the computer to do something.

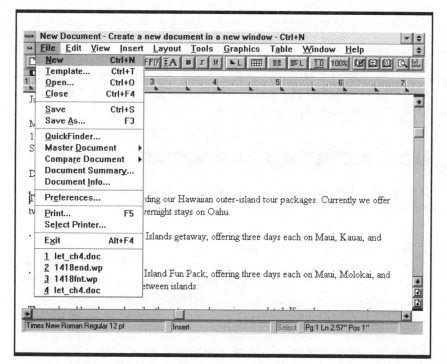

Figure 4.6

A pull-down menu on the screen displays "commands" to the computer from which you choose what you need. Each option in the menu bar at the top of the screen (e.g., File, Edit, Search, and so forth) has a separate pull-down menu from which you choose commands.

To choose an option from the menu, usually you can just click a mouse button or type in a key or combination of keys. Once you've made your selection, the command is carried out and the menu disappears, and you can see the text behind the menu once again. For example, if you were to choose Print from the menu shown in Figure 4.6, the letter on the screen would be printed, the menu would disappear, and the screen would become visible again, so that you would see the letter on-screen again.

Different programs work in slightly different ways but, generally, the basic procedure is the same. You type as you would with a typewriter, make changes and corrections as necessary, and print the final product whenever you are ready, using menu commands. It's all very quick and easy, once you get the hang of it, and not at all difficult to learn—even if you consider yourself something of a technoklutz.

Key Features: The Tools of the Trade

Not all word processing programs are created equal. Some are more powerful and flexible than others. It will be difficult for you to choose which word processing program is best for you if you don't know what features are available, and what they can do. So let's take some time to talk about what kinds of features you might want to look for when you go shopping for a word processing program.

Basic Typing Features

Typing is typing, but a good word processing program offers some features that make even the initial typing of the first draft a lot easier. Here are some key typing features to look for:

You're getting sleepy... sleeepy....

Print styles: Most word processors support basic print styles such as boldface, underline, italic, superscript, and subscript. For legal work, line numbering, strikeout, and redlining are also necessities. Other possibilities include double-underline, shadow, outline, and small capitals. Figure 4.7 shows examples of these different print styles. If you need these sorts of typographical characteristics, be aware that both your word processor *and* your printer must have the capability to print in the specific style.

Normal **Bold** <u>Underline</u>
<u>Double Underline</u> *Italic*
Outline **Shadow** Small Cap
Redline ~~Strikeout~~

Figure 4.7
Examples of print styles and special characters. If these will be useful in your work, you'll need both a word processing program and a printer that supports these features.

- • Bullet
- ○ Hollow Bullet
- ■ Square Bullet
- ☞ Right Pointing Index
- ✓ Check Mark
- ☐ Empty Ballot Box
- ☒ Marked Ballot Box
- £ Pound/Sterling
- ¥ Yen
- ¡ Inverted Exclamation
- ¿ Inverted Question Mark
- ¶ Paragraph Sign
- § Section Sign
- ® Registered Trademark
- © Copyright
- † Dagger
- ‡ Double Dagger
- ™ Trademark
- SM Servicemark
- ℞ Prescription (Rx)
- % Care of
- ‰ Per Thousand
- № Number (No.)
- ° Degree
- ♥ Heart

- ◊ Diamond
- ♣ Club
- ♠ Spade
- ♂ Male
- ♀ Female
- ✿ Compass
- ☺ Happy Face
- ☻ Dark Happy Face
- ☹ Sad Face
- ☎ Telephone
- ☻ Clock
- ⌛ Hourglass
- ↵ Carriage Return
- → Right Arrow
- ← Left Arrow
- ↑ Up Arrow
- ↓ Down Arrow
- ↔ Left and Right Arrow
- √ Bent Radical
- ± Plus or Minus
- ≤ Less Than/Equal

Special and foreign characters: Most word processing programs include a set of *special characters*, which fall outside the realm of the alphabetical and numeric characters on the keyboard. Some examples of these are shown beneath the print styles in Figure 4.7. If your work requires special characters, you will want a word processor *and* printer with these features.

Automatic hyphenation: With a word processing program you never have to worry again about the correct place to hyphenate a word at the end of the line. Is it comp-ute or com-pute? (It's the latter.) You can have an automatic hyphenation function that knows where to break words or you can turn this function off and not hyphenate the last words in your lines at all.

Tables: The ability to create and manage tables is a tremendously useful feature. A Table feature takes the guesswork out of setting up tab stops before you type your text into columns, because you can adjust the column widths to match the text *after* you've typed the text. Also, a Table feature usually gives you the option of using double- or single-lines, which lets you format professional looking tables, like the examples shown in Figure 4.8.

Equations: If your work involves writing or typing mathematical or scientific equations, you'll almost certainly want a word processing program with a built-in equations editor. Typically, you'll need a graphics printer as well. Incidentally, an equations editor will only let you type the equations—it won't solve them for you.

Editing Features

Once the first draft has been done, you may want to print it, check it, and mark it up to make some changes. Then you can bring the document back onto your screen and use the basic text insertion, deletion, and changing techniques to make your changes. Here are some other features that can help with editing and refining a document:

Cut and paste (or Moving and Copying): You can select ("highlight") any block of text, whether it is a letter, word, phrase, sentence, or several pages, and move or "copy" that text to a new place in the document, or to a different document. You can also delete that block of text.

Undelete: The ability to "undelete" deleted text is important. For example, suppose you select a large portion of text that you want to move to a different page, but you accidentally press the wrong key and delete the text instead. Yikes! With an undelete feature, however, you just press a key and presto, it's back!

Destination	Arrives	Ticket Price
Oceanside	8:30 am	$12.50
San Clemente	9:00 am	$17.50
Santa Ana	10:00 am	$37.50
Anaheim	10:30 am	$40.00
Los Angeles	11:45 am	$55.00
Malibu	1:00 pm	$70.00

Milk	A	Vitamin (mg)			
		B_1	B_2	B_6	B_{12}
Whole	307	.093	.395	.102	.871
Lowfat (2%)	500	.095	.403	.105	.888
Skim	500	.088	.343	.098	.926
Buttermilk	81	.083	.377	.083	.537
Condensed	1004	.275	1.27	.156	1.36
Evaporated	306	.059	.398	.063	.205
Chocolate	302	.092	.405	.1	.835

COMPARATIVE OPERATING EXPENSES

Division	1990	1991	% Change
North	1,980,870	2,780,870	40.4%
South	987,750	760,080	-23.1%
East	986,500	1,100,000	11.5%
West	1,275,000	987,000	-22.6%
Total	5,230,120	5,627,950	7.6%

Figure 4.8

Examples of documents produced with a Tables feature. The lines are attractive (but optional), and, most importantly, you can easily change the column widths to suit the text after you've typed the text. (The bottom table also incorporates different fonts, which are discussed later in this chapter.)

Undo: Although this feature sounds similar to "undelete," it's not. Undelete lets you recover only deleted text. Undo, on the other hand, allows you to "undo" any recent change to a document. For example, if you changed a whole document to uppercase, undo would let you change it right back.

Search and replace: This feature finds a given word or phrase and replaces it with another. For example, if you accidentally misspelled the name "Smythe" as "Smith" throughout your document, you could tell your word processor to "replace every Smith with Smythe," rather than go through the document line-by-line and make each change yourself.

Spelling checker: This is an extremely useful feature. It not only points out your misspelled words but can also help you find the correct spelling.

Thesaurus: This feature helps you find the right word without having to look it up in a paper thesaurus or a dictionary of synonyms and antonyms. A handy tool for writers.

Product at a Glance

WordPerfect 6.0 for Windows and WordPerfect 6.0 for DOS

Publisher:
WordPerfect Corporation

Suggested Retail Price:
$495-Windows/$495-DOS

Upgrade Price:
$99-Windows/$129-DOS

Windows Requires:
80386 processor or higher
6MB RAM
Windows 3.1 or later
32MB free hard disk space for full installation
VGA or better graphics monitor
Mouse recommended

DOS Requires:
80286 processor, 80386 recommended
520K RAM
DOS 6.0 or memory management software
16MB free hard disk space
VGA or better graphics monitor

Description:

These full-powered programs are now the most widely used word processors. They have the greatest range of features in the industry, including Grammatik, fax support, footnotes, equations, tables, math, WYSIWYG fonts and graphics, labels, multicolumn layout, legal formatting, and large document assembly. They also have pulldown menus, mouse support, and excellent technical support. Versions are available for Macintosh, Apple II, and Amiga systems as well as Data General, VAX, and Unix-based systems. Foreign language versions are also available.

Formatting Features

A good word processor offers many features for formatting the appearance of a document. In addition to the basic margin, tab stop, and spacing settings available in most word processors, you might want to look for the following features:

Automatic page numbering: A good package will let you number pages automatically and place those page numbers anywhere that you specify on the page.

Headers and footers: This feature lets you put a header or footer (text that identifies the manuscript) on every page, or a different header and footer on facing pages, and have that header and/or footer automatically appear on every printed page that follows.

Justification: You don't need to count letters and spaces to automatically left-, right-, center-, or fully justify text if you use a word processor. Just press the proper keys or buttons, type your text, and let the program do the work.

Large document assembly: If you create large documents with tables of contents, tables of authorities (used in legal documents), indexes, bibliographies, figure lists, table lists, and so forth, you'll want a word processing program that makes it easy for you to create and manage these various elements. The best ones let you place a "hidden mark" on words, headings, phrases, figures, and tables in the text as you work, to identify the current word(s) as a table of contents entry, or whatever it happens to be. When you have finished creating and editing your document, you press a couple of keys and presto: the program generates the table of contents, index, lists, and so forth, automatically. Even if you later insert or delete text, and the page numbers change, that poses no problem. You just press the magic key or button again, and all the lists will be updated.

Footnotes and endnotes: Every typist agrees that footnotes and endnotes (particularly footnotes) are a bane. If the documents you create require footnotes or endnotes, be sure to get a word processing program that supports these features—they're worth their weight in diamonds. For example, with a good footnoting feature, you just type your footnotes into little hidden boxes at the point in your text where the footnote is referenced. Later, when you print the document, the program automatically figures out how much room is needed for all of the footnotes on a page, and correctly prints the footnotes where they belong. Insert another footnote and the program renumbers the ones that follow for you. Add or delete text in a footnote and the program adjusts the pages so that everything's on the correct page.

Nonstandard page sizes: If your printer has the ability to handle nonstandard page sizes, such as envelopes, legal-sized paper, labels, checks, and half-sheets, you'll want your word processing program to be able to use these features as well.

Print preview: As mentioned earlier, your screen can show only about three-quarters of a page at a time. A print preview feature lets you see how an entire page, or several pages, will look when printed. For example, Figure 4.9 shows facing pages as viewed on the Word for Windows print preview screen.

Figure 4.9

A Word for Windows print preview screen display of facing pages in a sample document. This screen lets you see what complete pages look like, so you can make any necessary changes before printing.

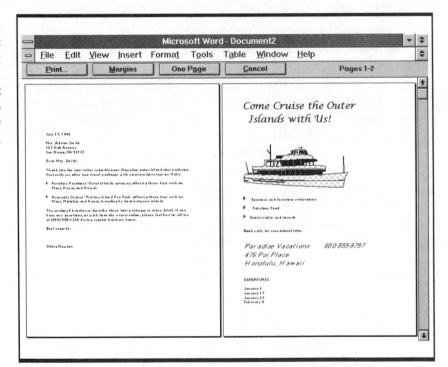

Desktop Publishing Features

Recently, the distinction between desktop publishing programs (see Chapter 5) and word processors has become a lot less clear. Today, word processing programs offer most of the features previously found only in desktop publishing programs. Figures 4.10 and 4.11 illustrate two versions of the same document. Figure 4.10 is a plain word processing document; Figure 4.11 is the same document spruced up with desktop publishing features, including fonts, columns, and graphics.

```
                    Another BRIGHT IDEA from BulbCo

                       A Lightbulb Guaranteed
                        to Last a Lifetime

Your life or the bulb's (we're betting on the bulb, by the way).
That's right, with BulbCo's new Perennial Lightbulb you and your
descendants will never again need to replace another lightbulb.
Sure, these babies cost almost $300 apiece, and we don't recommend
juggling with them, but think of the savings!

                    They Pay for Themselves in
                      Just Ten Years (Or So)

Waitaminit! you're thinking now, these lightbulbs we're talking
about here cost a fortune!  Well, sure they do, at first.  You can
get a lightbulb from one of the other guys for just over one-
hundredth of the cost but just think, in six months to two years
(see chart, above), you'll be browsing through the hardware store
looking for another replacement.  Add it up for yourself,  in
twenty, twenty-five, fifty years ...tops... our Perennial bulbs
will have paid for themselves.

                    Breakage Insurance Available

So, what's in it for BulbCo, you may wonder.  Well, first, we
should point out that we're going to do land-office business with
this product.  Planned obsolescence? Pfuui!  Give us a good, solid
(unbeatable, that is) product and just let us sell 'em one at a
time.  Of course, however, you are going to want to protect your
investment.  We'll guarantee these lightbulbs for a lifetime, yours
or theirs, as we've asserted, but we'll only guarantee that they'll
continue operating as long as they remain intact.  If that sounds
to you like that might be a big if, you're right.  You drop one of
our Perennials on the linoleum and you've dropped about three
hundred dollars and smashed them into shards all over your kitchen
floor.  Give one of our Perennials to baby to use as a rattle.
Shake, shake, shake, and there goes the filament.  We build 'em
sturdy, but, face it, they're lightbulbs.

                          Easy Terms

So what are we going to do for you?  Glad you asked.  We'll insure
every single one of your lightbulbs for a small premium, ranging
from $.50 a year for the 30-watt model to a still-negligible $1.97
a year for our superpowerful 250-watt bulbs.  See the table to the
left for details.
```

Figure 4.10

A sample word-processed document shown without any desktop publishing features.

Figure 4.11

The sample word-processed document spruced up with desktop publishing features, including fonts, graphics, and tables.

Another *BRIGHT IDEA* from *BULBCO*

A Lightbulb Guaranteed to Last a Lifetime

Your life or the bulb's (we're betting on the bulb, by the way). That's right, with BulbCo's new Perennial Lightbulb you and your descendants will never again need to replace another lightbulb. Sure, these babies cost almost $300 apiece, and we don't recommend juggling with them, but think of the savings!

They Pay for Themselves in Just Ten Years (Or So)

Waitaminit! you're thinking now, these lightbulbs we're talking about here cost a fortune! Well, sure they do, at first. You can get a lightbulb from one of the other guys for just over one-hundredth of the cost but just think, in six months to two years (see chart, above), you'll be browsing through the hardware store looking for another replacement. Add it up for yourself, in twenty, twenty-five, fifty years ...tops... our Perennial bulbs will have paid for themselves.

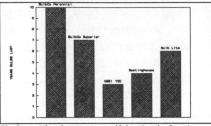

The Perennial outlasts even our old favorite, the Superior, and makes mincemeat of the competition. (The chart only shows ten years projected, but the Perennial will, of course, last forever.)

Breakage Insurance Available

So, what's in it for BulbCo, you may wonder. Well, first, we should point out that we're going to do land-office business with this product. Planned obsolescence? Pfuui! Give us a good, solid (unbeatable, that is) product and just let us sell 'em one at a time. Of course, however, you are going to want to protect your investment. We'll guarantee these lightbulbs for a lifetime, yours or theirs, as we've asserted, but we'll only guarantee that they'll continue operating **as long as they remain intact.** If that sounds to you like that might be a big if, you're right. You drop one of our Perennials on the linoleum and you've dropped about three hundred dollars and smashed them into shards all over your kitchen floor. Give one of our Perennials to baby to use as a rattle. Shake, shake, shake, and there goes the filament. We build 'em sturdy, but, face it, they're lightbulbs.

Easy Terms

So what are we going to do for you? Glad you asked. We'll insure every single one of your lightbulbs for a small premium, ranging from $.50 a year for the 30-watt model to a still-negligible $1.97 a year for our superpowerful 250-watt bulbs. See the table to the left for details.

Insurance Rates

Model	Premium	Deductible
30 watt	$.50	$25
75 watt	$.75	$35
100 watt	$.99	$50
150 watt	$1.49	$70
250 watt	$1.97	$99

Fonts: Basically, a font is a typeface. For example, Courier is a "type-writer" style font. Newspapers often use the Times font for text, and Helvetica for headlines. Invitations, announcements, and display ads often use more decorative fonts (see the examples in Figure 4.12). In general, word processing programs come with a range of fonts already installed. In addition, your printer may be equipped with additional fonts and you can buy as many others as your heart desires and your pocketbook can bear.

Graphics: If you want to create documents that include graphics, then you must be sure to choose a word processing program that allows you to embed graphics in text (unless you have a desktop publishing program to do this for you). Most programs come with a selection of sample graphics. You can create or obtain additional graphics from other sources including scanners, video "frame grabbers," clip-art libraries, paint programs, spreadsheets, and graphics programs. (See Chapter 6 for more on graphics programs.)

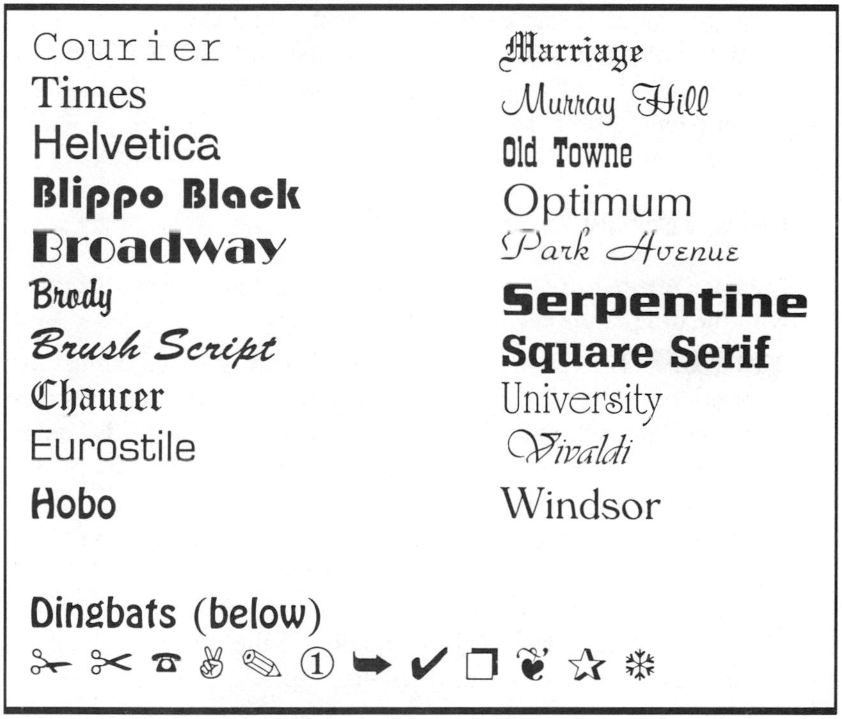

Figure 4.12
This figure illustrates examples of various fonts.

Courier
Times
Helvetica
Blippo Black
Broadway
Brody
Brush Script
Chaucer
Eurostile
Hobo

Marriage
Murray Hill
Old Towne
Optimum
Park Avenue
Serpentine
Square Serif
University
Vivaldi
Windsor

Dingbats (below)

Multiple columns: A word processing program that supports columns can greatly simplify the task of formatting text into *newspaper style* (snaking) columns (used in newspapers and newsletters), or parallel columns (as in this book, where the main text is in this column, and the notes are in the margin columns.)

Style sheets: A style sheet lets you define a style for each element of your document. For example, if you are writing an article that uses main topic and subtopic headings, you could define the following three styles for your document:

Main Heading	Helvetica Boldface 18 pt.
Subheading	Helvetica 16 pt.
Body	Times Roman 12 pt.

In this case, each style is actually a font (typeface, style, and point size). As you write your article, you simply activate the styles as you need them—turning on the Main Heading style before typing a main heading, and the Body style before typing the body text. If you decide you don't like the look of your main headings, you don't have to go back to change each one. Instead, you make the change in the style, which will automatically change all the main headings in your document. It's a terrific feature for making finished documents with consistent, repeated design elements.

Interface Features

Interface features are those that have to do with the way that you work with the program. They include the following:

On-line help: A good on-line (built-in) help system is a must for beginners and just as useful for experienced users who need reminders on how to use obscure features. On-line help typically comes in one of two varieties. *Context-sensitive help* means that when you press the Help key, you receive help with whatever feature you happen to be using at the moment. *Indexed help* requires you to look up a feature on an alphabetical list, just as you'd look up information in the index of a book. Context-sensitive help is better because it doesn't require you to guess what name the program's designers have given to the problem you're having.

Multiple documents: This feature lets you work on two or more documents at the same time. This can be extremely useful if you want to compare an original version with a revised version, or if you often want to copy text from one document to another.

Math: If you type financial reports, invoices, or other types of documents involving calculations, a built-in math feature for basic totals, subtotals, and other such calculations is very handy. You just type in the numbers and the program calculates and displays the results automatically.

Import/Export files: If you share text with people who use a different kind of word processor than you do, this feature's ability to import text from, and export it to, other word processing programs' formats is important.

Background printing/spooling: Background printing (or print spooling) is practically a must with word processing. It means that your whole program does not come to a grinding halt and become unusable while you are printing a document. Instead, the program just stacks up all the documents that you've decided to print and allows you to continue writing and editing other documents while it prints those that are in the printing queue.

Macros: Basically, a macro is a set of prerecorded keystrokes that you can play back at any time. For example, if you constantly need to type your company name, address, and phone number into your documents, you can record those keystrokes as a macro. Then, you attach that macro to some short name or special keystroke, such as Alt-C. In the future, when you need to "play back" those recorded keystrokes, you just press Alt-C. Using macros saves a lot of time and labor.

Mail/Document merge: This feature allows you combine information from two documents into a new, third document. One very common use for this feature is to combine a form letter with a name-and-address list so the final letter can be individually addressed to a large number of people.

Which Features Do I Need the Most?

The answer to that question depends mainly on the type of word processing you intend to do. The following list should help you to decide your answer:

Home/Personal: If you just write occasional letters, short school papers, memos, menus, diaries, and other such small documents, you don't need a fancy or expensive word processing program. The important features to look for include a good on-line help menu, simple editing/formatting menus, and perhaps a good spelling checker.

Office/Secretarial: For the office, where you need to produce letters, memos, short documents, and so forth, you can probably get by with the same basic features that will satisfy the home/personal user, but you also may want to look for a macro feature to help speed your repetitive work. If you frequently mail form letters, look for a merge feature, and also look for a word processing program and printer that will support printing envelopes and mailing labels. A laser printer might also be a good investment, to create a more professional appearance for your documents.

Legal/Attorneys: Legal word processing requires special formats used by lawyers, legal secretaries, and paralegals. In law offices, the emphasis often falls on making very quick changes to existing legal documents. Look for a word processing program (and printer) that supports redlining, strikeout, and special characters. Automatic cross-referencing (particularly Tables of Authorities and line numbering) will be very useful. For repetitive invoicing, mail merge and macro features might prove extremely useful.

Academic/Scientific: Students and professors who publish in professional journals create some of the most heavily referenced documents in our culture. Look for automatic referencing features such as tables of contents, indexes, footnotes, endnotes, page numbering, headers, footers, justification, and tables. If your work involves mathematical or scientific equations, an equations editor is a must.

Writing/Publishing: For writing, you'll want a good spelling checker and thesaurus, and perhaps a grammar checker and readability program. For technical documentation, you may need tables, special characters and print styles, and perhaps an equations editor. If you are responsible for producing the final copy, look for desktop-publishing features including graphics, fonts, and multicolumn formats. And be sure to get a good printer.

How Am I Going to Learn All This?

Now that you've looked at these lists of capabilities, you're probably horrified at the prospect of learning all this stuff. But it's not nearly as difficult as you might think. Remember, you don't have to learn everything at once. For example, you can learn all the basic typing and editing techniques in a fairly short time. That alone will increase your productivity dramatically.

From there, you can focus on more advanced features on an as-needed basis. Every feature, be it formatting, graphics, fonts, or whatever, usually just takes a few simple steps to implement—there really is no complicated programming or weird technobabble that you have to master.

Text versus Graphical Interface in Word Processing

Like operating systems (and everything else) in the ongoing computer revolution, word processing programs are available either in a text-based or a graphics-based interface. If you have a graphics-based system, such as a Mac or a PC with Windows, you will probably want to choose a GUI (graphical user interface) word processor.

NOTE

For more information on icons and the general differences between graphical and text-based interfaces, see Chapter 3.

Word 2.0c for Windows and Word 6.0 for DOS

Product at a Glance

Publisher:
Microsoft Corporation

Suggested Retail Price:
$495-Windows/$450-DOS

Upgrade Price:
$129-Windows/$99-DOS

Windows Requires:
286 processor
640K RAM plus 256K extended
Windows 3.0 or later
5MB free hard disk space
Mouse recommended
DOS Requires:
8088 or 8086 Processor
384K RAM
DOS 3.0 or later

Description

Microsoft Word has long been the most popular word processing program for the Macintosh and has been very successful on IBM-compatible computers since its introduction to those systems. Word has consistently been a leader in both sales and computer magazine reviews. It is, in a Word, a powerhouse word processing program that offers just about any feature that you could possibly need for working with short or long documents. Word provides style sheets, multicolumn text flow, strong drawing tools, outlining, fast envelope printing, and graphics capabilities.

Word 5.1 for Macintosh

Product at a Glance

Publisher:
Microsoft Corporation

Suggested Retail Price:
$495-Macintosh

Requires:
5MB free hard disk space
Mac Plus or better
1MB RAM for System 6.0.x, 2MB for
** Grammar Checker**
3MB RAM for System 7.x, 4MB for
** Grammar Checker**

Description:

Long the standard in word processing programs for the Macintosh, Word continues to add features as fast as users can ask for them. Word has consistently been a leader in both sales and computer magazine reviews. It is, in a Word, a powerhouse word processing program that offers just about any feature that you could possibly need for working with short or long documents. Word provides intelligent toolbars, text annotations, QuickTime support, bundled Microsoft Graph, outlining, fast envelope printing, even/odd page printing for 2-sided printouts, battery usage meter for use with PowerBooks, and graphics capabilities.

The main advantage of a graphical word processor is that you can see the fonts and graphics on your screen as you add them to your document (see Figure 4.13). In a text-based word processing program, you have to switch to "Print Preview" mode to get a reasonable facsimile of your printed page.

On the other hand, of course, if fonts, graphics, and other desktop-publishing features are not important in your work, you can probably save a lot of money on both hardware and software by using a simpler text-based word processing program, and a relatively inexpensive (nongraphics) printer.

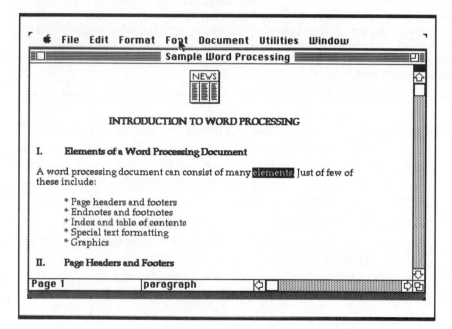

Figure 4.13

A graphical user interface lets you see fonts and graphics right on the edit screen. This figure shows Microsoft Word on the Mac. Similar programs are available for PCs using Windows.

What Are the Popular Word Processing Programs?

There are lots and lots of word processing programs available, as a trip to your local software or computer store, or a quick glance at the ads in a

Ami Pro 3.0 for Windows

Product at a Glance

Publisher:
Lotus Development Corporation

Suggested Retail Price:
$495

Upgrade Price:
$99.95

Requires:
DOS 3.1 or later
5 MB free hard disk space
286 processor
2MB RAM
Windows 3.0 or later

Description:

This program offers a full range of word processing features. In addition, Ami Pro does more to help the user create a document than any other program on the market and it offers such strong drawing and charting features that you might be able to get by without separate packages for these needs. It can even improve on some imported graphics by adjusting contrasts and smoothing edges. It also has strong table and file management functions.

NOTE

See our "Product at a Glance" reviews sprinkled throughout this chapter for some ideas about what's currently available on the market.

computer magazine, will prove. And like all software products, their features can range from the "no-frills" bare minimum to the ultra-powerful. In price, they can range from $50.00 to $500.00 or more, with the price as a fairly good indicator of how many features the product has, and how much hardware you'll need to run it.

One fact is clear: There's a word processing program available to suit just about everyone, whether you use the program for personal, corporate, legal, professional, or publishing applications. With a little research, you can find one that's within your budget and right for you.

Five

Desktop Publishing

* * * * * * * * * * * * * * * * * * * *

Until the advent of the computer revolution, much of the work of publishing was done by hand. Type was set on a machine but the actual creation of a page was done on a table by a person wielding typeset galleys, glue, and a razor blade.

The modern publisher has streamlined the publishing process and cut costs and production time by using a computer and desktop publishing technology. Using text from a word processor's file, the publisher arranges it with computer-generated graphics to create publications of professional quality. All of the cutting, pasting, and cropping formerly done by hand are now done electronically inside the computer with the use of the mouse and keyboard. Different typefaces, leading, columns, page designs, and virtually everything else that goes into the typesetting and page layout process can be done with desktop publishing software.

What Is Desktop Publishing?

Desktop publishing (DTP) is done with specialized software that can take nearly everything else produced by other programs on your computer—words, pictures, charts, graphs, and tables—and combine them into fully designed pages. DTP provides all the tools required to design and typeset anything from a newsletter to a book. Figure 5.1 shows a typical desktop-published document.

In this chapter, we'll cover the basics of DTP and the programs that do the basics and more.

In a typical DTP program, you can do the following tasks:

- Bring in text from a word processing program.
- Bring in pictures and drawings from graphics programs.
- Create documents that are many pages long, with the text flowing automatically from page to page.
- Display a single page, part of a page, or facing pages on the screen to see how they will look when you print them.
- Set up headers, footers, page numbers, logos, and anything else that you want to repeat automatically on every page.
- Use built-in drawing tools to create lines, squares, circles, rectangles, and fill patterns to dress up any page.
- Specify different typefaces (e.g., Helvetica, Times Roman), type sizes (e.g., 10-point, 12-point), and type styles (e.g., bold, underline, italic, expanded, condensed) for individual words, sentences, paragraphs, or throughout the entire document.

If you read Chapter 4, you know that everything in the above list is available in many word-processing packages. However, if you want to do high-level graphics editing, color separations, and color printing, you may need the specialized tools provided by a DTP program.

INSECT LOVER

Figure 5.1

With DTP software, it's easy to design professional-looking documents, such as newsletters. (We are using Latin so that you can see the format without being distracted by the text.)

Butterflies are Back!

In se perpetuo Tempus as revolubile gyro Iam revocat Zephyros, vere tepente, novos. Induiturque brev Tellus reparata iuventam, Iamque soluta gelu dulce virescit humus. Fallor? an et nobis redeunt in carmina vires, Ingeniumque mihi munere veris adest? Munere veris adest, iterumque vigescit ab illo (Quis putet?) atque aliquod iam sibi poscit opus.

Castalis ante osculos, bifid umque cacumen oberrat. Pyrenen somnia nocte ferunt. Concitaquuq arcano fervent mihi pectora motu, Et furor,

et sonitus. Head 1 Me sacer intus agit. Delius ipse venit. Iam mihi mens liquidi raptatur in ardua caeli, Perque vagas nubes corpore liber eo. Perque umbras, perque antra feror, penetralia vatum; Et mihi fana patent interiora Deum. Intuiturque animus toto quic agatur Olympo, Nec fug-iunt oculos Tartara caeca meos.

Quid tam grande sonat distento spiritus ore? Quid parit haec rabies, quid sacer iste furor? Veris, io! rediere vices; celebremus honores Veris, et hoc subeat Musa perennis opus. Iam sol, Aethiopas fugiens Tithoniaque arva, Flectit ad Arctoas aurea lora plagas. Head 1 Est breve noctis iter, brevis est mora noctis opacae, Horrida cum tenebris exulat illa suis.

Iamque Lycaonius plaustrum caeleste Botes Non longa sequirtur fessus ut ante via, Nunc etiam solitas circum Iovis atria toto Excubias agitant sidera rara polo. Nam dolus et caedes, et vis cum nocte recessit, Neve Giganteum Dii timuere scelus.Perque umbras, perque antra feror, penetralia vatum; Et mihi fana patent interiora Deum. Intuiturque

Uses of Desktop Publishing

DTP programs can be used for any project in which the final goal is a well-designed page. These include business cards and reports, letterhead stationery, fliers, newsletters, printed forms, proposals, advertisements, annual reports, brochures, posters, manuals, and last but not least, magazines and books.

What Do I Need for Desktop Publishing?

DTP combines several computer-produced documents. Thus, it has the most extensive and usually the most expensive hardware/software requirements. A DTP system should include the following (starred [*] items are optional):

- a DTP program
- an operating system that will run that program
- a fast and powerful computer
- as much computer memory as you can afford, but certainly no less than 8MB
- a hard disk with 120MB or more of storage
- a high-resolution graphics screen and a video card with 1MB of RAM
- a keyboard
- a mouse
- a small hand-held scanner to copy pictures*
- a laser-quality printer
- a compatible word processing program
- a graphics program to produce pictures and drawings
- a spreadsheet/graphics program to produce charts and graphs*
- clip art pictures to import into your documents
- a font program to tell the printer which typefaces to print*

For more ambitious projects requiring sophisticated output, you should consider the following items as well:

- a full-page or two-page graphics monitor
- a full-page scanner
- color graphics capabilities
- a font editing program
- an image enhancement program to touch up photographs
- a full-blown laser printer with PostScript capabilities
- a professional-quality typesetting machine*

Now, let's find out what can be done with DTP and how we can use it.

Mac vs. IBM

Desktop publishing was created with the arrival of the Apple Macintosh in the early 1980s. *PageMaker* for the Macintosh introduced the concept of creating finished pages that integrated text and graphics. As the best-selling DTP program of all time, PageMaker is routinely used as the standard against which other desktop publishing programs are measured.

In the past few years IBM-based DTP programs have greatly improved—they are easier to use and have more attractive user interfaces. By exploiting the power of new graphic interfaces, IBM-compatible programs such as *Ventura Publisher* and the IBM-compatible version of *PageMaker* itself have made the IBM a viable DTP system. Today, the IBM-based programs offer the same power and ease-of-use pioneered by the Mac.

Although file types are fairly standard on the Macintosh and can be imported into DTP software, no such standard was developed for IBM-based programs. As a result, you need to make sure that your DTP program and graphics program(s) will work together *before* you make your purchase.

Using a Desktop Publishing Program

NOTE

It's a good idea to take a look at professionally produced publications, such as magazines, books, brochures, and newspapers, to get a feel for how graphics and text best go together.

The easiest way to explain what a DTP program can do is to show you. This section will illustrate how to create the simple newsletter that was shown in Figure 5.1. We will use *PageMaker* as the DTP tool, and we'll go through some basic steps to show how DTP programs work.

Page Setup

The first step in page design is to decide what the page size and the margin widths are going to be. Figure 5.2 shows a page in PageMaker. The bar across the top is a ruler measured in *picas,* which is a common measuring unit in typesetting. However, DTP programs allow you to use just about any measuring system you want.

Figure 5.2

The first page elements you design are the paper size and margins.

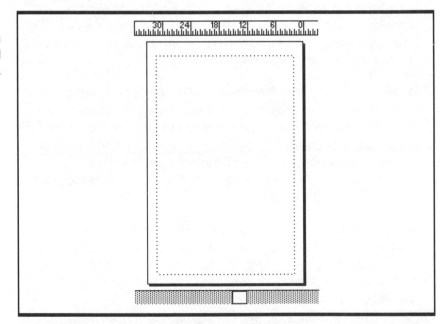

Setting Parameters

Once you have the basic outline for a page, the next step is to set the page's boundaries, margins, and graphics locations. This involves deciding where the text and graphics will be placed. A good DTP system displays nonprinting lines on the screen to guide your placement of text and graphics.

Making a Masthead

Once your basic page design is established, the next step is to put in all of the text and graphics. Most of the text in the body of the document will have been done on a word processor, but special design elements such as mastheads usually are done with a text tool provided in DTP software. The masthead for our fictional newsletter was done within the guidelines we had laid down. To create it, we used a boldfaced font and made the four middle letters of "Insect" into superscript. Using another block of text, we added the word "Lover." The spacing in "Lover" was stretched by using the spacing functions in PageMaker as shown in Figure 5.3.

Figure 5.3
Using the DTP program's text tool, a masthead is created.

Creating Styles

One of the time-saving features of DTP programs is the ability to create a style and then use it over and over again. In Figure 5.4, the headline is created as a style and placed in an on-screen style palette. This makes it easy to switch from style to style without having to redefine all of the elements that make up the style. By selecting the paragraph and clicking on a style with the mouse pointer, any style that you have defined will change the text to that style's parameters. For example, the headline in our sample newsletter uses a 30-point, Avant Garde, boldfaced, centered style.

Figure 5.4
Once you have defined a style, you can use it over and over again.

Importing Text

Once a page has been designed, most of the remaining work for any DTP program is to import the text into your document. A DTP program like PageMaker will allow you to enter text either one page at a time or as multiple pages. Figure 5.5 shows how two blocks of text in our sample newsletter were imported from a word processor.

Placing Graphics

Like text, graphics can be imported from compatible graphic files. Desktop publishing software can resize and crop graphics that are too large or too small when imported. Figure 5.6 shows a butterfly that is far too large to fit into the space we've left on the page. However, as you'll see, not only can we easily rearrange the text and position of the space, we also can resize and crop the butterfly to fit the space.

Final Cutting and Pasting

Now all that's left to do is to get the butterfly in place and add a caption. The text has been rearranged by lifting the bottom of the text block on the left and letting it automatically flow into the right column. This creates a space in the left column. Using the available tools, we shrink the butterfly to fit into the space. Also, even though there is no drawing seen, part of the graphic overlaps to the right column. So using the cropping tool, we cut the graphic area. (We could have cropped the butterfly image itself if we wanted.)

Figure 5.6

Graphics imported into a DTP
page may not be the correct
size for the document.

Finally, we write a caption under the butterfly. We don't need to worry
about specifying its font, placement, and so on, because we have a style
that defines these characteristics for all captions. Figure 5.7 shows the final positioning and the tools used to complete the page.

Figure 5.7

All of the tools provided in
DTP software give the user
ample power to complete
professional-looking documents.

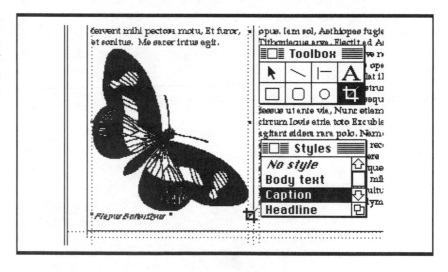

Key Features: The Tools of the Trade

Desktop publishing programs have hundreds of tools for designing final documents like the sample newsletter. Nearly all of these tools are geared toward manipulating words, pictures, and pages until the user sees on the screen the document that will be sent to the printer as a finished product. Let's examine these important tools.

Document Layout Features

In desktop publishing, the goal is a polished final document. The features examined here are those that are used to create the overall look and style of the document:

Column formatting: The ability to separate a single page into several columns, much as newspapers do. Columns don't have to be the same size. The number and size of columns, along with margins, depend on the page size, the type of publication, the audience, and the "feel" that you want to generate.

Automatic text flow: The process of allowing the text, usually your main story, to flow automatically from page to page and around pictures, headlines, and anything else you want to put on a page. Some DTP programs use a "linked block" format in which the user tells the program to have the text go from this box to this box to that box. Other programs create a single multipage master document and the text automatically flows from one page to the next and around any boxes that have been set aside for pictures or graphs.

Automatic page insertion: DTP programs can accommodate added material in either of two ways. Some automatically create as many pages as are needed to hold the text that you import initially, and then add pages automatically as you add text or graphics. Others ask you to define a total number of pages and then hold any text that doesn't fit in an "overflow" file for later manipulation.

NOTE

When first starting to design a document, remember that less is usually better. No more than two or three fonts should be used in a design. You don't want your publication to look like a ransom note.

You're getting sleepy... sleeepy....

Automatic numbering: A feature to automatically number pages, chapters, figures, tables, charts, graphs, and other elements.

Repeating elements: These items are set up once and then repeated on every page or every other page of the document. Headers and footers are examples of a repeating element.

Page sizing: You can have either a *portrait* orientation (higher than it is wide) or a *landscape* orientation (wider than it is high). You can have it printed either way on a standard $8\frac{1}{2}" \times 11"$ sheet of paper. Or you can design a page that will be reduced to 6" wide × 8" high or any other dimensions you specify. Some programs even allow you to create a document larger than you can print, such as a poster, and then print it in page-size pieces called "tiles" that can be pasted together.

Tables of Contents: Some DTP programs will create tables of contents automatically. If you add or delete section heads, you simply instruct the program to generate a new table of contents.

Indexing: Some DTP programs create an index. You must specify whether you want an entry to be a main entry or a subentry under something else. When you give the command to create an index, the indexing routine will go through an entire manuscript—including linked files—and create an index for you.

Footnoting: The ability to link footnote material to a word in the page text above. If you insert other text, and the word to which the footnote is linked moves to another page, then the footnote also moves.

Widow/Orphan control: Widows are single words or lines at the end of a page or column, and orphans are single words or lines at the beginning of a page or column. Both detract from a page's appearance and can be automatically prevented by most DTP programs.

Rulers: Rulers are graphical displays that look just like real rulers. Typically, they display across the top and down the side of the page to help you position objects. Figure 5.8 shows one example of how rulers are used.

Snap-to-grid: A method for creating guides on the page for text or graphics. The snap-to-grid command causes any text or graphic to line up with the grid lines. This is very handy for aligning text and graphics to create clean, precise pages. The grid lines are used to lay out the page, but they do not print.

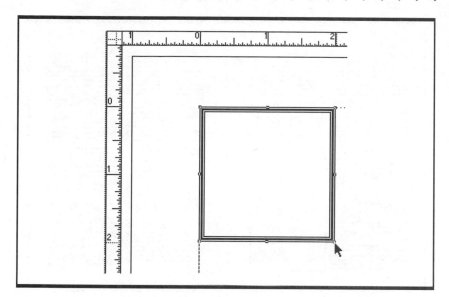

Page display (and zooming): A menu option that displays your document in different views: normal size, enlarged size, reduced full-page size, or further reduced facing-page size (this last option lets you "stand back" and look at your pages together). Figure 5.9 shows a facing-page view in one desktop program. Some programs also provide a zooming feature that allows you to magnify part of a document to work on small changes.

NOTE
To fine-tune a page and place the components exactly where you want them, zoom in to enlarge the page to 200 percent.

Text Features

Much of the power of DTP lies in the ability to change the size, style, and look of the words in the document. Because most DTP programs require seamless integration with a word processing program, it's very important that the two programs work well together. How the DTP program works with all the typefaces available is of even greater importance. Most of the features that are discussed next are related to working with the text in a DTP document:

Screen fonts: It's important to understand that the fonts you see on-screen are only rough representations of what you will see on the printed page. In fact, it's best to think of having two different sets of fonts, one for your screen and another in your laser printer. Programs

Figure 5.9

This figure shows a view of facing pages in a DTP program, which is very useful for seeing what individual pages look like opposite each other. In this case, the user might well decide that one or more of the graphics should be moved to achieve a better balance.

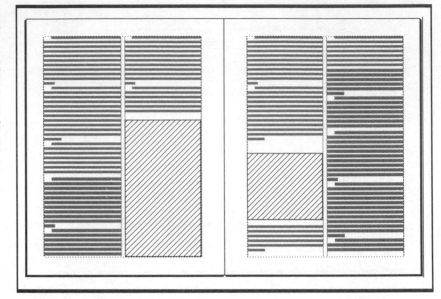

like the Adobe Type Manager, used with both IBM-compatibles and Macintoshes, help you see more clearly on the screen what will be printed, but remember that a laser printer's output looks a lot better than what you see on-screen.

Retention of word processor formats: How well does the DTP program retain the basic formatting codes that were set up by the word processor? Does the DTP program retain the tabs, indents, typefaces, and basic type styles? If it doesn't, it can make your life a lot tougher.

Text styles: Even when the DTP program retains type styles from the word processor, there's usually a need to make further changes once you see the text on-screen in a page format. Nearly all DTP programs allow you to set type in many different formats.

Style sheets: A DTP program's style sheet works like a word processor's. Essentially, it defines the characteristics of paragraphs. If the style sheet is applied to the paragraph, all of the previously defined characteristics of the style sheet are applied automatically to the selected paragraph. If a change is made in the style sheet, every paragraph with a given style sheet definition will change as well. This allows the user to easily make changes throughout a whole document.

Chapter 5: Desktop Publishing

About Fonts

One of your DTP design considerations will be which font to use. A *font* is a set of letters, numbers, and other characters having a consistent style and size. The size of a typeface is measured in points, with a point being $1/72$ " high. A 10-point font is $10/72$" high.

The instructions that tell a printer how to print a particular font can come from any of three sources:

- they are built into the printer when it's made
- from cartridges that are inserted into the printer
- from software programs that tell the printer what to print

Fonts are drawn by special computer languages called "page description languages." The most powerful language is called Post-Script, and the best laser printers can use a large library of PostScript fonts. Most Hewlett-Packard printers use a language called "PCL" (Page Control Language) that creates fonts for Hewlett-Packard and compatible printers. When considering the purchase of a printer, be sure to find out what type of page description language it uses.

A newer font technology, called TrueType, now competes with PostScript fonts. It offers the advantage of being able to print on PostScript and non-PostScript printers, as well as being able to show you on-screen what your font looks like. Most PostScript fonts are only printer fonts; they will not appear on-screen unless you are running Adobe Type Manager.

Be forewarned: the acquisition of fonts can be addictive! I personally know poor wretches with *hundreds* of fonts on their hard drives and still they search for more. It's sad but true.

Feed Me

Letter spacing and kerning: The design of each font includes a certain amount of space between the letters of a word. The program fine-tunes this space to justify lines of type, but you may also have to adjust it for aesthetic reasons. You can do so either locally or (in some programs) for the font as a whole. *Kerning* is an adjustment, also controllable through software, between pairs of letters whose shapes cause the standard letter spacing to look too tight or too loose.

Line spacing (leading): Most DTP programs give the user control over just how much space there will be between one line of text and the next line.

Word spacing: Most DTP programs allow the user to reduce or increase the spacing *between* words to create a tighter or looser look.

Text rotation: This is the ability of a program to shift the alignment of text, usually in 90-degree increments. For example, instead of having a headline running across the top of a page, it could run down the side of the page, and you would have to turn the page on its side to read it. Figure 5.10 shows how rotated text can be used in a flyer.

Greeking: This is a way to display text on-screen so that you see just the relative shape of the text lines (or graphic) but not individual letters. (The body text in Figure 5.10 is an example of Greeking.) This is a fast way to view the "look and feel" of the overall page because

Figure 5.10
Flipping the text vertically, the flyer announcement is right in the middle of the flyer to get the reader's attention.

the program doesn't have to stop and draw each character. With most programs you can set the type size for this process. For example, you can specify only characters that are typewriter sized (10-point) and larger to appear on-screen. All smaller type is Greeked. (Many programs also allow you to Greek pictures so that the program doesn't have to stop and draw them, which is an even greater time saver.)

Spell check: This will find all the misspelled words in your document and, like word processor spellers, most programs will offer you spelling alternatives for each word. This can be extremely important because often you have to add text to a document after it has been imported from a word processing file, and a further spell check ensures correct spelling in the final publication.

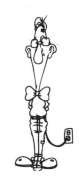

Hyphenation: Most DTP programs will insert hyphens automatically in words at the end of a line to make the line break properly at the right margin. Most programs perform hyphenation using either a hyphenation dictionary or grammatical rules. Usually, you can also tell the program not to hyphenate any words at all. But because full left-right justification is the most popular DTP format, most users use hyphenation to avoid wide gaps between words.

Table generation: A table is any amount of text and numbers formatted in a row and column fashion. Many desktop programs can create tables with any number of lines or text formats. You can either bring in the table entries from a word processing program or enter them into the desktop table directly. Some DTP programs can import data directly from database and spreadsheet programs and create a table around that information. Figure 5.11 shows a table created by a table utility that is shipped with PageMaker 4.0 on both the IBM-compatible and Macintosh versions.

Graphics Features

Graphics tools give you the ability to dress up your pages with lines and boxes and gray screens. They also give you the ability to enhance and improve many of the pictures and drawings that you bring into the desktop program. Here are some of the common graphics tools available:

Drawing tools: These let you draw lines, squares, rectangles, ovals, or circles on the screen. You can usually fill the interior and/or the

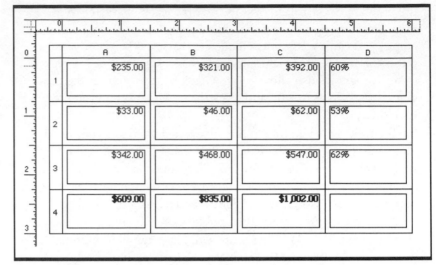

Figure 5.11

This sample shows a table created by a DTP table utility using numbers imported from a spreadsheet. This automatic table generation can save a tremendous amount of time for the user, who would otherwise have to insert each number and line one at a time. The formula-generated results in Column D and Row 4 are preserved from the spreadsheet.

	A	B	C	D
1	$235.00	$321.00	$392.00	60%
2	$33.00	$46.00	$62.00	53%
3	$342.00	$468.00	$547.00	62%
4	$609.00	$835.00	$1,002.00	

border of what you've just drawn with a fill pattern or color, and designate just how wide you want each of these lines to be. One common use for drawing tools is to make frames for large capital letters as shown in Figure 5.12.

Figure 5.12

The box around the drop cap was created with a square-making tool from a DTP program.

UO IN SE perpetuo Tempus as revolubile gyro Iam revocat Zephyros, vere tepente, novos. Induiturque brev Tellus reparata iuventam, Iamque soluta gelu dulce virescit humus.

Fallor? an et nobis redeunt in carmina vires, Ingeniumque mihi munere veris adest? Munere veris adest, iterumque vigescit ab illo (Quis putet?) atque aliquod iam sibi poscit opus. Castalis ante osculos, bifid umque cacumen oberrat.

Fill patterns: A fill pattern is used to fill in the enclosed region of a graphic or text object. In addition to patterns, you can also fill a graphic area with a color.

Reversing: This allows you to take text, pictures, lines, whatever, and reverse the colors to get a white image on a dark background.

Scaling: The process of adjusting text or graphics according to a proportion. For example, if you scale a graphic at 50 percent, it will be made half as large as the original; if you scale it at 200 percent, it will be made twice as large as the original. Some programs also let you change the proportion of any picture or drawing (see Figure 5.13) from, say, 3" × 3" to 3" × 6". That, of course, distorts the original picture. So it works pretty well with black-and-white drawings, but rarely with photographs.

Cropping: The process of removing unwanted portions of a picture is called cropping. During cropping, you "zero in" on the focal subject of your photo. Usually, the way you do this is to enlarge the picture bigger than the box it's in and move the picture so that only the part you want shows.

NOTE

Even word processors that can do most of the things that can be done with DTP don't scale graphics as easily and in as many different ways.

Figure 5.13

In this screen shot, we can see that Ali Baba was put on a diet and reduced in the right-hand graphic. The right side of the original, undistorted graphic was pushed in, causing the distortion.

Printing Features

The key printing feature is the number of different printers that you can use with your program. There are, however, a few other useful features to look for, including the following:

Background printing: This means being able to do other work on-screen while a document is being printed in the background. It's an extremely valuable feature because desktop pages have an incredible number of codes that must be sent to the printer to get all the type-faces and pictures printed. Some DTP programs require several min-utes to print one highly designed text-and-graphics page, and it's nice to be able to do something else while that's happening.

Print-order control: This is the capability to order either one page, several pages, or the full document to be printed, and the ability to or-der that only odd-numbered or even-numbered pages be printed. It's also the ability to print either the first page first or the last page first (the latter giving you a document with pages in the right order when the print job is completed). Figure 5.14 displays a portion of a desktop print menu.

Color printing: If you are designing a color document, it's necessary to have a DTP program that can recognize and deal with colors when printing. Such a program, if printing to a color printer, prints the whole page in the right colors. If you're sending the job to a service bureau with high-quality image setters, you must separate

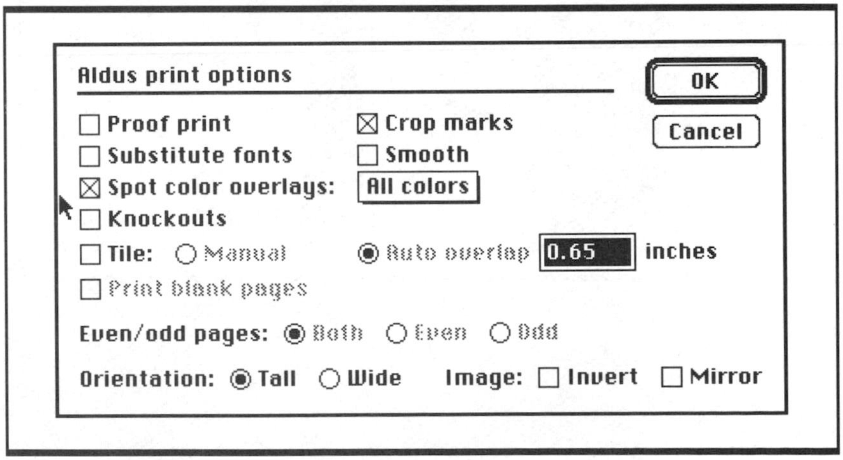

Figure 5.14

This sample of a desktop print menu shows some of the control choices available to a user. Notice that you can print any even or odd pages, different orientations, plus several other options.

Aldus print options | OK | Cancel

☐ Proof print   ☒ Crop marks
☐ Substitute fonts   ☐ Smooth
☒ Spot color overlays: [All colors]
☐ Knockouts
☐ Tile: ○ Manual   ● Auto overlap [0.65] inches
☐ Print blank pages

Even/odd pages: ● Both   ○ Even   ○ Odd

Orientation: ● Tall   ○ Wide   Image: ☐ Invert   ☐ Mirror

the colors into blue, red, and so forth. If you print a color job on a black-and-white laser printer, you must convert your colors into gray scales.

Printer support: The issue here is how many types and brands of printers the program can use to print its documents. The more types it "supports," the more choices you have. A good DTP program should be able to print to a wide assortment of laser, dot-matrix, ink-jet, and color ink-jet printers. Laser printers are most commonly used for desktop publishing.

PageMaker 5.0 for Windows and Page Maker 5.0a for Macintosh

Publisher:
Aldus Corporation

Suggested Retail Price:
$895–Windows/$895–Macintosh

Upgrade Price:
$150–Windows/$150–Macintosh

Windows Requires:
80386 processor or better
4MB RAM
Windows 3.1
VGA graphics adapter

Macintosh Requires:
68020 Macintosh or better
4MB RAM
System 6.0.7 or later

Description:

PageMaker is the most popular DTP package in the world and has long been the yardstick against which to measure other desktop programs. PageMaker lets you create both short and long documents (up to 999 pages). PageMaker also lets you place text and graphics anywhere on a page. Once placed, both the words and art become independent blocks that can be manipulated easily with a full array of layout, text editing, and graphic tools. The program's user-designed style sheets and master pages allow text to flow automatically to successive pages. The newest versions provide the Book feature for connecting successive chapters that would otherwise exceed the page limits, a spellchecker, and Pantone color selection for consistent control over the colors used by an outside service bureau. Text and graphics can be rotated around an axis anywhere in the document, providing more design flexibility. Whether you use PageMaker on a Mac or an IBM, PageMaker produces consistently high quality output.

Import Features

As mentioned previously, one of the key capabilities that a DTP program must have is the ability to *import,* or bring in, text, pictures, and other data produced elsewhere. This section offers guidelines on what features a DTP program should be able to import from other programs:

Word processors: DTP programs really don't need too much from a word processing program other than the words themselves. Still, it's reasonable to expect the program to be able to import both text and some simple formatting commands, such as tabs, from most of the widely used word processors.

Graphics programs: DTP programs need finished products, such as pictures, drawings, charts, and tables, from graphics programs. Thus, a good program should be able to read most graphic formats. This is more of an issue with IBM-compatibles than with the Macintosh line.

Spreadsheets: You will want a program that allows you to preserve the tabular layout of your spreadsheet in the document to which you import.

Database programs: Here, again, you will want a program that lets you keep the tabular layout of your database intact. So when you import the data, you won't have to move or shift data around; nor will you need to create the tables from scratch.

NOTE

By planning ahead with graphics and text, it's possible to minimize the time spent reformatting materials in the DTP program.

How Do I Learn Desktop Publishing?

There's no denying that using DTP programs requires a great many detailed skills, but, again, you don't have to learn it all at once. Once you have the word-processed and graphic files completed, using the DTP program itself is actually pretty easy. Always remember to break down a complex task into simpler ones. If you follow these ten steps, you will be able to master desktop publishing.

1. Learn how to start your program and create a new blank chapter. As you do that, learn how to save it to disk so that you'll always have a permanent record.

Calling in the Pros...

Designing a good-looking page requires knowledge of design rules more than knowledge of a DTP program. If you wish to publish a professional, commercial publication, it's definitely a good idea to hire professionals to do the basic design. Once you have that, you can go ahead and add new text and graphics on an as-needed basis. For example, if you are publishing a monthly newsletter that you sell, you want the design to be first-rate. Once your design template is completed by a professional, you only need to "refill" that template every month using the designer's suggested font styles and positions for graphic elements. You can save a lot of time and money by not using traditional methods of typesetting, and your results will look like the professionally designed product they are.

2. Practice creating a page design of one-column, two-columns, three-columns…, whatever you feel like, to get a feel for designing a page.

3. Play with some practice text and explore the Text Menu's options to get a feel for how to cut, paste, and move things around.

4. Learn how to change typefaces. Make some headlines either by changing some type sizes or by typing them in larger type. Try changing your paragraph type styles to get an idea of what the different choices look like.

5. Try creating additional text blocks somewhere and import a second text file so that you'll know how to work with more than one document in a publication.

6. Practice importing a graphic file picture and use the tools for cropping or enlarging it.

7. Now that you have everything together, experiment with the drawing tools. Draw some lines and squares and circles.

8. Try putting some gray screens on top of text and filling in blank spaces.

9. Save your work to disk. In fact, save it periodically—particularly every time you finish doing something that you don't want to have to do again.

10. Print your work. Take a look at it, and keep playing with it until you like what you see on the paper.

Work your way through the ten steps above and you'll be up and running with your desktop program pretty quickly. You can learn the fancy details from the instruction books as you need them. These basics are all that you really need to begin your own publications.

Text or Graphical Interface?

In desktop publishing, there really isn't any question about this—at least on the hardware side: You need a high-resolution display monitor (preferably VGA or Super VGA) to see your text and graphics on the screen exactly as they will appear when printed, and you need a printer (preferably a laser printer) capable of printing graphics and text at whatever resolution (print quality) your work requires. Although you will probably find it easier if the operating system or environment also presents a graphical interface, there are DTP programs that can run in text-based operating systems. For example, you can run Ventura Publisher (profiled in this chapter) under the text-based DOS 3.1 or higher. A quasi-graphics environment is utilized, but in a more limited form than for applications designed to run under the Windows graphical environment. The advantage of running Ventura under a text-based operating system is that it's usually faster than the Windows version.

What Do I Need to Know If I'm Going to Buy?

Although we mentioned it in the section on what you need for desktop publishing, it's worth repeating that the first thing you need to know is that DTP programs require a good deal of computer memory and disk storage space. If you're thinking of complex projects with lots of pictures, charts, and graphs (and that's really the only reason for getting a DTP program), then you are going to have to take a much sharper look at the chapters in this book on hardware.

As for picking a desktop program, there are varieties of DTP packages that range from around $200 to just under $1,000. The degree of control over text, fonts, and graphics is roughly proportional to the price, but you don't have to buy at the top of the line to get everything you need.

Quark Express for Windows and Quark Express 3.2 for Macintosh

Publisher:
Quark Inc.

Suggested Retail Price:
$895–Windows/$895–Macintosh

Windows Requires:
80486 processor
4MB RAM
Windows 3.0 or later
DOS 3.1 or later
Postscript printer recommended

Macintosh Requires:
Macintosh Plus or better
3MB RAM
System 6.0.5 or later

Description:

Quark XPress has long been a favorite DTP application for Macintosh users and has now migrated to the Windows environment. Using Pantone, TruMatch, or Focoltone color systems, you can add color to any of the elements of your publications. The word-processing capabilities now include style sheets and tab refinements, while the typographical abilities include flexible spacing, alternative hyphenation, ligatures, and single word justification. Using the Picture Update Preview, you can view TIFF and RIFF images before deciding whether to include them in your publication.

A Final Note

The heart of desktop publishing is the ability to combine text and graphics with ease. In Chapter 4 we discussed what is necessary to get your text arranged in a word processing program. In the next chapter, we will discuss what is available in graphics programs, how to create and change graphics, and the nature of graphics files.

As we saw with word processing, there is a good deal more to it than just typing in words. In the same way, there is a good deal more to graphics than drawing and painting. With a computer, not only can you draw and paint, you can also do all kinds of other things. If you have been reading consecutively, you are all set to begin learning something about computer graphics. For quite a few readers it will be the most useful aspect of their computer use—and fun too.

Six

Graphics

• •

Graphics are pictures, including charts, cartoons, logos, mastheads, drawings, graphs, and digitized photographs. In computer technology, the term "graphics" means almost anything that is not a word or a number. Computer-created images are all around us. You see them in newspaper ads, television commercials, movies, books, magazines—everywhere.

What Is a Graphics Program?

Graphics programs are those that create images, pictures, or designs that can be seen on-screen and printed. Figure 6.1 shows some of the simpler things you can produce with a graphics program.

Uses of Computer Graphics

Computer graphics are used wherever a picture enhances text or is more suitable than text. There are software packages to produce any kind of image for any purpose, including multicolor paintings; black-and-white or color line drawings and cartoons; company logos and stationery letterheads; pie, line, and bar graphs (in 2-D and 3-D); organizational flow charts; advertisements; maps and architectural drawings; and three-dimensional modeling. You name it, there's undoubtedly a program to do it.

Bitmap versus Vector Graphics

Graphics programs create images on the screen or printer either as *bitmapped* images or as *vector* images. The difference is that bitmapped pictures are made up of groups of dots, while vector pictures are created with mathematical formulas that provide smoother curves and sharper edges. They each have their strengths. If a bitmapped font is made larger, it looks like the "S" on the left in Figure 6.2, while the vector (or scaleable) "S" will always retain its smooth edges no matter how large you make it.

However, if you want an image that looks like a photograph, a bitmapped screen will give you the best result since bitmapped images are made up of dots very much like a photo is.

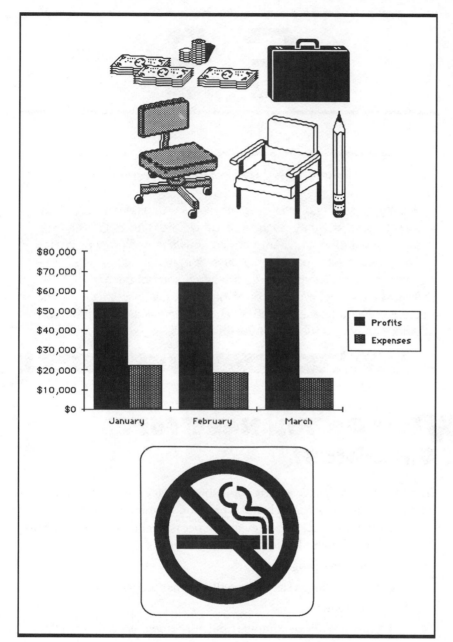

Figure 6.2
The letter "S" on the left is
bitmapped. The one on the
right is a vector image.

S S

Paint versus Draw Programs

Paint programs and draw programs work with different tools in different ways, but they each produce pictures, drawings, and designs. Paint programs can produce drawings and draw programs can produce paintings. These days, it may not matter which one you use, because you can do the same sorts of things with both. The key difference is that paint programs usually work with and create bitmap images, while most draw and illustration programs work with object-oriented or vector images.

What Do You Need for Graphics?

Graphics programs have a fairly sophisticated list of hardware needs, but much depends on how much and what kind of graphics work you want to do. On the low end, just to create an occasional cute drawing or picture, you'll need the following:

- a graphics program
- an operating system that will run that program
- a computer
- at least 640K of computer memory (more is even better)
- a hard disk with 80MB or more of storage

- a high-resolution graphics monitor such as a VGA or a MultiSync monitor
- a keyboard
- a mouse
- a printer that can print graphics
- some clip art pictures

For heavy-duty graphics work, you might also consider purchasing the following:

- a video accelerator board
- a math coprocessor (to speed the graphics calculations)
- a hand-held or full-page scanner
- a high-resolution color monitor
- a color printer (or a color laser printer if you can afford it)
- a plotter (for printing engineering drawings)
- a sketch pad tablet
- a video camera and digitizer

NOTE Macintosh computers all have a graphical interface. Microsoft Windows on IBM-compatibles is also a graphical interface.

There are two main issues to consider when setting up a computer to do graphics work. One is that each graphic file occupies a lot of room when it's stored on disk—anywhere from 15K to 1MB or more. The second issue is that the computer itself has to do a lot of manipulation to get those images onto the screen and to the printer. This brings up the related issues of computer speed, computer memory, and hard disk storage space.

If you wish to create pictures only occasionally, you don't have to worry about needing a lot of hardware. Your basic off-the-shelf computer with 1MB (Macintosh) or 640K (IBM-compatible) of memory, a screen good enough to see your work, and an 80MB hard disk should be able to handle it.

On the other hand, if you're going to do a great deal of graphics work, or use your graphics in a desktop publishing system, then you need a very fast computer, probably several megabytes of computer memory, and a hard disk with from 100MB to 200MB of storage. Whether you're going to store 30, 50, or 100 graphic images on your hard disk for easy access, you'll need a lot of disk storage room.

Paint Programs

Actually, the term *paint programs* is a bit of a misnomer. Paint programs are usually used to create drawings, charts, and pictures for purposes such as company logos or newsletter mastheads. And, just as often, they are used as graphics editors to change images that already exist in computer-readable form.

NOTE

It's important to keep in mind that what is finally printed may look quite different from what you see on the screen.

Paint programs are best for creating images with photographic details, fine shadings, or brush stroke effects, and for working with scanned and other bitmapped images.

Product at a Glance

FreeHand 3.1 for Windows and FreeHand 3.1.1 for Macintosh

Publisher:
Aldus Corporation

Suggested Retail Price:
$595–Windows/$774–Macintosh

Upgrade Price:
$150–Windows

Windows Requires:
80286 processor
2MB RAM
Windows 3.0 or later
EGA or better graphics adapter

Macintosh Requires:
Mac Plus or better
2MB RAM
System 6.0.5 or later

Description:

FreeHand is among the most popular graphics packages in the world. Whether you want to create a piece of classic art, a logo, business cards, or whatever, you will find that the tools in FreeHand let your imagination go. Text and graphics can be combined and manipulated on-screen and then printed out on any quality printer. Clip art, patterns, and typefaces can be created and edited to suit your imagination. You can save your creations and use them in most of the major DTP, word processing, graphics, spreadsheet, and other business packages on the market.

How Do They Work?

Paint programs work by simulating an artist's tools on a computer screen. Figure 6.3 shows a sample paint program screen with a drawing pencil in the middle. At the top of the sample screen are the names of pull-down menus, such as the File menu, that let you do things like load an existing picture, store the image to disk, and pick a typeface. Along the left side are icons of the various tools used for creating images on-screen and selecting lines of different thicknesses. Along the bottom are patterns you can use to fill in shapes.

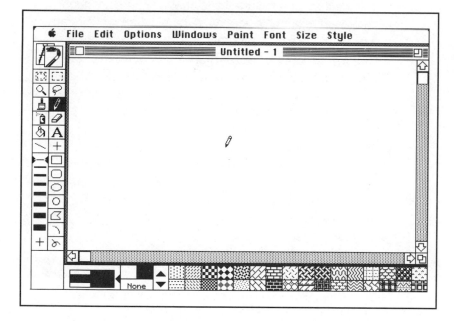

Figure 6.3

A sample screen of SuperPaint, a Macintosh program that has both painting and drawing capabilities.

To show you how a paint program works, let's create an invitation card for a baby shower. We will use SuperPaint. It runs on the Apple Macintosh and is a combination paint and draw program. Even though different paint programs give you different tools, the tools we'll use to create the card are common to virtually all paint programs.

Using Other Art Sources

When working with graphics programs, it's a common practice to use pictures that already exist in computer-readable form. You can see these pictures on your screen and change them any way you want to. You can also use a part of a picture in another picture, in the same way that you can cut a small drawing of a house from a magazine and paste in on a housewarming announcement.

The main sources for this ready-to-use art are:

- **Scanned images:** Produced by running a device called a *scanner* over a picture that's on paper. The scanner creates an electronic version of the picture that you can use in your graphics program.

- **Clip art libraries:** Pictures that either have already been run through a scanner or were created by professional artists. When you buy these, you get a disk with computer-readable pictures and printouts that show what the pictures look like.

- **Your own work:** Once you've created something in your graphics program and saved a copy of it on disk, that copy may provide just what you need for another creation. For example, you can turn a housewarming party announcement into a birthday party announcement just by changing a few words.

Here are some typical steps for creating a graphic image:

1. **Open a blank page**. This is simply loading the program. Most programs appear initially with a blank screen, as shown in Figure 6.3. Some may show the image you worked on the last time you used the program. If that is so, just clear the image from the screen so you'll have a blank "page."

2. **Import some artwork**. As stated earlier, working with existing art is often the easiest way to begin. In this case, suppose

you happen to remember a Happy New Year picture with some details in it that might be useful for the current project. To open the file containing the picture you want to use, pull down the File menu and select the Open command. Next, from the pop-up dialog box, select the name of the file you want to open and double-click on it. That file's graphic will appear on the paint program screen, as shown in Figure 6.4.

Figure 6.4
By going to the File menu and clicking on the file name, a Happy New Year picture has been imported onto the graphics program screen and is now ready for editing.

3. Magnify and erase. Next, magnify the drawing, and erase the parts that you don't want to use in the baby shower card. By magnifying the drawing, you can remove the unwanted portions more accurately. Figure 6.5 shows how this looks on the screen.

4. Zoom back and inspect. Now that you have seen the picture close up, zoom back and see if the baby looks the way you want. (See Figure 6.6.) If it needs more work, zoom in on those areas.

Figure 6.5

Both the regular size and magnified images show at the same time, so you can best see what needs erasing.

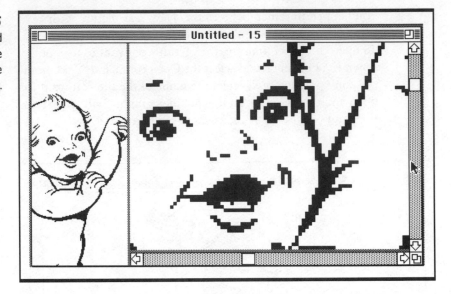

Figure 6.6

By backing up, you can see if you made all the changes you need. The Zoom feature in paint programs is very useful.

5. **Draw something.** Now we're ready to enhance our picture with drawings of our own. Using the oval tool (see the left side of the screen in Figure 6.3), we will draw a caption balloon. After the oval is drawn, we will erase a corner and draw a pointer pointing to the baby. Using the circle tool, we will make a rattle and then fill it with a fill pattern. A line inserted in the baby's hand will complete the rattle.

6. **Add text.** To complete the card, add the text, using the text tool provided with the program. The completed image for the card is shown in Figure 6.7.

7. **Save the file.** Now it's time to print it and see what it looks like on paper. It's also time to save this image to disk so that it will be available for future use just as the Happy New Year image was. You do this by choosing the Save As command from the File menu. The finished image can be called "Baby-shower," which will help you find it the next time you need it.

As you can see, painting and drawing programs are not hard to use, although they do take some practice to master.

NOTE

Most good computer programs can undo a mistake in a graphics program.

Figure 6.7

The completed drawing gives the viewer no clue that the image originally was a New Year's baby that had some simple changes made to it.

Key Features: Paint Program Tools

Painting programs have become very powerful and flexible. The following list describes some of the tools and features that you'll find in paint programs:

Marquee and lasso: Elect areas of your picture. The marquee selects a rectangular area; the lasso is like an elastic band that can wrap around irregular shapes. Once an area is selected, you can move, copy, trace, or perform some other special effect on it.

Hand tool or "grabber": Moves the picture around, somewhat like moving a piece of paper around on the desktop so that you have easier access to a portion of your drawing.

Text tool: Lets you add words to your picture, such as headlines, labels, and identifying text. You can control font, color, size, and style of the text.

Paint bucket: Fills any fully enclosed region of your picture with a color or pattern. If you fill a rectangle with a brick pattern, it will look like a brick wall.

Product at a Glance

SuperPaint 3.5 for Macintosh

Publisher:
Aldus Corporation

Suggested Retail Price:
$199

Upgrade Price:
$69

Requires:
Mac Plus or better
System 6.0.5 or later
2MB RAM (4MB for Color)
32-bit QuickDraw for Color

Description:

SuperPaint is one of the few programs that can edit both bitmapped (paint) and object-oriented (draw) art. You can draw smooth geometric shapes in draw mode, and then, with a click of a button, you can switch to paint mode to fill in intricate details such as shading. Features include autotrace, freehand Bezier curves, text and object rotation, an airbrush, editable arrowheads, and dash patterns. Plug-in tools let you draw 3-D boxes, calligraphic designs, and lines that look like toothpaste squeezings, bubbles, and stars. The program also supports color preview and printing.

Spray can: Sprays color or patterns on your picture. You can usually adjust the flow, pattern, and shape of the spray nozzle.

Paintbrush: Strokes color and patterns onto your electronic canvas. Most programs allow you to customize the shape of the paintbrush.

Drawing tools: Create lines, rectangles, rectangles with rounded corners, ovals, polygons, and so forth. A key drawing tool is usually called the *pencil*. With it, you can draw lines and figures of any shape and width. You can also undraw lines by turning the black dots white again. The pencil is often used for detailed dot-by-dot editing.

Eraser: Works like a pencil eraser and often is used to delete relatively large areas of the picture.

Pattern palette: Lets you select fill patterns, colors, or screens.

Flexible airbrush: Adjusts diameter and density of the paint flow (like a spray can), but it can also continue to spray dots even when it's not moving.

Blend tool: Also called a charcoal or smudge tool. Lets you soften the edges of solid shapes for a mistier look.

Symmetrical polygon: Lets you specify the number of sides for equilateral polygons.

Zoom: Lets you zoom in and edit a small portion of your picture as if you were working with it under a high-powered magnifying glass. It's very useful for close work. Of course, you can also "zoom out" to get a bird's eye view of your picture.

Exporting files: Paint images often are used as raw material for desktop publishing programs. Thus, it's important that a program be able to store its images on disk in several formats so that other programs can read them. A good paint program should be able to save files in more than one format.

Importing files: This is the opposite of *exporting*. It's important that your program be able to load and use many different graphics formats.

NOTE

When drawing or erasing fine points, it's a good idea to magnify the image on which you are working.

NOTE

Before making a final decision on which graphic file you should use, test print different types on your printer.

Draw Programs

Drawing and illustration programs manipulate object-oriented graphics. They remember each shape you draw and allow you to edit any shape without disturbing others, even if that shape is lying on top of or beneath another. You can create, edit, scale, and otherwise manipulate distinct forms and geometric objects such as rectangles, circles, and polygons.

Strictly speaking, a drawing package is designed for those of us who need a computer to help us create shapes. Illustration packages, on the other hand, are for artists. Artists use a program to draw more easily and faster and to test new ideas quickly.

About File Formats

A *file format* is the data structure used to record an image onto a disk. It's of particular significance in computer graphics because there are so many different graphics formats. Your word processing or desktop publishing program must be able to recognize the formats you want to import.

- **TIF** (Tagged Image File): This format stores bitmapped images in various resolutions, shades of gray, or colors. It is recognized by its .TIF extension (the extension being the last three letters after the dot in a file name).

- **EPS** (Encapsulated PostScript): This is the standard for graphics with PostScript code. Sometimes these files are simply programs that draw pictures when printed but cannot be seen on the computer screen. They are recognized by their .EPS extension.

- **PAINT**: Paint files have a .PNT extension. Graphics saved in Paint format are stripped of any high-resolution, object-oriented flexibility, gray-scale values, and color.

- **PCX**: This PC Paintbrush format is for bitmapped graphics. Images are stored as rectangles of black and white dots in various resolutions (300 dots-per-inch is the most common). PC Paintbrush files handle gray scales and colors, and are recognized by a .PCX extension.

- **GEM**: GEM draw/paint programs handle various resolutions, gray scales, and colors. GEM saves its line drawings with a .GEM extension and its image files with an .IMG extension.
- **PIC**: The standard format used by the Lotus 1-2-3 spreadsheet program for saving its graphs and data to disk when they are to be further enhanced by graphic programs. It is recognized by its .PIC extension.
- **PICT**: PICT can hold higher resolution bitmaps (more than 72 pixels per inch), but many applications convert these bitmaps to 72 ppi anyway.
- **PICT2**: This is an extension of the PICT format that can hold bitmaps and objects with up to 16.7 million colors, including shades of gray. Like PICT, there is no limit to the resolution of the bitmaps, except that imposed by the applications creating them. PICT and PICT2 are exclusively Macintosh file formats.

How Do They Work?

Like paint programs, drawing and illustration programs replace traditional tools with electronic ones to create computerized illustrators' tools. Paint and draw programs work similarly, often starting with or incorporating a piece of art that already exists. The main difference between them is that draw programs tend to be more powerful in their ability to manipulate the lines and curves on the screen.

Key Features: Draw Program Tools

Tools used by draw programs resemble those of paint programs, but it's almost magical how these tools can stretch and twist images. On a draw screen, everything from figures to text to borders is fair game for being manipulated into another form. It helps if you think of everything on the screen, including letters, as rubber figures that can be pulled into any shape, angle, or curve.

Drawing tools usually are called up by clicking the mouse on little icons. Some of the key tools in drawing programs are the following:

Pick tool: Selects objects or groups of objects on-screen. Once selected, the images on-screen can be moved, stretched, copied, scaled, rotated, skewed, flipped upside down, or deleted.

Shape tool: Changes screen images by moving, scaling, and stretching. It can round the corners of rectangles, turn a circle into a half-oblong, change the shape of a curve, and stretch letters. Figure 6.8 shows an example of the kinds of changes available with the Shape tool, which is often used in conjunction with other menus.

Zoom tool: Changes the viewing area and the magnification of the image you're working on. Most programs give you the ability to select any sized area, and that area will expand to fill the entire screen. You can also use this tool to see the image in the exact size it will print or to see what the whole page looks like.

Pencil or pen: Draws lines in any direction. Usually, you can draw a perfectly horizontal or vertical line. You can also set the line thickness and color.

Rectangle tool: Draws rectangular shapes. Again, you can set line width and color, or force the shape to be a perfect square. You use the mouse to click one corner and then move the mouse pointer at a 45-degree angle to the opposite corner before releasing the mouse button. You see what you are going to get as you go. For drawing lined-up rectangles for an organization chart, this tool is a gem.

Figure 6.8

Draw and illustration programs can do as much with text as they can with graphics.

Circle tool: Draws circles and ovals of any line width and color. It works the same way as does the Rectangle tool. You pick one side of the circle, move the mouse to the other side, and, when satisfied with the shape, you release the mouse button.

Text tool: Adds words to your graphics. Most programs come with several fonts or typefaces. You can set them for different type styles, such as bold or underline, and in any size. You first pick the type characteristics, position the cursor on-screen where you want the words to begin, and start typing. The words become part of the graphic and can be reshaped later if needed. Figure 6.9 shows an example of text uses when the text tool is selected.

Eraser: Wipes out anything you don't want. For large areas, however, you'll usually form a box on the screen and tell the program to eliminate everything inside the box. For detailed dot-by-dot edits, you'll want the eraser.

Outline tool: Picks the width or color of a line. That line could be either the outside border of a figure or the outside rim of a letter. If it's thick enough to be worth it, you can also pick a pattern— the line can be solid, or dotted, or whatever you want it to be.

Fill tool: Fills the inside area created by an outside line. Using a Fill tool, you can make the area solid black, a gray shade, or a color. In some programs, you can even have a fill pattern that changes from dark to light as it goes from one side to another. This is called *graduated shading*.

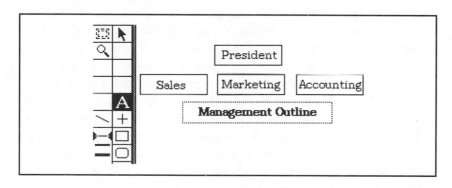

Figure 6.9

With the text tool selected, the user can type in information in graphic images.

NOTE

A PostScript printer or software interpreter is necessary to print Encapsulated PostScript (.EPS) files. However, their quality is so good that it may be worth the extra cost.

In addition to the basic tools, draw programs have many other features that permit you to create images that, not long ago, could only be done by professionals. These include the following:

Exporting files: As in paint programs, draw images are often used as raw material for other programs such as desktop publishing. On an IBM-compatible, a good draw program should be able to store its images to disk in at least a half dozen formats. Because draw programs usually work with both bitmap and object-oriented images, they can save files in more formats than paint programs can.

Importing files: Importing files is the opposite of *exporting*. It's important that the program can load and use many different graphics formats. Usually, draw programs can read more file formats than paint programs, because they can work with both bitmap and vector images.

Layering: Some programs let you design your picture in layers. This can speed up your work because you can have the screen redraw only the layer you're working on instead of the entire picture. It can also help you to produce desired effects by moving layers in front of or behind one another, hiding particular layers, and similar layering applications.

Libraries: Some programs allow you to store frequently used images or parts of images in separate libraries for quick retrieval. You might have one library of car pictures and another of boat pictures. A library allows you to get images from the disk more quickly because you don't have to sort through dozens (or hundreds) of file names.

Blending: Blend tools allow you to define a starting shape or color and an ending shape or color, and choose the number of intermediate shapes or colors that you want. The program automatically calculates and creates the transition shapes or colors. (See Figure 6.10.)

Preview mode: This allows you to split the screen so that you can edit a drawing in one window and watch the results at the same time in the other window. In many programs, the working version is often incomplete. The reason for this is speed. It takes a long time to draw the full version. So, with this you can keep working on the raw image of the outline without waiting for the full image to catch up. When it does, you'll see exactly what you have.

Slides/transparencies: This is the ability of a program to export a drawing into another program that can turn it into a slide or an overhead transparency.

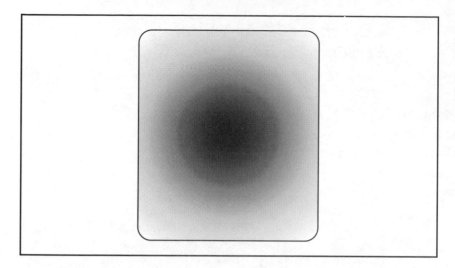

Figure 6.10
This is a radial blend,
beginning with a dark core
and spiraling outwards to a
light shade.

Snap-to-Grid: Normally a draw program makes rectangles and circles exactly the size you've drawn them. When you need to draw to exact specifications, you can call up an on-screen "grid" with points at some interval you've specified (for example, every 0.1") and your drawing will "snap to" the appropriate points.

Style sheets: These let you assign particular attributes such as color, and then apply them to your drawing. A change to the style sheet will be reflected in your drawing immediately. This is far more efficient than having to alter every element individually when you change your mind.

Presentation Graphics

Presentation graphics is the term used to describe line graphs, bar graphs, pie graphs, how-to-charts, and pep talk diagrams—whatever visual aids you would want if you were about to walk into a meeting to make a presentation. These kinds of graphics and charts are also useful when you are putting out publications with lots of numeric or abstract data. Such data are understood more easily when they are presented in graphic formats.

The major task of presentation graphics is to simplify. No one wants to look at pages of numbers without interpretation, but turn those numbers into a bar chart and suddenly everyone understands that sales are rapidly

Adobe Illustrator 5.0 for Windows and Adobe Illustrator 5.0 for Macintosh

Publisher:
Adobe Systems, Inc.

Suggested Retail Price:
$695–Windows/$595–Macintosh

Upgrade Price:
$149–Windows

Windows Requires:
80386 processor
Windows 3.0 or later
DOS 3.1 or later
4MB RAM

Macintosh Requires:
Mac Plus or better
System 6.0.7 or later
4MB RAM with System 6.0.7
4MB RAM with System 7

Description:

If you're an artist, you'll love using Illustrator. It's a digital version of all the art equipment that gives you precise control over every drawing detail, either in black-and-white or color. The program supports Pantone Matching System, True Match, Toyo, and Anpa color matching and can produce color separations. You can scan in a drawing or import existing digital artwork, and then use Illustrator's autotrace tool to smooth and enhance the bitmapped images. Draw tools include freehand, pen, rectangle, oval, blend, scale, rotate, reflect, and shear. There's even a graph tool that charts numbers automatically. Designers who work with type will especially like the program's sophisticated type handling and font editing features, using TrueType and all Type 1 fonts.

slipping in the northeast and rising in the south. Presentation graphics pull the hidden meanings out of huge columns of numbers, and focus an audience's attention on the most significant points. Figure 6.11 illustrates the difference between a table and a chart. They exhibit the same data, but it's much easier (and faster) to see the differences in the bar chart than in the table.

Presentation graphics programs are a boon to business people who must put together persuasive presentations easily and quickly. The saying that "a picture is worth a thousand words" is even more pertinent in business situations. There, you must get your message across quickly to people who are usually in a hurry.

	A	B	C	D
1		1992	1993	%Change
2	Clothing	$123,456	$148,147	20%
3	Autos	$104,938	$192,591	84%
4	Lumber	$89,197	$250,369	181%
5	Gold	$75,817	$325,479	329%
6	Food	$64,445	$423,123	557%

Figure 6.11

(a) The spreadsheet data shows changes in various categories for a two-year period and the percent of change. (b) The data shown in (a) have been graphed, using the built-in graphing capability of the spreadsheet program. Microsoft's Excel was used to create this bar chart, but Lotus 1-2-3, Quattro Pro, and other spreadsheet programs have built-in graphic capabilities as well.

With a complete presentation graphics package, you can create all phases of your presentation from outline to finished overheads, 35mm slides, audience handouts, flip charts, and speaker's notes. Also, you can use the same charts and graphs as the raw material for a paper publication prepared by a desktop publishing program. Figure 6.12 shows a sample of the images that presentation graphics programs can produce.

There are two main types of programs that produce the charts and graphs we've been discussing. They are the following:

Presentation graphics: Presentation graphics programs (discussed above) are designed specifically to create graphs or text charts from data entered manually or taken from a database, spreadsheet, or word processing program.

Spreadsheet programs: Although the main task of spreadsheets is to crunch numbers (see Chapter 7), nearly all spreadsheet programs

NOTE

If you don't have the equipment to turn a computer image into a photographic slide, there are commercial services that will do it for you.

Figure 6.12

Here's a sample of presentation graphics that mixes straight graphics with letters manipulated with Aldus Free Hand.

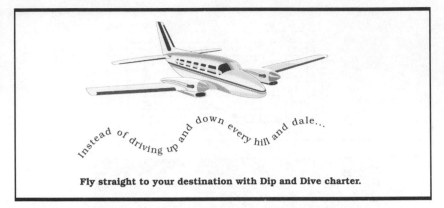

Instead of driving up and down every hill and dale...

Fly straight to your destination with Dip and Dive charter.

also have strong graph-making features. If you create graphs with a spreadsheet program, you can import them into your presentation.

How Do They Work?

Most presentation graphics programs operate on the same principle. First you decide what kind of graph you want, enter the numbers that will be represented in the graph, and the programs will turn those numbers into that graph.

If you change your mind about the effectiveness of a certain style of graph for conveying your information succinctly, you only have to change the type of graph requested and the program will use the same information to create another kind of graph.

Choosing the Right Graph

The type of graph you choose usually depends on the kind of analysis you want to perform.

Line graphs: These are best for showing patterns and trends over time—to track sales, for example. (See Figure 6.13.)

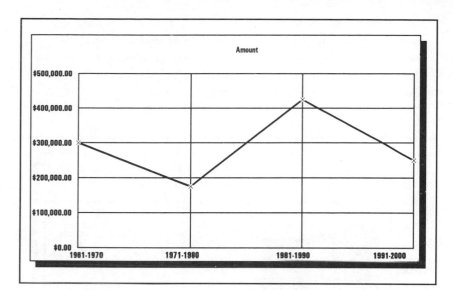

Figure 6.13
Line graphs are good for
tracking values over time.

Bar and column graphs: Bar graphs are good for comparing values of different items at specific times, for example, to contrast monthly commissions by each salesperson. (See Figure 6.14.)

Stacked bar & area graphs: These are used to show the relationship between individual values and the total, for example, to show how

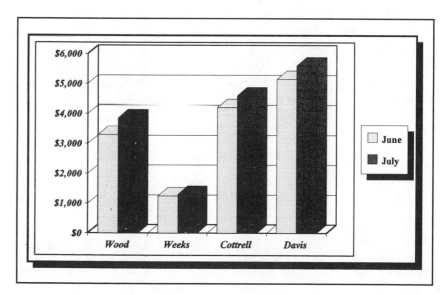

Figure 6.14
A column graph (shown here in 3-D) is used to compare salespersons' commissions over a two-month period.

total sales are divided among regions. (See Figure 6.15.) Because area graphs use lines to track values, they are even better than stacked bars for showing patterns over time. Stacked bar graphs are best for plotting values in one series, such as salary, against those in another, such as length of employment.

Figure 6.15

Stacked graphs can be used to compare expenses for two separate years to reflect where the company's greatest expenses were during selected periods.

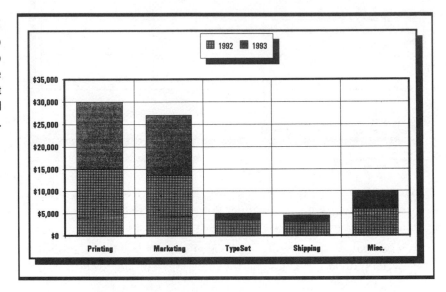

Pie charts: Used to show how a part affects the whole; for example, to show how yearly expenses break down into separate categories. (See Figure 6.16.)

High-low graphs: These display vertical lines that represent the difference between corresponding values in two series. Most high-low graphs are used to track daily stock prices, but you can use them whenever you want to compare the difference between pairs of values.

Text charts: These are good when you need to present textual information with bulleted items to illustrate each major point in an accompanying talk.

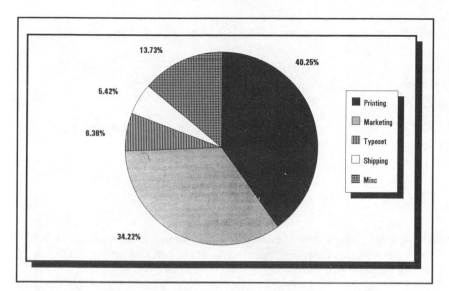

Figure 6.16
Using a pie chart to examine
a single year gives a clear
indication of where the money
was spent. Compare the pie
chart with the stacked graph
in Figure 6.15.

Key Features: Presentation Graphics Tools

Different graphics programs offer different tools for shaping your drawings. Some useful features that give you precise control over your final product include the following:

Color conversion: Allows you to convert a color graph to black-and-white causing the different colors to become various shades of gray. This is useful when you have created a color graph on the screen, but need to see what it will look like before it goes to a black-and-white printer.

Exploding pie charts: Lets you pull a wedge of the pie away for emphasis. Some programs determine the distance between the pie and the wedge automatically. Others let you determine this distance. (See Figure 6.17.)

Exporting: Allows you to save graphic images in a number of different formats so you can use them with other programs.

Graphs: Lets you create an assortment of bar, line, and pie graphs. You want to be able to set the width of graph lines individually, and to have the graph reflect as many different data points (the numbers that are being graphed) as needed. The general rule is to use as few data points as possible to avoid clutter and confusion.

NOTE
If you have software that
can do color separations,
you can use your black-and-
white laser printer to prepare color camera-ready
copy. It won't actually
print in color, but you
can do the "plate" for someone else to print the color.

Persuasion 2.1 for Windows and Persuasion 2.1.2 for Macintosh

Publisher:
Aldus Corporation

Suggested Retail Price:
$495–Windows/$495–Macintosh

Upgrade Price:
$99.95–Windows/Macintosh

Windows Requires:
80286 processor
Windows 3.0 or later
2MB RAM
EGA or better graphics adapter

Macintosh Requires:
Mac Plus or better
2MB RAM with System 6.0.5
4MB RAM with System 7

Description:

Use Persuasion to create handsome 35mm slide and overhead presentations in record time. Short notice? No problem! Just type in an outline and let Persuasion do the work of formatting the text into professional-looking visuals. It comes with built-in designs, or it will use your own designs. It can create or import logos, technical diagrams, and illustrations. It can also be used to produce charts, tables, and pie/bar/line graphs, or design and edit organizational charts. The program provides all outlining, word processing, drawing, charting, and formatting tools you might need for black-and-white or color work. It also produces speaker's notes and audience handouts automatically.

Figure 6.17

An exploding pie chart will show the biggest slice at a glance or a particular area you wish to emphasize. Compare this to Figure 6.16.

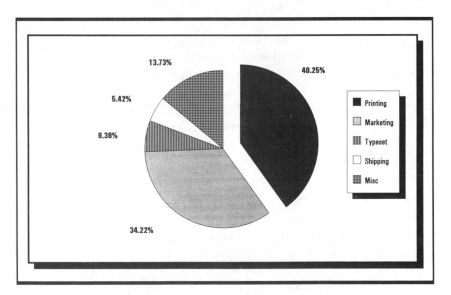

Gray-scale control: Lets you change the shade of grays in a color conversion. If two colors translate into the same shade of gray, this tool will let you differentiate them.

Importing: Lets you receive files and data from other programs so that they can be used to create charts and graphs. A good program will be able to read most graphic formats and raw data from spreadsheets and database programs.

Screen shows: Allow you to save images to a floppy disk and run them on any compatible computer without having to load the whole program that created the images.

Slide transition: Provides wipes, fades, blinds, falls, cascades, dissolves, spirals, and other ways to change images on-screen.

Speakers' notes: Allows you to split the screen so that you can see both the graphic and about a half-page of text. The text is often about the relationships shown by the graphic. For example, the text might explain which sales regions a graph represents.

Spreadsheet links: Allows you to view both a worksheet file from a spreadsheet and a graph created from that data in the graphics program. You can change numbers in the spreadsheet and see an immediate update of those changes in your graph.

Chart gallery: Lets you enter raw numbers, then call up an already existing chart format from a library and see the numbers reflected in that type of chart. It saves you from having to recreate charts every time you have new data.

Style sheets: Lets you use chart styles and templates to create graphic images.

Text charts: Allow control of typefaces, styles, and sizes. You want to be able to put the words anywhere on the page. Most programs can create automatic bullets, circles, or squares before a paragraph or sentence and can also create numbered lists.

Thumbnail sketches: Lets you show several story images in miniature on one screen or printout. They are helpful in providing an overview of your work.

Videoshow: Arranges the graphics, and shows them one at a time as in traditional slide show presentations.

How Do I Learn How to Create Graphics?

Even if you're a novice who has difficulty drawing decent stick figures, you can master the basics in just a few hours. Here are a few steps to get you started with paint or draw programs:

1. Learn how to use your mouse. You'll need it to draw, select, move, and change the shape of all the artwork you create. If you've been working on a Macintosh or with Microsoft Windows even for a little while, you're probably already a mouse master!

2. Learn how to get your program started.

3. Learn how to use the basic tools, such as the pencil, paintbrush, shape tool, text tool, patterns, paint bucket, selection tool, and the eraser. Practice making some pictures and erasing them. This is an amazing amount of fun and you can even pretend that you're working!

4. Learn how to load images from other programs.

5. Practice manipulating those images by erasing parts of them, adding new lines, or adding text.

6. Learn how to encircle a part of the drawing with the lasso or marquee; then try deleting and restoring that area, moving it, enlarging it, cutting it away, and pasting it back somewhere else.

7. Learn how to save and print your work.

8. Learn more advanced features on an as-needed basis.

 NOTE

Check your local college to see if they have classes in preparing graphics on a computer.

The starting point for presentation graphics is that you have some numbers that you want to show in a graph. For example, a simple practice session might involve a comparison of budgets and actual spending over a three-year period.

Here are some steps to get you started using graphics programs:

1. Learn how to start your presentation graphics program.

2. Learn how to choose the different graphs you can create: pie chart, line chart, and/or bar graph. Usually, each will give you a different format for entering numbers.

PowerPoint 3.0 for DOS

Publisher:
Microsoft Corporation

Suggested Retail Price:
$495

Upgrade Price:
$129

Requires:
IBM-compatible
80286 processor
(80386 recommended)
2MB RAM
Hard disk with 1MB free (8MB for all included software)
DOS 3.1 or later (version 5.0 or later recommended)
Windows 3.1 or later
One 1.2MB 5.25" or 1.4MB 3.5" disk drive
EGA or better graphics monitor
Microsoft or 100%-compatible mouse

Description:

Although none of the IBM-compatible presentation programs are dramatically better than most other programs, *PowerPoint* perhaps best uses the features of the increasingly popular Microsoft Windows environment. Geared toward a business user who wants to create presentations quickly with existing templates, the program helps the user create entire presentations. It produces overheads, speakers' notes, handouts, 35mm slides, and electronic presentations. It also comes with 22 TrueType fonts and 150 templates to get you started.

3. Learn how to enter the numbers you want the graph to show.

4. Learn how to enter graph titles, subtitles, footnotes, figure numbers, and other text onto the graph.

5. Learn how to manipulate the chart you have by, say, changing from a 2-D to a 3-D graph, enlarging or reducing text, or turning the graph on its side.

6. Learn how to use the drawing tools. Add a few lines, boxes, or circles that you feel might enhance the drawing.

7. Learn how to save and print your work.

8. Learn how to use the more advanced features as needed.

It'll probably take several days to try out all of the different kinds of charts available. But you'll have a lot of fun learning how to tweak, change, and enhance your graphs until you have just the images you want.

Text versus Graphical Interface in Graphics

You need a graphical interface if you want to create graphics. If you're thinking of pictures, figures, photos, graphs, clip art, or sophisticated charts, you'll need a high-resolution graphics screen and a graphics-based system.

It's important that you be able to see on-screen a close approximation of what you're actually going to get on the printer (or slides and transparencies). Otherwise, it's like working in the dark.

Product at a Glance

CorelDRAW 4.0 for Windows

Publisher:
Corel Systems Corporation

Suggested Retail Price:
$595

Upgrade Price:
$249

Requires:
80386 processor or better
Windows 3.1 or later
4MB RAM (8MB recommended)
VGA Video Display
CD-ROM drive optional but highly desirable
13MB free hard disk space for minimal installation
32MB free hard disk space for full installation

Description:

The 4.0 version of CorelDRAW adds a great many features to a program consistently rated by the computer magazines as the most powerful of the IBM-compatible draw programs. One of the niftiest features is the ability to view graphic files in directories before they are called up into the program. CorelDRAW 4.0 has all the draw tools needed to move, stretch, rotate, mirror, skew, or duplicate any image. It can import and export bitmapped graphics, or autotrace these (black-and-white or color) into object-oriented graphics, as well as access and open photographs stored on Kodak Photo CDs. This version includes four fully featured applications for charting, illustration, bitmap editing, and presentations. It comes packed with 750 TrueType fonts and 18,000 clip art and symbol images, all on two CD-ROM discs.

What You Need before You Buy

Buying a graphics package is very tricky. There are so many different kinds of graphics programs and so many different kinds of images produced by them that you really have to know pretty clearly what it is you need to do.

Is it going to be part of a desktop publishing operation? Then the key issues are the ability to create exactly the pictures you need for your publications. Furthermore, you want a graphics program that can deliver those images in a file format that your desktop program can read, use, and print.

Do you plan to hand out a lot of graphs and charts at business meetings? Then it might be good to review the section "Presentation Graphics." Do you plan to use graphics for slides or transparencies? Then you need to make sure that the graphics program you buy can export the images it makes to a program that can make the slides or transparencies you need. (You'll probably be going to a commercial printer or graphic arts studio for that.)

Do you expect to work in color? Then you should look at a program's ability to mix any color you need, and its ability to do color printing or color separations.

In short: Focus on what you need to produce. Narrow it down to programs that can produce what you want. Check out examples of how well those programs do what you want. Make sure the program is compatible with other programs on your computer. And, finally, consider costs and how many programs you actually need.

Shopping for a graphics program will probably take a long time because of the wide range of choices. Be aware that you may have to shop for hardware, in order to make sure that your computer has the resources to handle your graphics program(s), and that your printer lets you do something with the pictures once you've got them.

A Final Note

Graphics programs are terrific fun. It may take a little work to get proficient, but you're certain to have a good time in the process. Then all the techniques that have traditionally been the exclusive property of artists will be in your hands—quite literally at your fingertips.

Seven

Spreadsheets

· ·

Not so long ago, an accountant who was going to work with a spreadsheet would start with a large sheet of paper. It had a great many horizontal and vertical lines for rows and columns. The accountant would write in data and labels, and add up the long columns of numbers using an electronic or mechanical calculator. One tiny slip of the finger on the calculator meant going back over all those columns to find the error.

Computerized spreadsheets are much the same as paper ones, except that they are much more efficient. Because electronic spreadsheets use formulas to add totals, every time you change a number in a row or column, your totals will change simultaneously. And once you enter a number correctly, it *stays* correct. When the totals in accounts receivable get transferred to the general ledger, the computer *never* transposes a number.

For example, if you set up a formula to total everything in the Utilities row from January to December, as soon as you type in a new number, the Utilities Total (and the Total Total) will change automatically to include the new number. Figure 7.1 shows a sample of the computer-style spreadsheet that has largely replaced the paper version.

The ability to instantly revise totals, percentages, or any other calculated cell with the change of a single number is what gives computer spreadsheets both their power and their popularity. Today, the term "spreadsheets" is synonymous with computer programs that permit their users to work with numbers with amazing speed and accuracy.

NOTE

While you may meet the rare writer who longs for her old typewriter, you will **never** meet a bookkeeper who longs to have his manual ledgers back.

Figure 7.1

By using a computer spreadsheet, it's possible to find totals, percentages, differences, and several other calculated results very quickly. Moreover, if one figure in a matrix is changed, all of the other affected figures will change as well, thus saving a great deal of time.

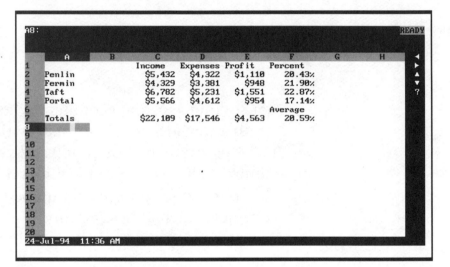

What Is a Spreadsheet?

A *spreadsheet* is a program that manipulates numbers by the use of formulas.

Spreadsheets are valuable both for calculating real numbers and imaginary "what-if" scenarios. If the numbers were a list of your business expenses and you wanted to add them, the spreadsheet would add the numbers and automatically place the total in the "Total" cell. Or suppose you wanted to see what the result would be if you increased or decreased the discount you give to wholesalers. By changing one single value on the spreadsheet, you would have every item on your spreadsheet changed, along with your projected profits.

You instruct a spreadsheet to do something by using formulas. Every spreadsheet program comes with dozens of built-in formulas for doing different kinds of calculations. It's just a matter of typing the formula, telling it what other numbers you want it to work with, and letting the spreadsheet do the calculations. The simplest example is the Totaling function—all spreadsheets have this. You simply have to know what formula your spreadsheet uses. You type in the formula, tell the program you want it to add all the numbers in your document from point A to point B, and the formula will give you the total of those numbers.

All spreadsheets can produce various types of graphs based on the numbers you provide. Figure 7.2 shows a simple pie chart created by a spreadsheet to show how a company spent its money.

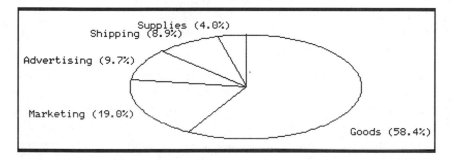

Figure 7.2

To create this chart, someone entered the dollar total of the company's expenses into a spreadsheet, and then activated the spreadsheet's graph-making feature to provide this visual breakdown.

The spreadsheet's ability to provide instant calculation, what-if analysis, and dazzling graphs has proven irresistible to computer users. It's a natural for producing financial reports for businesses, analyzing personal finances, and many other kinds of numerical operations. By 1988, spreadsheets replaced word processing programs as the best-selling single category of software in the country.

The latest trends for spreadsheets include the following:

- more functions to permit more kinds of calculations
- the ability to work with several documents at a time

NOTE

Spreadsheets are more than an accountant's tool. They are used by everyone— from teachers keeping track of class lists to paleontologists cataloging dinosaur bones.

- integration with other programs, such as desktop and graphic programs
- more dramatic graphs

A spreadsheet's basic function, however, is to work with numbers, and it does that in a way nearly everyone can understand. The key attraction is this: If you have to change a number or numbers, a spreadsheet will give you the new results in microseconds.

Spreadsheet Usage

NOTE

Frequently, spreadsheets are used to "look into the future" by changing many variables to see which ones are the most predictive.

Let's say a company has a spreadsheet that covers all income and expenses, with formulas to determine profits. Someone might ask, "What will happen if we hire three more salespeople?" So they key in the cost of three more salespeople's salaries. Someone else might ask, "What if that increases sales by 12 percent?" So they key in a sales increase of 12 percent. With each entry, the formula-derived profits figure will change. The final figure will help determine if hiring the new sales people makes good financial sense. Business decisions based on spreadsheet calculations like this one are made every day.

Spreadsheet documents, whether they are financial reports, cash flow statements, or accounts receivable ledgers, are used daily to help people make decisions or to understand the results of a survey, study, or any other type of numeric analysis. Both the numbers and the graphs are used as raw material for word processing, desktop publishing, and graphics programs.

What Do You Need for Spreadsheet Work?

Spreadsheet programs vary in size and complexity. Your typical computer set-up capable of working with these programs would most likely include the following:

- an operating system that will run your spreadsheet
- just about any size of computer
- at least 512K and optimally 640K of computer memory

1-2-3 Release 4.01 for Windows and
1-2-3 Release 3.4/2.4 for DOS

Publisher:
Lotus Development Corporation

Suggested Retail Price:
$495–Windows/$495–3.4 for
DOS/$495–2.4 for DOS

Upgrade Price:
$119–Windows/$119–3.4 for
DOS/$119–2.4 for DOS

Windows Requires:
80286 processor
 (80386 recommended)
Windows 3.0 or later
DOS 3.1
EGA or better graphics adapter
5MB free hard disk space

DOS Requires:

Version 2.4:
8088 processor or better
640K RAM
DOS 2.1 or later
EGA or better graphics adapter
5MB free hard disk space

Version 3.4:
80286 processor or better
2MB RAM
DOS 3.1 or later
EGA or better graphics adapter
5MB free hard disk space

Description:

One of the first programs available for the PC, 1-2-3 offers spreadsheets, charting, and "flat-file" database management capabilities in a single, integrated environment. Essentially, there are three different 1-2-3 programs available for PC users.

1-2-3 for Windows solidifies Lotus's position as a contender for the best spreadsheet in the Windows arena. It effectively uses the Windows graphical user interface common to all Windows applications and adds more @Functions and macro capabilities than any spreadsheet on Windows.

Version 3.4 requires at least an 80286 (AT) processor and a minimum of 2MB of memory, while adding three-dimensionality and the ability to link information across multiple spreadsheets.

Version 2.4 is the "basic" 1-2-3 program, capable of running on virtually any PC with 640K of RAM and just about any type of video display. However, a graphics monitor is required to view charts, and a graphics-capable printer is necessary to print charts.

- a hard disk
- a monitor (high-resolution color screen optional)
- a keyboard to type in your numbers
- a mouse (optional)
- a printer that can print spreadsheet graphs

If you think that all you will need is to look at the numbers on the screen, you can skip the graph-making capability. There are a few spreadsheet programs that can make graphs out of text characters, but the quality of these is similar to what you would achieve doing a pie chart or a line graph on a typewriter. To really take advantage of what spreadsheets are capable of doing, you need a graphics-based system.

Now let's take a look at the Excel program as it applies to the Macintosh. This is the Mac's most popular spreadsheet program because of its power and versatility. Its features are comparable to many stand-alone business graphics programs.

Product at a Glance

Excel 4.0 for Windows and Excel 4.0 for the Macintosh

Publisher:
Microsoft Corporation

Suggested Retail Price:
$495–Windows/$495–Macintosh

Upgrade Price:
$119.95–Windows/$95–Macintosh

Windows Requires:
80286 processor
Windows 3.0 or later
DOS 3.1 or later
2MB RAM

Macintosh Requires:
Mac Plus or better
System 6.0.2 or later
1MB RAM with System 6.0.x
4MB RAM with System 7

Description:

Microsoft Excel is the most popular spreadsheet available on the Macintosh and has gained great popularity in the Windows world. Combining a powerful spreadsheet with business graphics and a database, Excel can handle big jobs with its large work-sheet area of 16,384 rows by 256 columns. Its charting and presentation tools rival those of stand-alone business graphics packages—offering up to 256 fonts, variable row heights, shading, and more chart types than any other package on the market. Its 3-D "pages", strong file-linking, and ability to work with multiple documents are important features to consider. Excel provides file linking to Microsoft Word, extensive auditing tools, and an impressive macro language and macro editor.

Working with a Spreadsheet

Like their paper counterparts, spreadsheets are organized as *rows* and *columns*. Typically, columns are numbered with letters from A to AA to ZZ at the top, while rows are simply numbered on the left. Although you see only a few columns and rows on the screen at one time, normally, there are several thousand rows in a full spreadsheet, and you move around on the screen to see and use any part of the full spreadsheet.

The point where each column and row intersect is called a *cell*. The cell is the spreadsheet's basic building block. Each cell has a name. For example, in Figure 7.1, the word "Average" is in cell F6. The cell is so named because it's located in column F and row 6.

In each cell, you can enter one of the following three items:

words	to describe what you are keeping track of
numbers	to represent the raw information
formulas	to do something with those numbers

Formulas are the source of any spreadsheet's power and usefulness. You can use them to add, subtract, multiply, and divide numbers; to total columns and rows; to find percentages; and to determine averages. And that's just the simple stuff. More complex formulas can compute internal rates of return, depreciation allowances on an asset, payment schedules on loans, and much more.

Formulas take advantage of a spreadsheet's grid layout by working with cell locations rather than directly with the numbers they contain. That way, whenever the value in a cell changes, all the formulas involving that cell can be recalculated right away using the new value.

Here's an example: Cell C5 might contain the number 100. Cell D5 might have the number 200 entered in it. If you wanted to put a formula into cell E5 that would add those two numbers together and put the result in E5, you would not enter 200+100 there. Instead, the formula would look like this: **+C5+D5**. This tells the program that no matter what the numbers in C5 and D5 are, they are to be added together and the result displayed in cell E5. Thus, if you change the raw number in the cell named

NOTE

A matrix is any organized grouping of objects, be they numbers or words. Tic-Tac-Toe is one form of a simple matrix. An Excel worksheet is another matrix. It's the place holder for the numbers or the text.

C5 from 100 to 300, then the number in cell E5, where the formula is, will change instantly to 500 (C5's 300 plus D5's 200).

In the simplest terms, that is the way spreadsheets work. If you had another formula somewhere that used the result in E5, then that number would also change by 200. By the time a reasonably complex spreadsheet is finished, one small number change can ripple through dozens of formulas and change dozens of results.

What you see on the screen while all this is happening is one of three things: the word or the raw number that you enter, or the number that is the result of a formula calculating a value. You don't see the formula itself. It remains invisible in the background; however, you can go to a cell at any time and see the formula displayed at the top of the screen, and then change the formula any way you like.

Different spreadsheets show you what's in a cell in different ways. Nearly all have a place on the screen where, when you move the cursor into a cell, it will show you what formulas or words or numbers have been entered for that cell. In Figure 7.3, for example, a formula has been entered into cell E5 that is visible in the upper left-hand corner of the screen. It shows that the percentage value in E5 was derived by dividing the contents of D5 by the contents of B5. Then, the value in E5 was formatted to appear as a percentage.

Figure 7.3

When you place the cursor in the cell where a formula calculates a value, the formula appears somewhere on the screen. In Lotus 1-2-3, the formula is seen in the upper left-hand corner. However, when you print the results, the formulas remain invisible.

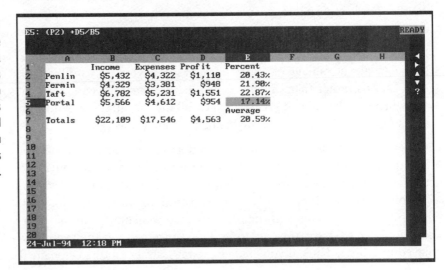

Quattro Pro 5.0 for Windows and Quattro Pro 5.0 for DOS

Publisher:
Borland International

Suggested Retail Price:
$99.95–Windows/$99.95–DOS

Upgrade Price:
$39.95–Windows/$39.95–DOS

Competitive Upgrade:
$49.95–Windows/$49.95–DOS

Windows Requires:
80386 processor or better
Windows 3.1 or later
4MB RAM available
EGA or better graphics adapter
10MB free hard disk space

DOS Requires:
8088 processor or better
DOS 3.1 or later
512K RAM
EGA or better for WYSIWYG
6MB free hard disk space

Description:

Quattro Pro was designed to compete head-on with Lotus 1-2-3 by giving users the familiar 1-2-3 interface with more features. Note the competitive upgrade price: if you have proof of ownership of a competing product, you can purchase Quattro Pro for only $49.95. Versions 4 and 5 no longer offer the 1-2-3 interface, but still provide full 1-2-3 compatibility. Quattro Pro for DOS provides a great deal of spreadsheet power without large hardware requirements. It has an easy-to-use windows format, draw tools for enhancing its charts, direct access to database files, enhanced analytical tools, and the ability to view numbers and charts in the same worksheet. Quattro Pro can open up to 64 files at one time, and has an extensive file-linking capability. This is a highly rated program for both the DOS and Windows environments.

Key Features: The Tools of the Trade

Various spreadsheets have hundreds of built-in formulas and tools to help you enter data, create formulas, format the document, and prepare graphs. This section will explore other features typical of spreadsheets.

Basic Functions

Spreadsheets come with dozens to hundreds of functions. Some frequently used functions are as follows:

Sum: Adds up the numbers in a given range of cells.

Average: Gives the average value in a range of cells. If one or more cells are blanks, they usually won't be included in determining the average.

Minimum & Maximum: Examine a range of cells (such as A5 to AZ5) and display the smallest or largest number found.

Round: Rounds off a number to whatever decimal point you specify. So, a calculation resulting in 5.15433 could be 5 or 5.2 or 5.15 depending on how many numbers you want to see after the decimal. Figure 7.4 shows an example of the output of many of these functions.

NOTE

Even for financial nonwizards, spreadsheets can help calculate various types of financial outcomes. They do all the work and math. You just have to know where to look for the results.

Figure 7.4

Functions can be used to calculate values for an array of different formulas, the results of which are seen in this figure.

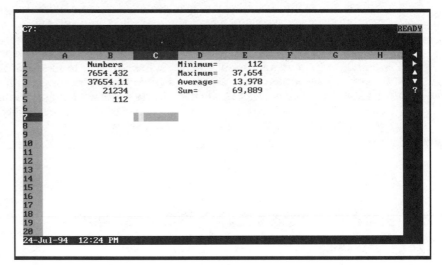

Other functions available in specialized areas include the following:

Mathematical: Determine sines, cosines, tangents; take a number to any power (3^4); give you a square root; compute logarithmic bases; reduce a number to its integer (5.14 to 5); tell you the remainder of a division; return pi (3.1415926); generate random numbers; or give you the absolute value of a number (-5 becomes 5).

How to Make It All Add Up

All spreadheets use the basic mathematical symbols, that is, a plus (+) for addition, a minus (−) for subtraction, an asterisk (*) for multiplication, and a slash (/) for division.

Another very important symbol is the parenthesis. You use parentheses to indicate what part of a formula you want done first. For example, 1+2*3 will give you 7, because programs tend to multiply before they add. If what you really want is to first add 1+2 and then multiply that sum by 3, which equals 9, you must use parentheses. To do that you use the formula (1+2)*3, and the program will do what is in parentheses first.

Most spreadsheets will tell you in what order they perform math functions. But rather than worrying about it, just get into the habit of using parentheses. For example, ((1+2)/3)*4 tells the program to *add, then divide, then multiply,* which is the exact opposite from the way the program would do it without the parentheses.

Financial: For accountants and financial officers. These functions provide information such as how long it takes for a fixed-interest investment to grow to a certain value; what the depreciation allowance on a value is; what the internal rate of return for cash flow values is; what the monthly payment on a loan at a given interest rate for a given period of time would be; and every sort of financial formula you can imagine and many you've never thought of!

Words: In computerese, any group of characters can be called a *string,* as in strings of letters. Spreadsheets include formulas that can act on words. These are called string functions and can compare words and word lengths, convert words to upper- or lowercase, copy a word as many times as you want, or remove extra blank spaces.

Dates: Convert dates and times to numbers so you can work with them in your calculations. Once you learn how to enter dates and times for any particular spreadsheet, these can tell you the month, day, year, hour, minute, and second of a specific date.

Database: You can use a spreadsheet as a database. You have commands to search for specific information (such as a name), copy a record or part of a record into a separate area of your worksheet, sort information, or delete a record. You also can get information from a database and perform spreadsheet functions on the data. Figure 7.5 shows a spreadsheet being used as a database.

Logical: Perform tests, comparing one value with another or determining whether a value is of a specific type (such as text or a number). For example, after a formula has found the average of a group of values, another formula might test the individual values against that average and label each one as Average, Above Average, or Below Average, accordingly.

Statistical: Totaling, averaging, and finding the minimum or maximum value in a list are considered statistical functions. More complex formulas can compute the standard deviation of values in a list on the basis of the square root of the variance.

As you can see, there are lots of formulas built into any spreadsheet to solve different mathematical problems. The average user needs less than a dozen—the others will stay out of the way and never bother you.

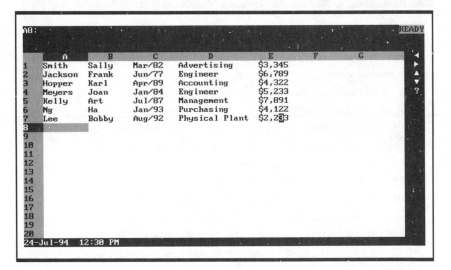

Figure 7.5

Used as a database, spreadsheets can organize fields by columns with each row showing data for given individuals.

Manipulation Tools

Manipulation tools are those tools that make it easy for you to create a worksheet quickly. They are used to manipulate on-screen data. They include the following:

Copy: Allows you to take any words, numbers, or formulas in one part of a spreadsheet and reproduce them in another part of the spreadsheet. The most common use is to copy a formula from one cell to produce similar formulas in other cells.

Move: Allows you to pick up a block of words, numbers, or formulas in one part of a worksheet and move them somewhere else. Typically, the formulas and the cells they reference don't change, and the space from which the block was removed becomes blank. Figure 7.6 shows an example of such a move.

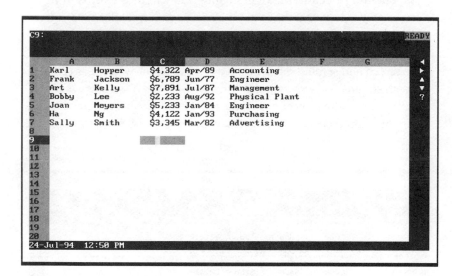

Figure 7.6

To illustrate a typical Move function, Figure 7.5 was rearranged so that the first name came before the last name and the monthly salary column followed the employee's name. Using the Sort function, the names were placed in alphabetical order by last name.

Erase: Lets you remove unwanted data.

Help: Gives you instructions at the touch of a key. The most useful Help menus are context-sensitive, that is, they will give you instructions for whatever feature you are working with at the time. Figure 7.7 shows a sample Help screen.

Figure 7.7

The Help screens will help you get the most out of your spreadsheet program. The Wingz spreadsheet for both IBM-compatibles and the Macintosh has an excellent Help program.

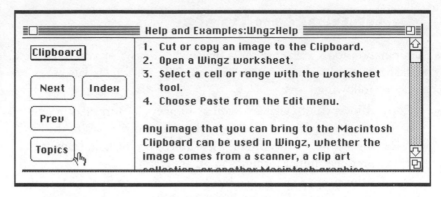

Movement: Because a full worksheet is much larger than the single screenful of data you see at one time, most programs offer you easy ways to move around. For example, in Lotus 1-2-3, a Tab will move you one full screen to the right, a Shift-Tab will move you a full screen to the left, and the PageUp/PageDown keys will move you a full screen up or down.

NOTE

Even spreadsheets of several screen-widths can be handled by scrolling up and down and left and right.

Freezing Titles: Allows you to lock one or more rows or columns on the screen and scroll the rest of the worksheet. For example, a 12-month summary of expenditures will be wider than one screen. If you lock your spending categories on the left side of the screen, you can still see which numbers go with which category. Figure 7.8 shows an example.

Figure 7.8

The labels in the first column are frozen. Several months have been scrolled off the screen, but the labels remain. When you have a wide or long spreadsheet with a sea of numbers, you'll be glad you have the locking feature. (Note the cursor under the 'K' column.)

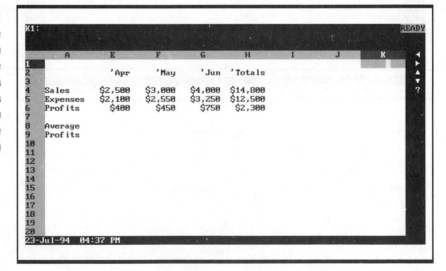

Product at a Glance

Microsoft Works 2.0 for Windows and Microsoft Works 3.0 for DOS

Publisher:
Microsoft Corporation

Suggested Retail Price:
$199–Windows/$149–DOS

Upgrade Price:
$79–Windows/$49.95–DOS

Windows Requires:
80286 processor or better
Windows 3.0 or later
1MB RAM
5.5MB free hard disk space
EGA or better graphics adapter

DOS Requires:
8088 processor or better
DOS 3.0 or later
640K RAM

Description:

Microsoft Works is an integrated package that offers word processing, database management, spreadsheets, and communications capabilities. Although not as powerful as its big brother, Excel, Works has just as many rows (16,384) and columns (256), and comes with a full range of mathematical, trigonometric, logical, financial, date/time, and special purpose functions to analyze statistics, manage finances, and develop forecasts. It also provides draw tools to enhance its pie/bar/line charts, and other tools to format cells with type styles, borders, and grids.

Product at a Glance

Microsoft Works 3.0 for Macintosh

Publisher:
Microsoft Corporation

Suggested Retail Price:
$249

Upgrade Price:
$79

Requires:
Mac Plus or better
System 6.0.5 or better
1MB RAM or 2MB RAM for System 7
2MB free hard disk space or two
   floppy drives
HyperCard 2.0 for tutorial

Description:

Microsoft Works for the Macintosh has all the integrated features of Works for Windows and DOS. It provides all the tools for most business and personal uses, and it can be run on a floppy-only system or a system with limited hard drive space, such as a PowerBook.

Formatting Tools

Formatting tools are those that let you change the look of your document in some fashion. They include the following:

Defaults: The way that programs look when they first load up is called the default setting. In spreadsheets, that has to do with how wide the columns are, whether numbers display automatically as 1 or 1.00, and so forth. Not only can you change each individual cell, you can also change the default settings for the program (or document) so that it comes up on-screen looking just the way you want it. (See Figure 7.9.)

Figure 7.9

The default settings of a spreadsheet can be changed to give you exactly what you need for your application.

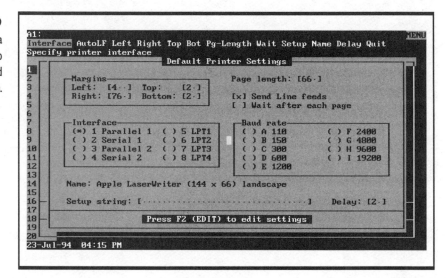

```
A1:                                                                    MENU
Interface AutoLF Left Right Top Bot Pg-Length Wait Setup Name Delay Quit
Specify printer interface
                          Default Printer Settings
1
2         ┌Margins─────────────────────┐    Page length: [66 ]
3         │ Left:  [4  ]  Top:    [2 ] │
4         │ Right: [76]  Bottom: [2 ] │    [x] Send Line feeds
5         └────────────────────────────┘    [ ] Wait after each page
6
7         ┌Interface──────────────────┐    ┌Baud rate─────────────────┐
8         │(*) 1 Parallel 1  ( ) 5 LPT1│    │( ) A 110       ( ) F 2400│
9         │( ) 2 Serial 1    ( ) 6 LPT2│    │( ) B 150       ( ) G 4800│
10        │( ) 3 Parallel 2  ( ) 7 LPT3│    │( ) C 300       ( ) H 9600│
11        │( ) 4 Serial 2    ( ) 8 LPT4│    │( ) D 600       ( ) I 19200│
12        └────────────────────────────┘    │( ) E 1200                │
13                                           └──────────────────────────┘
14        Name: Apple LaserWriter (144 x 66) landscape
15
16        Setup string: [·····························]   Delay: [2 ]
17
18           ┌──── Press F2 (EDIT) to edit settings ────┐
19
20
23-Jul-94  04:15 PM
```

Text: Word entries (also called labels) that you use for titles or descriptors also can be formatted to justify to the left, right, or center of any cell (and usually any page). Graphics-based programs also let you change the text to be larger, smaller, a different typeface, or a different type style (bold, italic, and so forth).

Columns: You can insert a new column, delete a column that's already there, or change the width of one or all columns at any time.

Rows: You can insert as many new rows as you need or delete rows that are already there. In graphics-based programs, you also can change the height of a row to allow for larger or smaller type. Text-based rows, however, always remain one-character high.

152 *Chapter 7: Spreadsheets*

Ranges: This is any rectangular block of cells. Once you've identified a block as a range, you can change the appearance of all the numbers in that area to a particular format; that is, you can use 1 or 1.000, $1.00 or $1, or 100%. Figure 7.10 shows an example of a range being defined. In many programs, you can name a range and just go directly to that range by giving the program its name.

	A	B	C	D	E	F	G	H
Enter name: Third

1								
2		98765	101728	104780	107923	111161	114496	
3		98963	101931	104989	108139	111383	114725	
4		99160	102135	105199	108355	111606	114954	
5		99359	102340	105410	108572	111829	115184	
6		99557	102544	105621	108789	112053	115414	
7		99757	102749	105832	109007	112277	115645	
8		99956	102955	106043	109225	112501	115877	
9		100156	103161	106256	109443	112726	116108	
10		100356	103367	106468	109662	112952	116341	
11		100557	103574	106681	109881	113178	116573	
12		100758	103781	106894	110101	113404	116806	

23-Jul-94   04:29 PM

Figure 7.10
The third column is being named "Third." In large spreadsheet applications, remembering a name for a set of data is easier than remembering the cell names.

Hiding columns: This allows you to hide some columns from view on the screen. This comes in handy for 12-month summaries, which usually are too wide for a screen. (See Figure 7.11.) By hiding six months of data, you can see descriptions on the left, totals on the right, and the six months you're in the middle of. The data are not gone; they are just hidden, and the numbers are still included in the totals.

Sorting: Nearly all spreadsheets give you the ability to change the look of a page by sorting the data. Let's say you have a list of stocks and want to know how they're doing. To read the page more easily you might want to sort the lines alphabetically by stock name or show the highest yield first.

NOTE
In addition to performing calculations, another major use of spreadsheets is the clear presentation of the calculated data.

Figure 7.11

Notice that columns C and D as well as F and G are not on the screen. Hiding columns and rows makes it easier to compare others next to one another. This is especially true in large spreadsheets.

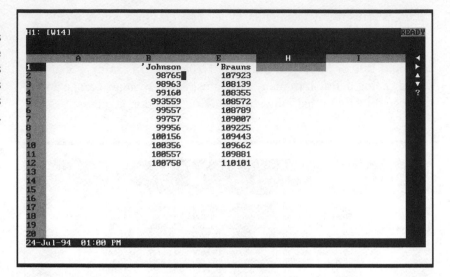

Page graphs: The newer programs will allow you to show both numbers and a graph on the screen. (See Figure 7.12.) If you change a number, the graph will change also.

Figure 7.12

Excel can show both the data and the chart on the same screen.

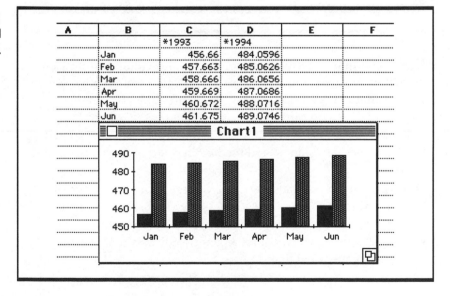

Graph Features

Most spreadsheets can create graphs of all types. The advantage of creating graphs from spreadsheets as opposed to using presentation graphics programs is that the numbers are already in place, whereas in many presentation programs you may have to type in the numbers. Factors to consider in evaluating the graph features of spreadsheets include the following:

Variety of graphs: The most common types of graphs include pie, line, bar, stacked bar, and Hi-Low-Open-Close (as in stocks). A good spreadsheet should be able to create all of these.

Color conversion: This feature lets you convert a color graph to monochrome so the different colors become shades of gray. Unless you have a color printer, you'll need this in order to produce readable graphs.

Exploding pie charts: This sounds like more fun than it is; it's just a pie chart with a wedge pulled out for emphasis. Some programs set the distance between the pie and the wedge automatically, while others let you determine the distance.

3-D perspective: Graphs with a three-dimensional view can provide dramatic illustrations. Such graphs, generated from spreadsheet data, can be very effective in reports or advertising. Figure 7.13 shows an example.

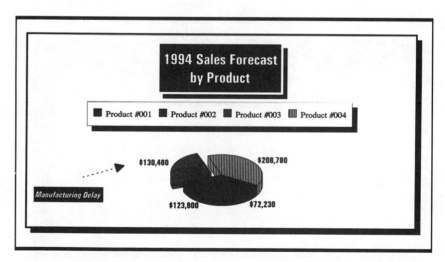

Figure 7.13
Many of the spreadsheets available provide an option for 3-D graphics.

Text formatting: All graphs use words to explain what the chart is about. If you plan to do a lot of charting, look for a spreadsheet that gives you plenty of flexibility in changing the font, type style, and type size in your chart. Graphics-based programs tend to offer more selections than text-based programs.

Draw tools: Sometimes graphs can use a bit of enhancing with extra lines, boxes, and circles. Some spreadsheets provide these basic drawing tools that you can use to enhance your graphs.

Ease-of-Use Features

Ease-of-use features are those that are generally useful, and the amount of such features is proportional to the usefulness of the spreadsheet. These features include the following:

Macros: A macro is a set of prerecorded instructions that you can use to automate your work. For example, suppose you find yourself working on a spreadsheet in which you must continually copy one full column to another. Manually, it may take you about 9 to 12 keystrokes to do that. With a macro, you set up the same sequence of keystrokes and give it a name like Alt-C. Then, every time you must copy a column, you just press Alt-C, and the macro will play back those keystrokes, copying the column. Figure 7.14 shows how a macro command is set up.

Figure 7.14

This macro was developed to examine the average of values in cells A1 through A5 and to assign a grade from A–F. Once this macro has been created, it can automatically be executed to determine grades.

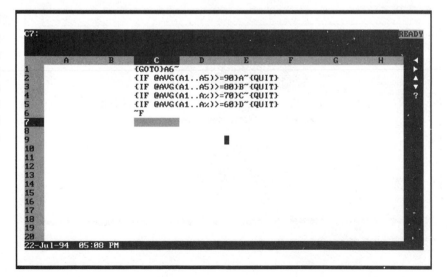

Word processing: Some of the newer spreadsheets offer more text-handling capabilities, such as line justification, font changes, and type-size changes. One test of a spreadsheet's versatility is how well it works with words to create actual pages, as opposed to just making worksheets and graphs. Graphics-based spreadsheets tend to do this best.

File combine/extract: All spreadsheets must be able to save files to disk and to retrieve them to be of any use at all. Most of these programs also allow you to copy a piece of one worksheet (extract), and then insert that part into another worksheet (combine). This is a way to move data between worksheets, such as a set of formulas, so you don't have to retype the formulas every time you need them.

File linking: This is a step above the file combine/extract feature. Here the program has the ability to link cells in different worksheets. This means that when you make a change in one worksheet, that same change is made in the worksheet to which it's tied. One common use of this is to link several financial detail worksheets to one master consolidated worksheet that displays overall totals. Most programs that can do this can also have more than one worksheet in memory at a time, so you can see the supporting worksheets while you work with the master.

Database connectivity: This feature takes advantage of the fact that spreadsheets and databases both work in a row-column format and allows spreadsheets to retrieve information directly from database programs.

Windows: This is the ability to display and use several worksheets in various windows on-screen at one time, as shown in Figure 7.15. You can resize, move, stack, and zoom in on each of the windows, making it possible to see all the information you need in multiple worksheets at the same time.

Passwords: This feature allows you to set a password, controlling who can see and who can change a spreadsheet.

Minimal recalculation: Usually, when you enter a number, the spreadsheet recalculates everything in the worksheet. This feature instructs the program to recalculate only the formulas affected by changes. In short, it speeds things up.

Three-dimensionality: Most worksheets are flat; that is, they have rows and columns. Some newer spreadsheet releases also have

NOTE

With a good spreadsheet program, you should be able to get data that has already been entered from other programs.

Figure 7.15

Wingz is a typical window-using spreadsheet. Here, three different spreadsheets are on the screen at the same time.

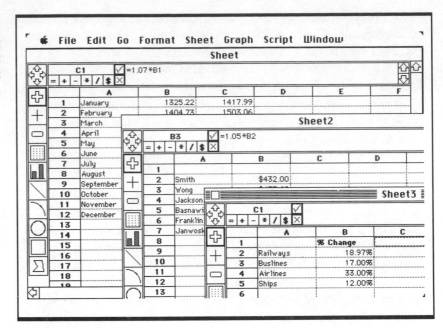

"pages," or other row-columns sheets *below* the top one. This three-dimensional effect allows you to define ranges spanning several rows, columns, and pages, and to manipulate data over pages.

.WK exporting: The extension .WK plus a number (.WK1, .WK2, etc.) is the file format of the Lotus 1-2-3 spreadsheet. Because 1-2-3 has been around so long, nearly all programs that import files have learned how to read it. So if you plan to use your spreadsheet data in word processing, desktop, or graphics programs, make sure your spreadsheet can save files in that format.

Notes: Some spreadsheet programs will allow you to write notes that are connected to cells. The most common use is to write yourself a reminder about a formula that you entered in a cell. This can be a very handy feature when you look back at a formula you wrote three months ago (or three *hours* ago) and don't remember what the formula is supposed to do.

Function paste menus: Instead of having to remember and type out a lot of different functions, many spreadsheets provide paste menus from which you select the formula you need. For example, Figure 7.16 shows the Macintosh Excel Paste menu offering 10 categories of spreadsheet functions (Business, Date/Time, and so forth).

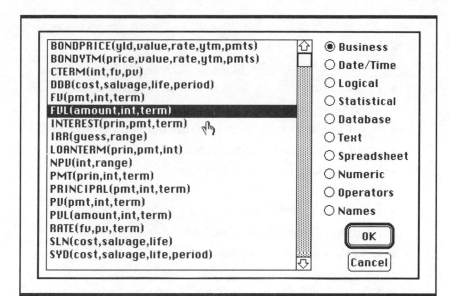

Figure 7.16
Paste menus are very handy in a spreadsheet program. By substituting values for the parameters of each formula, the user can quickly apply them.

How Do I Learn Spreadsheets?

The spreadsheet programs of today can seem very intimidating. After all, a program can have over 500 commands and 100 functions. This is one time when it doesn't pay to look at the big picture.

Like most software, you only have to learn a little at any given time. Unless you have some specialized needs, if you figure out a half-dozen basic formulas, that's probably all you'll need to know for the first few worksheets.

The easiest way to learn this is to practice by building an application— a worksheet—and in the process, look up the essential commands, functions, and other features that the software provides. Just as you can learn a foreign language faster by hearing it and trying to speak it, you'll learn these programs more quickly by trying to use them.

Here are some suggestions on how to learn to use spreadsheets quickly:

- Enter some data. Use both words and numbers.
- Create a few simple formulas, such as adding two cells.
- Practice using some of the basic functions previously described.
- Try copying some formulas.
- Learn how to change the appearance of numbers (1 or $1.00).
- Learn how to create percentages (change .5 to 50%).
- Practice changing the width of columns.
- Try inserting and deleting rows and columns.
- Learn how to save a worksheet as a file.
- Learn how to retrieve a worksheet.
- Learn how to print your document.

None of this is very hard. It may take you a few evenings to pick up this much, and that will probably handle about 95 percent of everything you'll need to do with any basic worksheet.

Once you understand these basics, then you're ready to move on to building your first graph. Pie charts are the easiest to work with and thus a good place to start. Then try creating other types of graphs. Each graph might take one evening to learn. Then explore the possibilities for enhancing your graphs. You can then start to explore the more complex functions as you need them.

In a week, you should know enough about both the numeric and graphic sides of spreadsheet programs to create anything you might need.

Text versus Graphical Interface in Spreadsheets

NOTE

All Macintosh computers have a graphical interface, and more and more IBM-compatible software uses a similar interface with spreadsheet programs. All Windows applications use a graphical interface.

Spreadsheets operate in dual roles. In worksheets, about all you'll ever see are characters. If all you need is to see text-only output, a text-based screen, computer, and printer will suffice.

But nowadays spreadsheet programs can create more than just text. In fact, the bar/line/pie charts they create have become ubiquitous in the business world. To do those, you will need a graphical interface that lets you see what you are creating. This is also known as WYSIWYG (What You See Is What You Get).

Today, newer versions of spreadsheets produce entire pages that include text, a worksheet, and a graph, as shown in Figure 7.17. To do these effectively, you will need a high-resolution graphics screen that can show you exactly what you are going to get from the printer, and a printer that can print what you see.

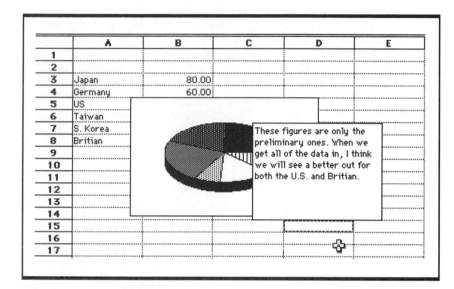

Figure 7.17
On this Wingz screen, you see the spreadsheet, the graphic, and a text sheet together.

What Do I Need to Know If I'm Going to Buy?

By this time, you should have a pretty good idea of how spreadsheets work and what they can do.

The key determining factors in what you buy include how fast the program runs, how much memory is required, how easy it is to learn and use, and what type of graphing functions are provided.

One unique thing about spreadsheet programs stems from the long domination of Lotus 1-2-3. Because people were so familiar with how Lotus 1-2-3 worked, most competitors created spreadsheets that worked almost the same way. They added features, improved graphics capabilities, and made the results prettier, but the basics remained the same.

So here are some factors to consider when you buy a spreadsheet package:

- **Hardware**: The boxes in which software is packaged usually tell you what kind of a computer you need to run that program. Because there's such a wide variation in systems needed by different spreadsheet programs, it's a good idea to find out if your computer system matches what that particular spreadsheet requires.

- **User help**: Most current spreadsheet versions come with excellent help menus, but often the best help you can get is from other users. So think of all those Lotus 1-2-3 users out there as a resource. Also, remember that other spreadsheets work similarly to Lotus and these programs have enthusiastic users, too.

- **Use with other programs**: If you plan to use spreadsheet data with other programs such as word processing, desktop, or graphics programs, you'll want a spreadsheet whose files can be read by the other programs you use.

- **Price**: Because all spreadsheets do the same tasks, your decision becomes a matter of choosing how many bells and whistles you can't live without.

- **Clones**: In software, a clone is a program that looks and works almost the same way as a more expensive brand name program. Because Lotus has been *the* spreadsheet for so long, there are a number of Lotus 1-2-3 clones around; some are even available as shareware and freeware. You might want to look for one of those if you want to test the waters before diving into a full-price version.

A Final Note

Spreadsheets are the number-crunchers of the computer world. With hundreds of built-in features and functions, they specialize in solving any kind of number-calculation problem and in preparing dazzling graphs that illustrate what the numbers mean.

They are not difficult to learn, and they all operate very similarly. Once you've mastered one program, you can probably learn to use any other spreadsheet in a matter of hours.

Eight

Database Management Systems

• •

ost of the program categories discussed in the preceding chapters—word processing, desktop publishing, and graphics—are tools designed to help you *present* information in a highly polished format, whether it's text, graphics, or financial reports. Database management is a tool to help you with a very different kind of task—keeping records of information. A typical database is a huge and continuously updated file of information, abstracts, or references on a particular subject or subjects.

In general, database management is the tool of choice for the "business" of running a business, including order entry and shipping, inventory control, accounts payable and receivable, and much more. It's a general-purpose information storage and retrieval tool for managing large amounts of information ranging from simple address lists to extremely complex business and scientific data.

What Is Database Management?

A *database* is simply an organized collection of information (data) stored in a computer file. A *database management system* (DBMS) is a program that allows you to enter the information into the computer file, find it, edit it, sort it, search it, view it, or print it in whatever form suits your needs.

Although you may not have thought about it in such terms, the chances are good that you've been managing databases for a long time—even if you've never touched a computer in your life.

For instance, a shoe box full of index cards with names and addresses of customers is a kind of database. A file cabinet with drawers full of file folders and documents is a database. Even your little black book is a database.

The more information you have to manage, however, the more you need a database program. For example, if you send correspondence to the same group of people from time to time, obviously it's time-consuming to type or hand-address each piece each time you send a mailing. When you use a DBMS, you need only type the names and addresses once. Also, you can add new names and addresses, and change existing ones as needed. When the time comes to send out the next correspondence, you can have the DBMS type all the form letters, envelopes, and mailing labels.

But managing a list of names and addresses barely scratches the surface of the kinds of things you can do with a DBMS.

What Can I Do with a Database Management System?

DBMSs can be used for both large- and small-scale record-keeping and information retrieval. The type of information you can store is limited only by your needs and your imagination. Here are just a few of the many common uses for DBMSs:

- Manage mailing lists and telephone directories.
- Manage customer, sales lead, and membership information files.
- Handle bookkeeping and accounting, such as general ledger and accounts payable and receivable.
- Manage orders and control inventory.
- Manage a personal or professional library.
- Build and keep track of schedules, such as students in classes or goals in a project.
- Store and analyze statistical and research data.

Virtually every business, from banks to retail chains to video rental stores, uses DBMSs to track customers, accounts, and inventory. Some of these systems are on large computers, but DBMSs on desktop computers offer the same powerful capabilities.

What Do I Need to Use a Database Management System?

To manage a computer database, you'll need a computer system complete with the usual hardware: monitor, keyboard, hard disk, and printer.

Memory: Because a DBMS generally works with large amounts of data stored on disk, the amount of memory required is determined by the program itself, not by the amount of information you wish to manage. Most PC DBMSs can operate on a "standard" configuration of 640K of memory, although you need to check the requirements of the specific database management program you're interested in to be sure. Also, because most DBMSs can store *some* information in memory, the more memory your system has, the faster your DBMS will operate.

Printer: Although it's possible to store and view information using just your monitor, you'll certainly want to print something from the database, whether it's mailing labels, form letters, invoices, or reports. If you want to print form letters for correspondence, use your company logo, or print other graphics, you'll want a laser printer. A simple dot-matrix printer will do for labels.

Hard Disk: As with most modern programs, a hard disk is a must for database management. The amount of hard disk storage you'll need is determined by 1) how much space the database management program itself requires, and 2) how much data you need to store.

It is important to determine how much disk storage you'll need for your database before you buy a computer, because you don't want to find yourself halfway through the process of building a database only to discover that you've run out of disk space. And you need to keep in mind that databases tend to grow with time.

Because storage capacity is measured in bytes, you need to think about how the information you'll be storing translates to bytes. This is fairly easy to do, because a byte is basically one character of information. So, let's suppose that you want to manage names and addresses with your DBMS. A rather large name and address might look like this:

Wanda Granolabar
Vice President, Marketing
Technobabble Institute
17047 Northwest Passage Rd.
Rancho Santa Fe, CA 92067

If you were to count all the characters (including blank spaces and punctuation) in that sample name and address, you'd come up with 115 characters. That is, 115 bytes.

If you plan to store as many as 100,000 names and addresses, you'd need 11,500,000 (i.e., 115 times 100,000) bytes. Divide that value by a million

NOTE

To learn more about memory and hard disks, see Chapter 14. To learn more about printers, see Chapter 16.

to figure out how many megabytes (abbreviated MB) of storage you would need just to store the names and addresses. In this case, you'd need 11.5MB.

But there's also some "overhead" to think about. Different DBMSs require different amounts of overhead, but doubling the initial value is probably more than sufficient; say 23MB to store all the names and addresses.

Of course, you'll also need to store the DBMS itself, the operating system, and any other programs you'll be using. It's always better to err on the side of having too much, rather than not enough, storage capacity. So you'd probably want to double or triple the value you arrived at before, and buy a hard disk with somewhere between 60 and 100MB of storage capacity.

To manage a database, you'll also need the appropriate software. In addition to the operating system, you'll obviously need a DBMS. We'll discuss some of the features to look for in a DBMS a little later in this chapter.

Using a Database Management System

As previously mentioned, one of the things that makes a DBMS unique is its record-keeping orientation. When you use a word processor, you start out with a "blank sheet of paper" on the screen, and then type, edit, and print your document. Once you've printed the document, you may or may not want to save a copy for future use. The job may be finished just as soon as the document is printed.

But with a database, storing data for future use is the whole objective. In fact, how the information *looks* on the screen is of almost no importance at all. Instead, your main concern is how the information is *organized* on the disk. After the information is organized and stored, you can display it in whatever format you wish, as form letters, mailing labels, envelopes, receipts, invoices, or financial reports, as often as necessary.

Virtually all DBMSs require that you organize the information that you want to store into a tabular format with rows and columns. For example, Figure 8.1 shows a list of names and phone numbers organized into a table.

There are some specific terms that go with database management to describe the components of the database table, as illustrated in Figure 8.1.

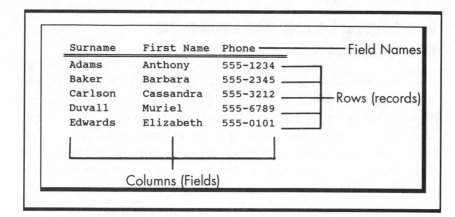

Figure 8.1
Sample database table of names and phone numbers. In database terminology, each row in the table is called a record, and each column is called a field.

They are defined below:

Field: Each column in the table, also called a *field*, represents a specific type of information. For example, the database table in Figure 8.1 contains three fields (columns) of information. These fields are named Surname (contains a person's last name), FirstName (contains a person's first name), and Phone (contains a person's phone number.)

Record: A row, or *record* in a database table is made up of all the fields, and each record in one database has the same fields. For example, in Figure 8.1, the first record contains the name and phone number for Anthony Adams. The second record contains the name and phone number for Barbara Baker, and so forth.

Table: The full collection of records, fields, and field names makes up one database *table* (also called a *database file*.)

Although some database programs limit how many fields and records you can have in your database as a whole, by and large a DBMS doesn't care how many fields or records your tables contain, or what the names of the fields are. It's up to you, as the user of the program, to figure out what information you want to store, and how to organize that information into the tabular format required by the DBMS.

To illustrate, let's look at the exact steps you might follow to set up a database, and then manage that database with your DBMS.

Design Your Database Structure

Before you even run your DBMS, it's a good idea to think about how you can organize the information you need to store into rows and columns. Basically, you want to store each "meaningful" item of information in a separate field. For example, suppose you're keeping track of information about customers, including each person's name, address, phone number, credit limit, and the date they applied for credit. In that case, you might want to break the information for each customer into the following fields:

    Surname
    FirstName
    Address
    City
    State
    ZipCode
    Phone
    CreditLimit
    StartDate

You may be wondering why we should bother to split people's names into two fields, Surname and FirstName. The reason is that the more fields you break the information into, the easier it will be to manage the data later on.

For example, storing each person's surname in its own field makes it easier to tell the program later to "put the information into alphabetical order by surname" or to "find Smith."

Separating the fields also makes it easier to determine exactly how you might want to print them later. For example, if at some point you want to print a list of customers in alphabetical order, you could easily tell the program to list Surname followed by a comma, followed by the FirstName, like this:

    Adams, Anthony
    Baker, Barbara
    Carlson, Cara

And, when using this same database to print form letters, invoices, mailing labels, envelopes, or whatever, it would be just as easy to tell the program to print the same information in a different format—for example, FirstName followed by a space and then Surname, like this:

Anthony Adams

Barbara Baker

Cara Carlson

Also, you need to plan how much space each field is likely to require. On the one hand, you don't want to shortchange yourself when making these decisions: for example, if you allot only 10 characters for the Surname field, you won't be able to store the hyphenated name *Livingston-Gladstone* in your database, because that requires 20 characters. On the other hand, you don't want to allot 100 characters per surname, because nobody's surname is that long, and you'd just be wasting disk space to give that much space to each and every surname in the table.

A good compromise here might be to assign the maximum length of each field in our sample database as follows:

Field Name	Length
Surname	20
FirstName	15
Address	30
City	15
State	2
ZipCode	10
Phone	14
CreditLimit	10
StartDate	8

The last step in designing a database concerns deciding what *type* of information is to be stored in each field. This is perhaps the least intuitive step in the process because we don't usually think about "types" of information in our day-to-day lives. If we do think about it, the "type" of information we're dealing with is obvious, and we don't need someone to tell us that "this is a number, and this is text, and this is a date."

But because computers store different types of information in different ways (and because they don't have any brains of their own), they *do* need to be told what type of information is in each field. Though the exact *data types* you'll have at your disposal depend on the specific database management program you're using, most require that you specify the following types of information:

Text (or Character, or Alphanumeric): Textual information such as names, addresses, and any other written text

Numeric: Any numeric information, such as quantities or dollar amounts, with which you want to do math operations such as totals and subtotals

Date: Any chronological dates that you want to be able to do "date arithmetic" with (for example, when you want to tell the program to "print out dunning letters for all accounts that are more than 60 days past due from a specific date")

Defining the type of information in each field in the database table not only determines how the database management program will store the information, it also determines what you can do with that information later. For example, defining StartDate as a "date" field means that later you'll be able to tell the database management program to do things such as "print a list of all customers who signed up a year or more ago" or "list all the customer names and addresses in chronological order."

So, at this stage of the process, our sample table design might look something like this:

Field Name	Length	Type
Surname	20	Text
FirstName	15	Text
Address	30	Text
City	15	Text
State	2	Text
ZipCode	10	Text
Phone	14	Text
CreditLimit	10	Numeric
StartDate	8	Date

Now you may be thinking "Wait a minute—you just said that the Numeric data type is for numbers. Yet you just made ZipCode and Phone the Text data type." That's true, and the reason is that neither Zip codes nor phone numbers are "true" numbers. That is, you would never want to "total up" all the zip codes in a database, or divide one phone number by another phone number. Besides, Canadian and other overseas zip-type-codes include letters in them. So, unless you specifically want to do math operations on the contents of a field, you don't need to define it as a Numeric data type.

Now, once you've figured out how to store the information you want to manage with your DBMS, the next step is to actually run the program, and to create the database table structure.

Creating the Table Structure

Most database management programs provide a simple screen for translating your "paper" database table structure into the real thing. For example, Figure 8.2 shows a database design screen for Paradox (a popular database management program for PCs) filled out to define the table structure we've designed thus far.

The letters and lengths next to each field name describe the type and length of each field. Notice the information box (labeled FIELD TYPES) shows the types of data that Paradox supports.

You may also notice in Figure 8.2 that the information box indicates that you can mark *key fields* with an asterisk. We'll talk briefly about "key fields" later in this chapter.

NOTE

Paradox and some other database management programs require that you specify the maximum length of Text (Alpha) fields only.

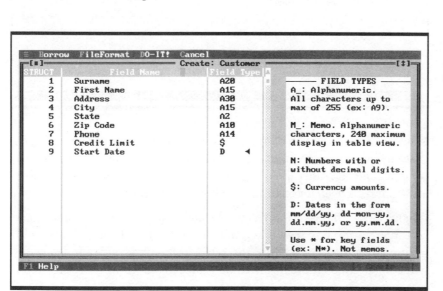

Figure 8.2

A sample database table structure defined in Paradox.

Entering the Data

Once you've defined the structure of your database table, you can easily enter information into the table. You can add new data, change data, and delete data at any time. Most DBMSs make this step very easy. When you're ready to enter information into your database, you just make a couple of menu choices, or press a couple of keys, and the screen displays a "fill-in-the-blanks" form for entering data into your database.

For instance, Figure 8.3 shows a sample screen for entering data into the database defined in Figure 8.2, with information for a single database record already keyed in next to each field name. (This figure shows a screen from dBASE IV, which is another popular PC DBMS.)

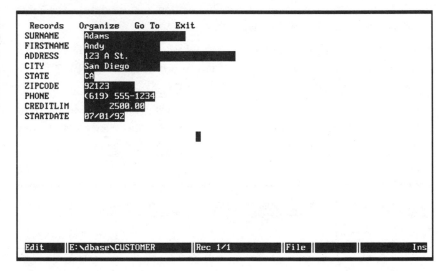

Figure 8.3

A sample screen for entering data into a database table structure. Shown here is the "one-record-at-a-time" data-entry screen for dBASE IV.

Many DBMSs also let you design your own custom data-entry screens. On a custom screen, you can order the fields however you want, create your own prompts, and add other useful information. For example, Figure 8.4 shows a customized screen for entering data into our sample database table.

Finally, most DBMSs also give you the ability to enter, view, change, and edit information one record at a time, as in Figures 8.3 and 8.4, or with multiple records displayed on the screen. Of course, a database usually will contain much more information than can possibly fit on-screen, but

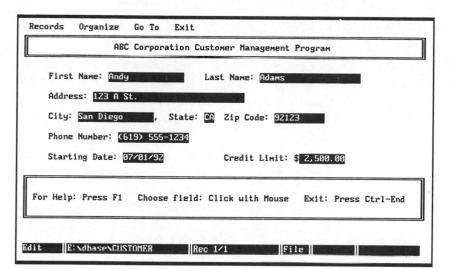

you can easily scroll across fields, and down through records, to "look around" while managing your database. Figure 8.5 shows an example, with a portion of some hypothetical data added to our sample database.

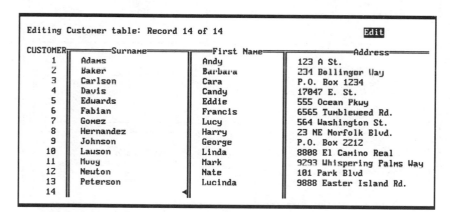

Figure 8.5
On this sample screen you can see multiple records in a database, but only as much as will fit on the screen. You can "scroll around" to find specific information.

Design the Reports

Finally, you'll probably want to print information from your database. The fact that you've *stored* the information in a tabular format doesn't in any way limit you to *printing* the information in that format. In fact, most

NOTE

If you want to print directly on envelopes from your database, both your DBMS and your printer must have this capability.

DBMSs give you the ability to define just about any format for printing the data in your tables.

Your DBMS will include a *report generator* that makes it easy to define exactly how you want your printed output to appear. Figures 8.6 and 8.7 show examples of data from our sample database table printed on a sheet of labels, and a form letter printed from a single record.

Figure 8.6

Mailing labels shown printed from a database table.

Andy Adams
123 A St.
San Diego, CA   92123

Barbara Baker
234 Bollinger Way
Encinitas, CA   92021

Cara Carlson
P.O. Box 1234
Alameda, CA   91234

Candy Davis
17047 E. St.
Waltham, MA   02123

Eddie Edwards
555 Ocean Pkwy
Dallas, TX   75207

Francis Fabian
6565 Tumbleweed Rd.
Cary, NC   26513

Lucy Gomez
564 Washington St.
Islandia, NY   17788

Harry Hernandez
23 NE Norfolk Blvd.
Elliot, KS   12345

George Johnson
P.O. Box 2212
Manhasset, NY   11030

Linda Lawson
8808 El Camino Real
San Francisco, CA   94543

Mark Moog
9293 Whispering Palms Way
Troy, MI   48084

Nate Newton
101 Park Blvd
Honolulu, HI   12345

```
July 24, 1994

Andy Adams
123 A St.
San Diego,  CA 92123

Dear Andy:

Welcome! ABC Corporation is pleased to have you as a new credit
customer. Your application for credit has been approved, and we
have opened an account in your name with a credit limit of
$2,500.00.

Our credit terms are explained in detail in the enclosed
brochure. Please let us know if there is any way we can be of
service to you. Again, ABC extends our warmest welcome to you as
one of our newest customers.


                                   Best regards,



                                   U.B. Sari
                                   Vice President
```

Figure 8.7

Sample form letter, printed from a single record in a database table.

Most DBMSs also let you define any required math calculations right in the report format. For example, if your database includes quantities and unit prices for orders, you could define the report format so that it automatically calculates the extended price (quantity times unit price), calculates and adds sales tax and shipping cost, and calculates the grand total for the invoice.

One of the main advantages of a DBMS is that you only need to define the format of your printed report one time. For example, once you've defined how you want your mailing labels to look when printed, you can print labels as often as you need them. You can always add and edit names and addresses in a database table throughout the month. Then, when the time comes to print labels, you just need to load the blank labels into your printer, tell the program to "print the labels," and you can go to lunch while the computer and printer do all the work!

Key Features to Look for in a Database Management System

When shopping for a DBMS, think about the features you'll need, both now and in the future. Some of the convenience features listed below are available only on the more advanced relational database systems, but some are available even on basic low-cost systems. Read the software package to see which features the program offers.

Structure and Size Limits

Some inexpensive "low-end" DBMSs place a strict limit on the number of records that you can store in a database, so you need to check this out before you buy. For example, if you'll be managing a membership list with 300,000 records, obviously you won't be able to do the job with a system that can handle only 2000 records.

Query-by-Example

Querying is the fundamental technique you'll be using to manage your databases. This feature lets you "ask questions" of your database, and isolate specific records for printing reports. For example, querying would allow you to do the following tasks:

- Print "welcome" letters only for new records in the database, instead of for all of the records in the database
- Select items from your master inventory indicating which are at or below the reorder point
- Print a summary of all sales, subtotaled by product or date
- Look up an address, phone number, or current account balance for a specific customer very quickly
- Print reminder letters for customers whose accounts are overdue

Paradox for Windows and Paradox 4.5 for DOS

Publisher:
Borland International

Suggested Retail Price:
$795–Windows/$795–DOS

Upgrade Price:
$199–Windows/$199–DOS

Windows Requires:
80386 processor or better
8MB RAM
Windows 3.1
DOS 3.1 or later
20MB free hard disk space for
**   installation**

DOS Requires:
80286 processor or better
2MB RAM
DOS 3.0 or later
5.5MB free hard disk space for
**   installation**

Description:

Paradox is very powerful and easy to use, whether you want to manage a single table or build a custom application with multiple related tables.

It offers Query-by-Example (QBE), custom forms, and the ability to print data in just about every format imaginable, including labels, free-form, and tabular. One of the database management systems also includes the ability to instantly create business charts from database tables.

For more advanced users, Paradox offers PAL, the Paradox Applications Language, for developing custom applications, as well as Personal Programmer, which is an applications generator for database management experts who have little or no programming experience.

A good DBMS will provide unlimited querying capabilities to let you isolate any records for whatever purpose you have. Different programs offer different techniques for querying databases. Most people agree that, of all the querying methods available, Query-by-Example (abbreviated QBE) is the easiest and most flexible.

In Query-by-Example, the program shows you the names of the fields in the table that you're asking questions about, and then you provide an *example* of what kind of information you're looking for.

For instance, let's say that you want to send a special offer to your clients who have at least a $5000 credit limit with your company.

To isolate database records with a credit limit of at least $5000 using the Query-by-Example method, you would go to the program's query screen, scroll to the field containing the credit limit, and enter the *search criterion*

>=5,000

as shown in Figure 8.8.

Figure 8.8

A sample Paradox Query-by-Example screen requesting records with credit limits that are greater than or equal to $5000.

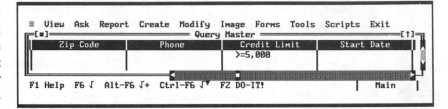

You could now tell the program to print the "special offer" form letter, and perhaps mailing labels, for those records that meet the search criterion.

Notice the *operator* >= (greater than or equal to) used in the search criterion. Most DBMSs provide a wide range of such operators making it possible for you to specify *any* search criterion. There's really no limit to the types of queries you can perform.

Data Entry Forms and Data Validation

NOTE

In database management, the term **form** refers to any display of information on the screen.

Being able to create your own customized data entry forms not only lets you create fancy, personalized screens, it can also help you simplify the job of entering and editing data. *Data validation* takes this a step further by checking for errors as you enter or change information. For example, you can have the screen check to make sure that a two-character state abbreviation entered into a field is indeed a valid abbreviation. Or you can have the screen ensure that a product code entered into a database is indeed a valid product code.

A DBMS that has this ability to validate data *before* it's stored in the database table greatly reduces the potential for confusion and inaccurate results down the road.

Indexing and Sorting

Indexing is an important feature if you'll be searching for individual records often. An example of indexing would be looking up customer information by customer number and then having the appropriate record appear almost instantaneously on the screen. Indexing creates an index file similar to an index in a book. When you want to locate a particular record, it's much faster for the program to check the index to find the record than it is to search through every record one by one.

Product at a Glance

dBASE IV 2.0 for DOS

Publisher:
Borland International

Suggested Retail Price:
$795

Upgrade Price:
$99.95

Requires:
80286 processor or better
DOS 3.1 or later
2MB RAM
3.5MB free hard disk space
 (6MB recommended)

Description:

A full-featured database management system, dBASE IV 2.0 (pronounced Dee-base four two point oh) offers the ability to manage single and multiple related tables, custom forms with data validation, flexible report formats for printing labels, free-form reports, and tabular reports, including some capabilities for taking advantage of laser printer fonts.

dBASE IV also includes an applications generator and a complete programming language for developing custom applications. Though considered complicated by many users, dBASE often is the product of choice for experienced programmers, because it provides a good deal of power and flexibility for managing data and building applications.

Label and Report Formats

NOTE

In database management, the term **report** refers to any information that is printed from the database.

The ability to print the data stored in your database in a wide variety of formats is an important component of any DBMS. Most high-end DBMSs offer a *report generator* or *report design screen* to help you define the exact format for your various printed reports. Some particular capabilities to look for, depending on your needs, include the following:

Label and envelope formats: Will the DBMS allow you to print data directly on mailing labels and envelopes?

Tabular formats: Virtually all DBMSs let you print data in simple tabular format, because this is the format in which the information is stored.

Free-form reports: Free-form reports provide the ability to print data in whatever format you wish. This is important if you want to generate form letters, invoices, and other types of nontabular printed reports.

CAUTION

Storing a graphic image with each database record greatly increases the amount of disk space the database needs.

Graphics: Some DBMSs let you display data and the results of calculations in a variety of business graphs, such as bar charts and pie charts. Others even let you store digitized graphics with each database record. For example, a real estate office could store a digitized photo of a house with each listing in the database, or a large business could store an employee's picture for a personnel database.

Programming Language and Applications Generator

The high-end DBMSs all include a programming language to let you develop database *applications* that are specifically suited to a given business. Using the programming language requires some programming savvy. But the resulting application can be designed so that staff members with little or no computer expertise can easily use the system to store and retrieve whatever information their jobs require.

An applications generator is a tool designed to help you develop custom applications with minimal programming. These days, a fairly experienced DBMS user with no programming experience can develop applications that rival the more sophisticated applications developed by programmers.

FoxPro 2.5a for Windows and FoxPro 2.5a for DOS

Publisher:
Microsoft Corporation

Suggested Retail Price:
$495–Windows/$495–DOS

Upgrade Price:
$129.95–Windows/$129.95–DOS

Windows Requires:
Microsoft-compatible mouse
80386 processor or better
VGA monitor recommended
DOS 3.1 or later
Windows 3.0 or later
4MB RAM
10MB free hard disk space

DOS Requires:
8088 processor or better
DOS 3.1 or later
640K RAM
1.5MB free hard disk space

Description:

FoxPro is the fastest database management program available, running through files of thousands of records in just a few seconds. Combine this speed with some of the best report, label, screen, menu, and window generators in the world, and you will be able to create your own applications for home or office in a short time. With FoxPro for Windows, you can use Dynamic Data Exchange (DDE) to swap and link data to and from other Windows programs such as Microsoft Word and Access. Other Fox database programs, such as FoxBASE+, are available on the Macintosh and Unix platforms and provide full compatibility with each for both the databases and the application code. Microsoft even provides the Transporter, a program that makes minor changes to program code when moved across systems. When different systems are connected using a network, such as Macs and PCs, one set of data can be maintained for both systems, keeping the data on only one server. An upgrade of FoxPro for the Macintosh is expected in late 1993.

Flat-File versus Relational File Systems

So far in this chapter we've discussed DBMSs as a single category of software. But, in truth, there are actually two major categories of DBMSs. One is the *flat-file* database management system, sometimes called a *file manager*. The other is the *relational* database management system.

A flat-file DBMS lets you access only one database table at a time. For many applications, such as simple mailing list management, a flat-file approach is sufficient.

But let's suppose you run a mail-order business and you want to keep track of your orders, your inventory, and your customers. Clearly these represent three separate "bodies" of information, and there's no way to combine that information into a single database table. Instead, you'd need to create three separate database tables.

You'd need one table to keep track of what you have in inventory. In Figure 8.9's example, each item in the inventory has a product ID number, description, and unit price. The quantity of that item currently in stock is also stored in this table. You could add other information about each product as it pertains to your business (as indicated by *etc...* in the figure), such as the reorder point, manufacturer information, or whether the product is taxable.

Figure 8.9

A sample database table containing information about the current inventory.

```
Inventory Database Table

Product Id    Description                    Unit Price    In Stock    etc...

   HP-123     HP Deskjet Cartridge             16.95         10

   HP-234     HP Paintjet Cartridge            27.95          5

   HP-235     HP Colorjet Cartridge            33.95          3

   HP-291     HP LaserJet Letter Tray          67.97         15

   HP-292     HP Laserjet Legal Tray           71.95         20

   HP-300     HP III Envelope Tray             78.95         25

   HP-500     HP Lower Cassette Tray          139.95         10
```

Another table could contain information about customers or accounts. In the example in Figure 8.10, the name and address of each customer is stored in a table. (Again, we've used *etc...* to indicate that you can include any other information you want about each customer, as pertinent to your business.) Notice that we've also assigned each customer a unique customer identification number (or account number), in the field named Cust Id. We'll explain below why each customer has been assigned a number.

Chapter 8: Database Management Systems

```
Customer Database Table

Cust Id   Surname     First Name   Address            etc...
  1001    Adams       Andy         123 A St.
  1002    Baker       Barbara      234 Bollinger Way
  1003    Carlson     Cara         P.O. Box 1234
  1004    Davis       Candy        17047 E. St.
  1005    Edwards     Eddie        555 Ocean Pkwy
  1006    Fabian      Francis      6565 Tumbleweed Rd.
  1007    Gomez       Lucy         564 Washington St.
  1008    Hernandez   Harry        23 NE Norfolk Blvd.
  1009    Johnson     George       P.O. Box 2212
  1010    Lawson      Linda        8808 El Camino Real
```

Figure 8.10

A sample database of customers, in which each customer is assigned a unique customer record (or account number).

Finally, a third database table could keep track of orders. In the example shown in Figure 8.11, each record defines who placed the order (via the customer's ID number), what was ordered (via the product ID number), the quantity ordered, and the date that each order was placed. (Once again, we've used *etc...* to indicate that you could add any other pertinent information to each record.)

Notice how compact the Orders database table is. It doesn't waste a lot of disk space by repeating information that's already stored in the Customer and Inventory database tables. Instead, it stores only the Customer ID, Product ID, quantity, and date of each order.

```
Orders Table

Cust Id   Product Id   Quantity   Date Ordered   etc...
  1001    HP-292         1         7/1/94
  1001    HP-300         1         7/1/94
  1001    HP-500         1         7/1/94
  1003    HP-235         5         7/1/94
  1004    HP-300         2         7/1/94
  1010    HP-123         1         7/1/94
```

Figure 8.11

A sample database containing information on incoming and fulfilled orders. The customer ID and product number fields indicate who placed the order and what was ordered.

Now, here's where the difference between a flat-file manager and relational database manager becomes apparent. If you used a flat-file manager, you could indeed manage each of these tables individually. However, there would be no way for the various tables to share information.

On the other hand, a relational database management system, which can manage multiple tables simultaneously, can do the following tasks:

- Print invoices and packing slips for current orders by combining information from the Customer, Inventory, and Orders database tables

- Automatically subtract the quantity of each item shipped from the Inventory database, so your Inventory table is always correct

- Have the Orders database table check to make sure there's a sufficient quantity of items in stock to fulfill the order, and if not, place the order on a "backorder list" table, to be fulfilled when the stock is replenished

In fact, you could "mix-and-match" the information from these various tables however you wish, to manage and get whatever information you need. The only real requirement is that the tables have to be designed in such a way that the DBMS can *relate* the information from one table to the appropriate information in another table. You use *key fields* to do that.

For example, the Cust Id field in the Customer and Orders table is the key field that uniquely identifies each customer. Thus, when processing orders, the program can find the name and address of a customer automatically by "looking up" the customer information from the Cust Id field. At the same time, the program can automatically retrieve pricing information, in-stock quantity, and product descriptions from the Inventory database table by looking up that information from the Product Id field.

I should point out that the process of dividing information into separate tables, defining key fields, and setting up all the relationships between multiple tables is not a skill you learn overnight. In fact, there are plenty of computer professionals who specialize in those very tasks. So unless you have a lot of time to learn this technology, you should seriously consider having a pro do it for you.

NOTE

The technique of breaking information into separate tables, and defining key fields that relate the tables, is called **normalization** in database management terminology.

FileMaker Pro 2.1 for Windows and File Maker Pro 2.1 for Macintosh

Publisher:
Claris Corporation

Suggested Retail Price:
$399–Windows/$399–Macintosh

Upgrade Price:
$89–Windows/$89–Macintosh (upgrade from 2.0 to 2.1 is $20)

Windows Requires:
80286 processor or better
DOS 3.1 or later
Windows 3.0 or later
2MB RAM

Macintosh Requires:
Macintosh Plus or better
System 6.0.5 or later
1MB RAM for System 6.0.x
2MB RAM for System 7

Description:
FileMaker Pro combines functionality with accessibility by using graphical tools to create databases and applications. Its graphical data entry tools, report facilities, script language, and cross-platform capabilities make it one of the most popular database programs in the Macintosh world.

4th Dimension 3.0 for Macintosh

Publisher:
ACI US, Inc.

Suggested Retail Price:
$895

Requires:
Macintosh Plus or better
System 6.0.5 or later
1.5MB RAM

Description:

4th Dimension (4-D) is a relational database manager that can handle everything from single tables to sophisticated, custom-designed applications with multiple related tables. The program includes three environments—Design, User, and Custom. The Design Environment lets the database developer set up database tables, custom data entry forms and reports, and relationships among files.

Most users will work in the User Environment, where they enter data, print reports, search, sort, and chart, all using built-in capabilities and information set up in the Design Environment.

The Custom Environment provides the ability to develop and run custom-designed applications that can include all the graphical features expected in the Mac, including pull-down menus, buttons, alert messages, and dialog boxes. 4-D features include layout design with fonts, styles, and graphics; picture storage; data sharing among network users; business charts; serial communications; and the extensive import/export capabilities of many popular Macintosh/PC database and text file formats.

Text versus Graphical Interface in Database Management

Probably most DBMSs that exist out there in the world are text-based. However, since the first edition of this book was published in 1992, the marketplace has been flooded with new Windows-based graphical DBMSs. Some of these PC database products are available only in a Windows version, like Microsoft's Access. Products available in both DOS and Windows versions include Paradox, FoxPro, FileMaker Pro, Approach, and DataEase Express. Because Windows has become so popular and comes installed on many new PCs, many more Windows versions of DOS products can be expected.

In the Macintosh environment, of course, all of the available DBMSs are graphical. However, many of those packages are "flat-file" database managers. So if you need to manage multiple database tables on a Mac, make sure that you find a product that can handle your needs.

Nine

Telecommunications

• •

Telecommunications is the *big* buzzword in computers today. You don't even have to read computer magazines—the business and home sections of the daily papers have regular articles on CompuServe, Prodigy, Internet, and the communications super highway. Many new computers are being sold with communications hardware already installed. And using telecommunications is now as easy for normal people as for the pocket-protector crowd.

These days more and more people are working at home, either as employees or as the self-employed. Using telecommunications and home computers, they transmit their work over a modem to an office or to others in the electronic chain.

Telecommunications are used now for hundreds of different applications. Investors routinely check their stock market holdings, pilots file flight plans and get weather briefings, and shoppers compare and purchase merchandise on their computers. You can call a local phone number and send and receive mail from all over the world, and electronic bulletin boards are used for everything from selling used cars to finding dates.

What Are Telecommunications?

Telecommunicating is done by simply linking your computer to a telephone line and contacting someone through a device called a modem. A modem changes computer information into sound impulses that can be transmitted over the telephone lines.

You can sign on to any number of commercial on-line services, special interest bulletin boards, or even dip your toes into the vast ocean of information known as the Internet. All these services are discussed in the following sections.

Bulletin boards are frequently free, because they are maintained by community-minded computer buffs. On-line services, on the other hand, usually charge you for the time you are connected, but in return they provide an amazing array of services. The largest services, CompuServe, America Online, and Prodigy, offer various pricing options. Most boil down to a flat fee for some basic amount of usage, with surcharges for additional services. Other on-line services, such as DUAT (Direct User Access Terminal) for flight planning and weather briefings, are federally funded and provide free services to specialized groups.

NOTE

With the variety of on-line services now available, there's a good chance that there's at least one you'll find useful or interesting.

Commercial On-Line Services

On a commercial on-line service, you'll find such diverse services as a low-cost stock broker, an airline reservations service, technical support personnel for hardware and software manufacturers, and access to massive databases containing all kinds of information. Some services are emerging that will allow you to take care of all of your shopping needs—even grocery shopping—on-line.

You'll be charged a basic monthly fee for access to a commercial on-line service (whether or not you access it) and an additional fee for special services such as the use of special databases, airline reservation services, and home shopping services. Note that these services can become expensive fairly quickly, particularly in the case of Dialog Information Services and Dow Jones News/Retrieval, which are the services used by investors. Because investors make money with the information they download, they don't mind paying a premium price.

There is insufficient space here to provide anything but a partial list of features for some commercial on-line services. But it should be enough to lead you to one or two services you'll want to try out. The initial investment is negligible, so poke around until you find a comfortable spot.

CompuServe

CompuServe offers a very comprehensive list of features that can be accessed 24 hours a day. When you become a CompuServe subscriber, you'll be provided with a list of local telephone numbers you can call to hook up with the service. If you're in an urban area, you'll probably incur no long distance charges. If you live in a small town or rural area, your long-distance charge will be only to the nearest city where the service is available.

NOTE

Using on-line services, it's possible to send mail across the country for the price of a local call and the time connected to the on-line service.

CompuServe currently charges $8.95 a month for its Standard Plan. With that you get unlimited access to their basic services, which include:

- News, weather, and sports: Associated Press On-line, Sports, entertainment and business news, National weather service
- Reference library: American Heritage Dictionary, Grolier's Encyclopedia, Consumer Reports
- Shopping, stock quotes, games, travel information, movie reviews, and more

And that's just the basic stuff. CompuServe goes on and on. Got skeletons in your closet? Try the genealogy forum. Bats in the belfry? Get advice on the Pets/Animal forum. Plus, every major software and hardware manufacturer (and most of the smaller ones) maintains an on-line service from which you can get excellent technical support and advice.

The list of services fills up a 96-page booklet that you get when you contact CompuServe at P.O. Box 20212, 5000 Arlington Centre Boulevard, Columbus, Ohio 43220.

The phone number in the U.S. is 800-848-8199.

Prodigy

Prodigy is a service provided by a cooperative effort between IBM and Sears. In its early days, the service grew very rapidly because of its ease-of-use and, especially, its low cost. Lately, Prodigy is undergoing some growing pains, the main symptom of which is a revamping of their fees. Once they were distinguished by the fact that they charged a flat monthly fee regardless of usage level. This appealing simplicity has been replaced by a monthly fee that covers basic services with hourly charges beyond a certain level. In return for the increased cost, however, Prodigy is now offering many more services.

Traditionally, Prodigy's services have been aimed particularly at shoppers and the needs of children. For adults, Prodigy provides the whole range of services from banking to shopping, as well as helpful document files from experts on managing money, computers, and other useful information. For children, there's an on-line encyclopedia, as well as adventure, science, and entertainment features. The entire system is set up to be simple and fun to use. It would be a good first service for a beginner, and you may discover that it provides everything you need.

The best way to get Prodigy is to buy a Prodigy membership kit at your local software store. Often the package is sold with a modem at a reduced price. The software is available for DOS or for the Mac. No Windows software is available—though Prodigy is working on it.

You can contact Prodigy at the following address: Prodigy Membership Marketing, 445 Hamilton Avenue, White Plains, NY 10601. The phone number in the U.S. is 800-PRODIGY.

You can sign on to Prodigy using any modem up to 9600bps with no surcharges for faster modems.

America Online

America Online (AOL) is a rapidly growing service. Like CompuServe, you can access AOL with either DOS and Windows-based software that AOL will be happy to send to you free.

AOL has a long list of available services, such as electronic mail, on-line newspapers, financial services, travel, and entertainment. It's not quite as comprehensive as CompuServe, but it does have the undeniable advantage of being cheaper. The monthly charge of $9.95 includes five hours of access time, with additional hours at $3.50 each. The disadvantage of AOL is its emphasis on on-line conferences and chats that can easily run up your bill. Also, the maximum modem speed available is 2400bps. You can, of course, access AOL with any modem, but it won't transmit data any faster than 2400bps.

To get the free software or any help with signing on, call 800-827-6364. Or you can write to America Online at 8619 Westwood Center Drive, Vienna, VA 22182-2285.

Internet

Internet is a truly amazing, loose network of thousands and thousands of computers all over the world. Every kind of information and every kind of person can be found somewhere on the Internet. You can access a NASA-funded computer full of space science, find out what books are in the Munich library, and participate in discussions ranging from cooking to the current tour plans of the Grateful Dead to concepts in higher mathematics.

The tricky thing about the Internet is getting on it. You can't just call up directly; you need to get an account on a participating computer, a service provider. But you may already have access. Most big companies are on the Internet. Ask the person who runs the network in your company. It may not be in your department, but perhaps the folks in the engineering or research department have a connection.

If you're a student at a medium to large college, go to the computer center and ask. Virtually every four-year school has an Internet connection and a way for students to get an account.

For an individual without a business or academic connection, you can join a service such as The WELL (Whole Earth 'Lectronic Link) for $15 per month plus $2 per hour. For information, you can call 415-332-4335.

Or try Software Tool and Die in Brookline, Massachusetts (617-739-0202). You can join Software Tool and Die for $5 per month plus $2 per additional hour over 5 or $20 per month plus $1 per additional hour over 20.

You can send and receive mail to and from people on the Internet through CompuServe and America Online (though not Prodigy). However, you will not have direct access to the many open computers on the Internet.

Dow Jones News/Retrieval

Dow Jones News/Retrieval is a service specifically for investors and others who require up-to-the minute business news. On this service, you'll find the transcript of this week's "Wall Street Week," a financial affairs program aired on PBS. You can see the New York Stock Exchange ticker tape, buy and sell stocks, read brief descriptions of companies, check on the sale and purchase of a company's stock by the officers of the company, and access similar information.

Dow Jones News/Retrieval is available through Tymnet and Telenet. You can contact them at 609-520-4000 or P.O. Box 300, Princeton, New Jersey 08543-0300.

GEnie

GEnie is a service owned and operated by General Electric (hence the capitalization of the first two letters of its name). It offers newswire and airline reservation services, but not Telex or MCI Mail. GEnie operates its own network of local telephone numbers. You can link up with Dow Jones News/Retrieval through GEnie. GEnie is a competitive service that increases its features frequently.

The interface with GEnie is through a program called Aladdin. It's not as cute as the other services' software, but it does get the job done. GEnie is also very inexpensive. You can call GEnie at 800-638-9636, or write to 401 N. Washington Street, Rockville, Maryland 20850.

MCI Mail

MCI Mail is the electronic version of the U.S. Postal Service. It's simply the nation's electronic mail drop/mail box. This service can be accessed from within other services, such as CompuServe.

You can contact MCI Mail at 800-444-MAIL, or write MCI Mail Registration at 1133 19th Street NW, Suite 700, Washington, DC 20036.

Local Bulletin Boards

NOTE

An extremely thorough and detailed listing of bulletin boards throughout the U.S. can be found in the monthly magazine **Computer Shopper.** You should be able to find it at any large magazine stand.

There are local bulletin boards sponsored by user groups, individuals, and businesses. Some set aside certain hours for new users to register. How do you find a bulletin board? Ask the salesman at your local computer store or a friend who is involved in telecommunications. Computer newspapers and newsletters (given away free at computer stores) usually include lists of local bulletin boards.

If the bulletin board requires registration, you'll be subjected to a friendly interrogation and required to enter your name, address, telephone number, and other information, such as the kind of computer and modem you are using. Then the system operator (called a sysop—pronounced SIS-op) will contact you over the telephone to verify your identity.

Once you're in telephone contact with the board, you can download (receive) artwork, games, and useful programs, or you can play games or "talk" to the other people on-line. Some bulletin boards even have multiple lines that allow you to chat in real time—which is like carrying on a conversation, except that all of the interactions are typewritten messages.

Don't forget your manners when you are using a bulletin board. If the board has regulated hours, you should respect them. If you upload (send) programs, make sure that those programs are shareware or public domain programs—those that specifically permit public access. Profanity is a no-no as is the uploading of false or illegal information (such as stolen credit card numbers).

Any bulletin board that's around for longer than the blink of an eye will be clean of such things and will also be thoroughly examined by the sysop for computer viruses.

User Groups and Services

User groups often operate bulletin boards as a service to their members. There you'll find libraries of shareware programs and computer books. User groups are a great place for beginners to learn from experienced users. User groups are usually organized around a particular computer or computer manufacturer. There are IBM/PC, Amiga, and Macintosh user groups in just about every good-sized city.

Software Manufacturer Help Services

Software manufacturers must answer questions about their products from thousands (to millions) of users. In order to meet the needs of all these users, most manufacturers provide technical support lines to respond to questions. Often, as a corollary to this service, a computer telecommunications service is established. These systems operate like bulletin boards. When you contact the service, you can type in your question and then reconnect the following day (or a few days later), and you'll find that your question has been answered by a technician.

These services are also available as part of many commercial on-line services.

What You Need to Telecommunicate

There are only a few things you need beyond a computer with a serial port and a telephone line to telecommunicate. (And internal modems don't require a serial port.) Specifically, you'll need a modem and some variety of telecommunications software.

Modems

The word "modem" is a contraction of the words MOdulator and DE-Modulator. Originally, modems sent information relatively slowly. Even a few years ago, 300bps (bits per second) was the standard speed for data transmission. That represented about 2K per minute. Now 2400bps is fairly standard, and 9600bps is common.

As previously indicated, a modem is simply a device that converts the electronic signals of your computer into sound impulses that can be processed by the telephone system. They are rated by bits per second. You can purchase a 2400bps modem for under $60 and a 9600bps modem for under $150. The new 14,400bps modems sell for about $300.

I should mention that some services charge more for using faster telecommunications equipment. However, the money you save on connection costs and the shorter connect time will more than make up the difference.

NOTE

External modems require particular cables, but they will work with just about any type of computer.

There are two basic modem designs: internal and external. An internal modem is inserted into a slot in your computer. It takes up precious room in your expansion bus—the slots in your computer where you can add cards—but it saves on desk space. Furthermore, an internal modem is usually $10 to $20 less than an external modem. (See Figure 9.1.) Most of this price difference is the result of the fact that an internal modem

Figure 9.1

If you get an internal modem, you take up a slot in your computer, but you save desk space and money. The modem pictured is a 14,400bps model manufactured by U.S. Robotics. Faster rated modems can handle slower transmissions, so you can still communicate with a 2400 or even 1200bps modem. (Photo courtesy of U.S. Robotics, Inc. Copyright 1991.)

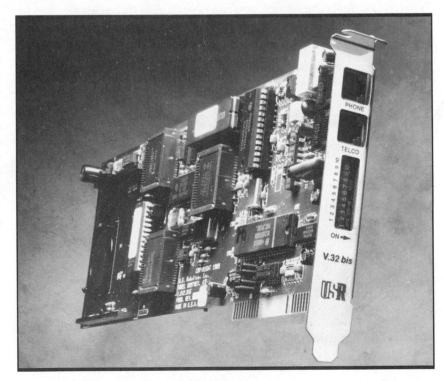

takes its power from your computer's bus and power supply while an external modem requires a separate power supply. (An external modem also requires another outlet near your computer and provides you with yet another wire to tangle up.)

Instead of inserting your modem into your bus, you may prefer to use an external modem. This route is best taken if your bus is full or nearly full, or if you've more than one PC that will use the modem. An external modem connects with your serial port. (See Figure 9.2.) Although most new computers are equipped with the handier 9-pin serial port, most modem connectors are set up for the 25-pin connector. Before purchasing a modem, you should know what kind of serial port you have and, if necessary, purchase an adapter at the same time as you purchase the modem. If you opt for an integrated package such as Microsoft Works for your telecommunications software (or if you use some other software that supports a mouse) and if you are using a serial mouse, you also may want to purchase a second serial card for your modem. This card will take up a slot on your bus. Unfortunately, there's no way for a mouse and a modem to share a serial port.

Figure 9.2
An external modem may take up space on your desk, but it saves a slot inside your computer. This is a 2400bps external modem manufactured by U.S. Robotics. (Photo courtesy of U.S. Robotics, Inc. Copyright 1991.)

Hayes Compatibility

Make sure that any modem you select is Hayes-compatible. Hayes was an early manufacturer of modems and it set the standard for telecommunications commands. There are other standards, but Hayes is the most widely used.

Hayes commands always begin with AT, which stands for Attention. It alerts the modem that a command will follow. The most likely command to follow is D, which stands for Dial, and then T or P, which stands for Tone or Pulse. Therefore, to contact a service, you might enter

    ATDP 5551212

which tells the modem to send the necessary pulses over the phone line to mimic a dial telephone. Most telecommunications software will do the dialing for you, so you may never use the Hayes commands directly, although your software will.

Telecommunications Software for On-Line Services

If you're going to be using the commercial on-line services, your software needs are fairly simple. For example, Prodigy requires that you use *their* (dedicated) software. You get it from Prodigy (or the local software store). It can't be used for anything but Prodigy, but it does work very well. America Online also requires dedicated software. Fortunately, it's free and easy to use.

CompuServe can be accessed using a number of packages. You can even sign on using the Terminal program in Windows. However, trying to navigate CompuServe with such a "program" is like crossing the Atlantic by rowboat. It's an enormous amount of work and you're very likely to get drowned.

The best programs for CompuServe are their own CIM (CompuServe Information Manager) and WinCIM (the Windows version of CIM). Once you're on CompuServe and want to move around even more quickly, you can download programs such as TAPCIS or OZCIS, which will give you the means to save money if you're on-line a lot.

General Telecommunications Software

For communicating with bulletin boards, other individual users, or the Internet, you'll probably need a general telecommunications package. There are a number of software packages available for telecommunications. You can look around for shareware (and some shareware is very good) or you can pick up a commercial product such as Cross Talk or Pro-Comm Plus for about $100.

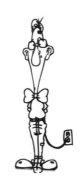

The newer telecommunications packages that include a modem and software are very friendly and easy to use. Gone are the days when you had to know all sorts of arcane modem commands just to get a dial tone!

Some communications packages come with predefined session profiles to connect you to various services such as GEnie, MCI Mail, and Dow Jones News/Retrieval service. All of them are easy to install, provide extensive technical support, and have a multitude of features.

Login Scripts and Macros

Some services and bulletin boards require that you enter a long string of commands before you can enter the area you want. Sometimes your use of a given service will be routine: Each day (or several times a day) you enter a given area, download some information, change to another area, download some more information, and then log off. Entering these strings of commands and passwords may become tedious and you may begin to long for a feature that would allow you to automate part or all of the procedure.

Login scripts are that feature. They are automated lists of commands that your software reads from a file and sends over the telephone lines to the on-line service. Frequently, the only action you need to take is to select the script from a list; the program will do the rest.

Macros are similar to login scripts, but they can be more complex and they can be used at any time while you are on-line. They're just like the macros used with spreadsheets that we discussed in Chapter 7. Some macros are simple key presses. You press a combination of keys, such as Shift-Ctrl-G, to enter the command GO GAMES, and you log on to the games area of the service. Of course, macros can be much more complicated than that. Remember that although macros may be a bit more complex to create, ultimately they tend to make operations simpler.

Supported Protocols

You can receive much more information from an on-line service than simple lists of bibliographies or encyclopedia articles. For example, you can download (receive) text files and graphics for your own creative work. The method for downloading information this way is called a "transfer protocol," and there are half a dozen common ones. For unformatted text transfers, a simple text or ASCII protocol is used. For most of your formatted text and/or graphics transfers you'll use protocols called YMODEM or ZMODEM. Even if you've got a lot of protocols, you'll find that you use only one or two, and almost assuredly it'll be one of these two.

If you have a good telecommunications program, your involvement in the procedure will be minimal. Simply select Send or Receive File from a Transfer menu, specify the protocol to use, provide the name of the file to send, or the name of the file to contain the downloaded information, and the machine will do the rest.

Terminal Emulation

You may want to have your computer emulate a terminal in order to deal directly with a remote computer. Terminal emulation allows your computer to pretend that it's a "dumb terminal" rather than a PC. This means that it relies totally on the remote computer for prompts and data storage. Common terminal types are VT-100 and VT-52.

Chat Mode

Chat mode allows you to have a dialog with another user or the sysop who runs the bulletin board by typing your end of a conversation on the keyboard and reading the replies on your computer screen. If you are transferring data between your computer and another with a modem, and not through a bulletin board, the chat mode is important for coordination. It's also fun just to chat via the keyboard.

Host Mode

Selecting host mode turns your computer into an answering machine, but only for calls from other computers. In host mode, your computer waits until your telephone rings. Then it answers the phone and sends a carrier signal that informs the calling computer that it's in contact with another computer.

Generally, host mode is used by the same person who would normally use the computer, but while he or she is away from the office. If you're in San Francisco and your computer back in Cleveland is in host mode, you can use your laptop to call your computer and download a list of clients you forgot to bring, or upload a list of orders for processing when you return. To keep unauthorized people out of your computer, the software may require that a password be entered correctly before it allows entry.

TIP

Some small businesses leave their telecommunications software in host mode and take orders over the modem.

Elements of Telecommunications

As with computer jargon, there's a language unique to telecommunications. Because telecommunicating is relatively new, there weren't any words to describe many of the things that it can do. As a result, many technical terms from engineering were coined to describe various processes in computer telecommunications. Terms such as "baud rate," "parity," and other words with specific meanings for telecommunications are not hard to learn. Some, such as "parity," have to do with settings that you set once and forget. As long as you know to set "parity" to "none," (or whatever is the appropriate setting), you don't even have to know what it means. Just as knowing how to turn the knob on a TV set to Channel 5 at 8 o'clock doesn't imply understanding how a TV separates and broadcasts the selected channels.

Don't be too concerned about learning the language beyond the terms discussed here. Once you start telecommunicating, you'll pick up the rest of the language by usage. If you run across a term you don't understand, just ask someone on-line.

Baud Rate and Bits per Second

The term "bits per second" (bps) has been used frequently in this chapter. It simply refers to the number of bits that can be sent (or received) every second. There are eight bits in every byte, or character, that you'll send, and every byte is preceded by a start bit and generally followed by a stop bit, which means that for every character, you must send ten bits over the line. You can easily divide the bps by 10 to provide you with a more realistic transmission rate of the number of characters per second. Therefore, 300 bps equals about 30 characters, or about six words of average length, per second. At that rate, a four-page text of 1000 words will take 166 seconds, or a little under three minutes to transmit. By comparison, a 2400 bps modem will transmit 240 characters per second, 48 words per second, and a four-page text in 21 seconds.

Parity

Part of computer telecommunications involves sending a set of characters. All computers use a character code known as ASCII (American Standard Code for Information Interchange), pronounced ASK-ee. This standard code is used so that all computers will agree that an A is an A and so forth.

The code for A, incidentally, is the number 65. When 65 is written in binary code, it looks like this: 01000001. That means that if you were transmitting the letter A and your ears were sensitive enough, you would hear coming over your phone line a low tone, a high tone, five low tones, and a high tone. At the other end of the line, the receiving computer puts all these tones together in a byte of information that represents the letter A.

How do the computers stay in sync with all the pulses traveling over the telephone lines? If you've ever called long distance, you are aware of how prone the long phone lines are to squeaks, squawks, whines, and sirens. These present little or no problem for telecommunications because before each character is sent, your computer sends a start bit, which says in

effect, "Here comes a character!" Then it sends the character, either in seven or eight bits, depending on the setting you make in your communications software. If you are sending seven bits, the eighth bit will be the parity bit. Your telecommunications program will add together all the bits set to one (in the example of the letter A—01000001—two bits are set). If you set your software for even parity, the parity bit would be added to the number of bits set to make the total even. Because two is already an even number, the parity bit for A would be a zero. If your software received the letter A over the phone lines and then discovered that the parity bit was set to one, it would know that the letter was received incorrectly and it would ask that the letter be sent again. If you set your software for odd parity, the parity bit would be used to make the value odd. In that case, the parity bit for A would be set to one. (See Figure 9.3.)

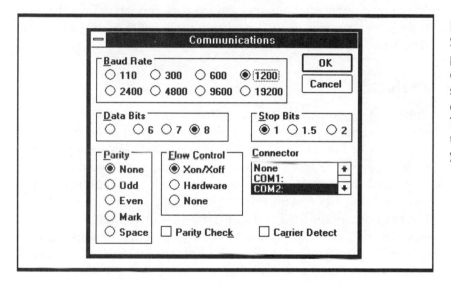

Figure 9.3

Setting your communications parameters is usually a one-time affair and fairly simple. This Communications dialog box from the Windows Terminal program requires only that you click the settings that you want.

Data and Stop Bits

In the example with the letter A above, the data would be transmitted in the following fashion:

- A one would be sent as the start bit.
- Then the data bits would be sent: either 1000001 would be sent (if you selected 7-bit) or 01000001 (if you selected 8-bit).

- Then, if you selected 7-bit and parity, a parity bit would be sent—either one or zero, for odd or even parity, respectively.
- Finally, if you set up your software to send a stop bit, a bit with the value of one would be sent over the line, signifying that the byte or character is now completed and the receiving computer should prepare itself for the next start bit to be sent.

Duplex

The term *duplex* refers to the ability of your program and hardware to send and receive information at the same time. *Simplex* telecommunications are one-directional communications: information goes from one computer to the other. Half-duplex means that each computer can communicate with the other, but only one can communicate at a time. Full duplex means that one computer can receive information from the other at the same time as it sends information to the other. Nearly all systems are capable of full duplex communications.

Protocols

Human interaction is regulated by a set of norms that allow us to interact with a minimum of stress, most of the time. This set of norms is called etiquette when it governs relations between individuals and protocol when it governs relations between nations. The term "protocol" is also used in telecommunications. It means that each computer behaves in a predictable manner, and provides information in an understandable way. The most commonly used protocols are 2400-n-8-1 (2400bps, no parity, eight data bits, one stop bit) and 2400-e-7-1 (2400bps, even parity, seven data bits, one stop bit). If these don't work for you, check the documentation that your on-line service sent.

What the Manuals Don't Tell You

The documentation sent by on-line services can be relied upon to give you much information that you'll need to find your way through the service. But there are always hard-earned bits of information only a crusty, old tele-communicator can tell you.

- Never simply hang up or shut off your computer while you are on-line. It may take a long time for a commercial on-line service to recognize that you've left, and you'll be charged for all the intervening time!

- Take notes while you learn the structure of a new service. Then you'll have a map of your progress, making it easier to escape and to find your way back to that point next time you call.

- The first time you contact an on-line service, log on and off a couple of times to make sure you know how it's done.

- If there's a help command, use it. It'll assure you that you're not missing some neat feature.

- Feel free to experiment. Try sending and receiving files using different protocols. (Do yourself a financial favor and do this on a free bulletin board.)

- Early on, download the shareware program PKZIP. Register it. This program can save you lots of connect time by shrinking files down to a manageable size for transfer. Even if you're rolling in dough, you'll need PKZIP to expand the zipped files that others send to *you*.

- If you enter a service and your program seems to stall, the remote program may be waiting for some assurance that there's a person on the other end. Press the Enter/Return key a few times if this happens. That should get things rolling.

Computer Viruses and Telecommunications

Telecommunicating is, in many ways, still in its infancy but already there are dangers lurking out there. A big danger comes from the nasty little computer vandals who devise programs known as viruses. Once on your system, these programs can cause everything from a minor annoyance to full-fledged disaster.

One way that viruses reproduce is through programs that are downloaded from bulletin boards. This doesn't mean that you'll endanger yourself by downloading a program. Simply downloading an infected program will not infect your computer. You must *run* the program on your computer for the virus to be activated.

Therefore, you must have an anti-virus program to run on the program first. You can download the famous shareware program SCAN from McAfee Associates (408-988-3832). Pay the registration fee immediately and always have the latest version. This program will scan every program file on a disk, as well as the boot sector, looking for known viruses. By running SCAN each time you download a program, you can protect yourself from viral infection.

Or you can use the anti-virus software that comes with DOS 6 (either the Microsoft or IBM version) or use some other commercial anti-virus program. The actual risk of acquiring a virus from a well-managed bulletin board is fairly small—but the consequences can be so dire, it's definitely worth taking precautions.

A Final Note

Telecommunicating is an effective and entertaining way to use your computer. There's a wealth of information available on bulletin boards and on-line systems. Nowadays, many people use electronic mail (e-Mail) rather than mail letters, and more and more businesses are using telecommunications in their daily procedures. In publishing, advertising, marketing, and virtually every other business and profession, telecommunications have made complex procedures more efficient. In the home, telecommunications provides information and entertainment that would be unavailable, scattered in several different locations, or very expensive.

Ten

Application-Specific Software

• •

S uppose you fly an airplane, practice law, run a small business, or want to learn a foreign language and you've started to wonder whether a computer can help you. What you really want is something specifically for your job or your hobby. You want a program that will work out a flight plan, determine financial support in divorce cases, track revenues and expenses in your business, maintain past and current information about clients or patients, print invoices and checks, and/or teach you to speak Russian.

Or perhaps you want a program that can count calories and give you nutritional advice. Or you want to trace your family tree, track the tides, plan a garden, keep an electronic address book, or design your dream house.

Can a computer perform those specialized tasks for you?

No matter what your specific needs are, the answer is definitely *yes*. There are programs for managing law, dental, medical, and sales offices, beauty salons, churches, bowling alleys, construction companies, wineries, auto repair shops, and just about any other business imaginable. Several companies market software for making flight plans for pilots (see Figure 10.1), and you can get software that speaks to you in foreign languages.

All these programs fall under the broad category of application-specific software—that is, software designed to provide a specific purpose, often for a specific business.

Figure 10.1

This program computes a flight plan for pilots. The pilot enters the waypoints, wind direction, and speed, and the program automatically computes the heading, time of flight, ground speed, and the number of miles between waypoints.

```
=================================================================================
FROM  TO    FREQ     WINDS    MILES   COURSE  HDNG    G\S    ETE    TOTAL
            (Mhz)    (TRUE)   (NM)    (MAG)   (MAG)   KTS           (HR & MIN)

CRQ   OCN   115.3    120/7       10    302     302    157     4     0    04
OCN   SLI   115.7    120/5       46    303     303    155    18     0    22
SLI   MRY   118.4    100/9      251    298     299    159    95     1    57
      TOTAL MILES= 307
=================================================================================
Type  R  for Return  C    New trip  H  for Hardcopy  E  to End.
```

What Is Application-Specific Software?

As the name implies, application-specific (or A/S) software is designed to perform some specialized task, be it running a particular kind of business, handling payroll, or scheduling appointments. Figure 10.2 shows a typical A/S program that provides nearly all of the tools needed to run just about any kind of business.

NOTE

There are catalogs of shareware that have several A/S packages for very low prices.

In general, A/S software is written for a small, distinct market, or for a particular business, or to perform a single task. Because consumers have so many specialized needs, inevitably, application-specific software is a huge

```
┌─────────────────────────────────────────────────┐
│   ┌───────────────────────────────────────┐      │
│   │                                       │      │
│   │     O P E N   A C C E S S   I I I     │      │
│   │                                       │      │
│   └───────────────────────────────────────┘      │
│                                                   │
│   ══════════════════════════════════════════     │
│     Multi-function software to manage your growing business. │
│   ══════════════════════════════════════════     │
│                                                   │
│  Relational Database: Easily manage your accounting, customer records, or │
│                       any other such application using OA III's friendly │
│                       menu-driven, forms-oriented approach. │
│ Programming Language: Tie your databases together with menus, windows, and │
│                       advanced procedural statements. │
│          Spreadsheet: Makes quick work of any numerical analysis task, such │
│                       as budgeting, forecasting, or statistics. │
│      Word Processing: Tailored expressly for the needs of the busy manager, │
│                       helping produce professional letters and reports. │
│   Telecommunications: Connect your computer with a wealth of resources, │
│                       including weather, stock, and travel reports. │
└─────────────────────────────────────────────────┘
```

Figure 10.2
This screen outlines some of the various features of a general business program called Open Access III. Useful for any business, it gives the user the ability to switch between spreadsheet, word processing, telecommunications, and database functions. The program also can generate graphs from information in the database.

market. In sheer numbers, there are more special-purpose software programs than all other kinds of programs combined. We all have special needs (see Figure 10.3). Why shouldn't there be programs out there to fulfill those needs? Luckily, there are.

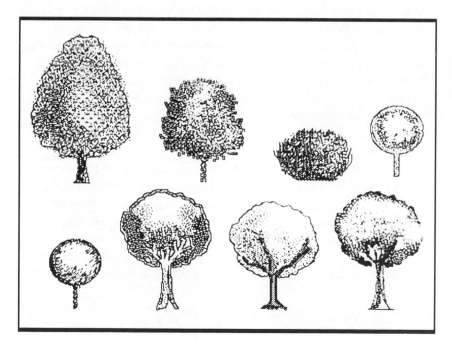

Figure 10.3
There are several clip art libraries for specific audiences. For example, this figure shows clip art for landscapers.

In the preceding chapters, we looked at general-purpose software such as word processors, spreadsheets, or database programs—mass market products that are designed to do a little something for everyone. This chapter focuses on specific programs that are written to meet unique needs.

How Application-Specific Software Differs from General Software

How does A/S software differ from general purpose software? Primarily, the difference lies in its focus on a single task or serving the special needs of a particular industry. A/S software comes with different sections (called modules), each of which perform a particular aspect of the task the software is built to do. The following list describes some of the characteristics of A/S software, especially those packages that are designed to solve the specific needs of particular businesses:

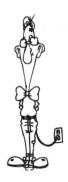

Ready to go: Because A/S software is built to do a particular task, usually it's much better prepared to do that job right from the start than general purpose software. For example, suppose you need to manage medical office data. You couldn't unpack a general purpose database and expect to track patient histories or to file insurance claims immediately. You'd have to design your own databases to accomplish those tasks. But you can buy A/S medical office software, unwrap it, install it, and be ready immediately to "fill in the blanks" with your patients' names, insurance carriers, and so forth.

Some limitations: Naturally, because it's so task-specific, A/S software also tends to be less versatile than general purpose programs. Suppose you want to use a different invoice form or billing calculation than the one provided in the package. A general purpose database or spreadsheet program would probably let you make the changes you want, but an A/S program might not. Or suppose you want to write a letter to a friend. Your payment-reminder letter module could hardly be expected to fulfill that function, and you would have to switch back to your general word processor. Consequently, you may need both A/S software and general purpose programs.

Less computer learning time: With general purpose software, you must spend a certain amount of time learning how to set up your programs and how your hardware works. With A/S software, most of this is done for you. Most A/S programs know how to set themselves up automatically on the computer. And as most A/S programs are designed to run on a particular type of computer, you don't have to pay much attention to the hardware.

Customizing: You might ask, "Why would I need to customize a package that is already designed for my specific application?" There are many reasons, but most come down to differences between the way you actually operate and the way that the package developers thought you would operate. For example, let's say you calculate fees on a sliding scale, depending on the difficulty of the job, while the A/S program allows you to enter only an hourly rate and number of hours. Customizing means you can change the way the program calculates fees. It's the most critical feature to shop for because the alternatives are expensive. You might have to pay the developer to revise the program, or you might have to buy another piece of software.

Templates: Some A/S "software" isn't really a computer program at all. Instead it's a predesigned template created to work with a general purpose program, such as a database, spreadsheet, or word processing program. These templates serve as models for you to load into your general purpose package, and then to fill in your own data. For example, you can buy sample business letters for a variety of word processors, or predesigned spreadsheet templates for general accounting and other business or personal uses. To use these add-ons, you will need both the A/S part (i.e., the template) and the general purpose software (i.e., the spreadsheet, word processing, or database program) for which the template was designed.

Supplied by less "famous" companies: Most likely you have heard the names of companies such as Microsoft, Lotus, WordPerfect, or Borland, because they produce and promote well-known general purpose software. With A/S software, you're less likely to recognize the developer's name. That's neither good nor bad. In fact, it can be an advantage. For example, if you have a company that just produces medical software, then the company probably knows more

NOTE

Templates require that you have the specific software made for them. Be sure to check whether the A/S software you purchase is a template and, if it is, that you have the program it requires.

about medical programs than big name manufacturers. (It's worth checking, however, just how long the company has been doing business, and listening to what other people in the field have to say about its track record.)

Uses of Application-Specific Software

What are these A/S programs used for? They're everywhere that a need is being met by a computer. If you run a packaging company, the software can determine the dimensions of packaging materials. If you have a construction company, the software can determine a competitive bid and calculate your profit. If you fly an airplane, it can determine the heading and distance between waypoints.

Consider this chapter a quick tour of A/S software. Listing all the programs available would take the rest of this book and a few more books besides. It's too big a field to try to cover exhaustively.

So, we'll do an overview for the various kinds of special-purpose software and give you an idea of what's available. If you don't see what you are looking for, that doesn't mean it doesn't exist. You may have to do some research to find the program you need, but it's undoubtedly out there somewhere.

The A/S categories that we'll discuss in this chapter include the following:

- Accounting and bookkeeping
- General business and office management
- Educational
- Personal and home
- Vertical applications (programs for specific industries)

Accounting and Bookkeeping Programs

No business can afford to be without some kind of accounting or bookkeeping system. Programs in this category can help you to compute your taxes and measure the overall health of your business. You should have no trouble finding good general accounting packages; they are widely available by mail order or at your local software store. They are also frequently reviewed in computer magazines. Usually accounting/bookkeeping programs can perform accounting for almost any business. (See "Vertical Applications" below, for accounting programs for specific businesses.)

Often programs in this category require more time to learn than those in other A/S categories. That's only to be expected because automated accounting, especially with integrated software that feeds data from one module to the next, deals with large amounts of data, sometimes tricky calculations, and relatively complex (for many of us) accounting concepts.

Your full-fledged accounting system should provide several different modules, including the following:

General Ledger (G/L): The G/L module contains all accounting functions that summarize financial performance, and essentially provides an overview of an organization's financial condition. Figure 10.4 illustrates a typical accounting package showing several different tasks performed for different companies.

Accounts Payable (A/P): Your A/P module records the money that you owe to your suppliers. In addition to recording financial transactions, most A/P modules keep track of supplier terms, discounts for

NOTE

An accounting program will not **teach** you accounting. It may help, but you'll need some knowledge of the basic principles to use an accounting program effectively.

```
┌─────────────────────────────────────────────────────────────┐
│ ┌───────────────────────────────┐                           │
│ │ MILLER'S JEWELERS             │                           │
│ │ INVENTORY REPORT       Prestige Manufacturing, Inc        │
│ │                           I N V O I C E                   │
│ │ Product                                                   │
│ │ 1000  Wedding Ring      Beckman Bootery                   │
│ │ 1010  Jade Bracelet     100 Main Street                   │
│ │ 1020 ┌────────────────────────────────────┐              │
│ │ 1030 │ Hunny Tree Restaurant              │              │
│ │ 1040 │ General Ledger Transaction Listing │ Terms Ship Via│
│ │      │ For the 4 periods ending 01-31-1990│ Net 30  UPS   │
│ │                                                           │
│ │ 1200 │ Acct#          Debit    Credit │ Price   Total     │
│ │ 1210 │ 5775  Food/Non Perishable  598.90 │ 1.23  236.16   │
│ │ 1220 │ 5830  Kitchen Supplies  249.36 │    .25    9.00    │
│ │ 1230 │ 1001  Cash In Bank          848.26 │  .89    8.90   │
│ │ 1240 │    Mr. Bee's Honey Farm │                          │
│ │      │    Check # 93821        │ order ──→  $254.06       │
│ └──────┴────────────────────────────────────┘              │
└─────────────────────────────────────────────────────────────┘
```

Figure 10.4

Different parts of an accounting form can be generated and integrated. The sample shown here illustrates how one A/S software package can be used for different companies' accounting needs.

prompt payments, and automatic checkbook reconciliation. They also print checks.

Purchase Orders (P/O): The P/O module is closely allied with Accounts Payable. Typically, this module tracks all purchasing activities from purchase requisition to final receipt of the order. Once the order is filled, the P/O module sends the information to the A/P module, which ultimately pays your supplier.

Accounts Receivable (A/R): The A/R module represents the other side of the purchasing coin. It tracks the money that people owe you. A/R programs also print invoices, calculate sales taxes automatically (sometimes for multiple cities and states), let you establish customer payment terms and billing cycles, handle recurring invoices, age past-due accounts, and print payment-reminder letters.

Payroll: In addition to printing paychecks, a Payroll module should handle sick and vacation time, shift differentials, bonuses and commissions, hourly and salaried pay, and it should calculate all federal and state payroll taxes.

Inventory: An Inventory program lets you track and value your inventory as it moves through your business, from initial purchase or manufacture to final sale. Most Inventory packages support LIFO (Last-In-First-Out), FIFO (First-In-First-Out), Specific Unit, Standard, and Average costing methods. Many also allow you to track serial and lot numbers.

Fixed Assets: Fixed Assets programs are used to manage your company's fixed assets, such as cars, computers, trucks, and buildings. You can use this program to keep tabs on the location of assets and their yearly depreciation.

Job Cost: Job Cost modules let you determine the costs and profitability of different jobs. Computers are particularly good at complex tasks such as determining the costs of building a shopping mall or writing a computer program, and they are also good for simpler jobs such as determining the cost of installing carpet. Some programs also can help you to schedule jobs.

Report Writer: Most accounting programs come with a variety of "canned" or predefined reports. Some also provide a special module called a Report Writer that lets you develop custom reports, modify predefined reports, present data in graphical format, and transfer information to popular database or spreadsheet programs.

General Business and Office Management Programs

General business and office management software includes just about any business program that doesn't handle accounting and bookkeeping. Here you'll find software for making proposals and quotes, flow-charting, managing your employees, designing and printing forms, managing and scheduling projects, tracking sales orders (Figure 10.5), and printing mailing labels.

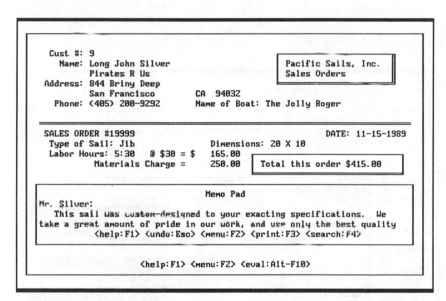

```
    Cust #: 9
      Name: Long John Silver          ┌─────────────────────────┐
            Pirates R Us               │ Pacific Sails, Inc.     │
   Address: 844 Briny Deep             │ Sales Orders            │
            San Francisco    CA  94032 └─────────────────────────┘
     Phone: (405) 200-9292   Name of Boat: The Jolly Roger

   ─────────────────────────────────────────────────────────────
   SALES ORDER #19999                      DATE: 11-15-1989
     Type of Sail: Jib          Dimensions: 20 X 10
     Labor Hours: 5:30   @ $30 = $    165.00
            Materials Charge =         250.00  ┌────────────────────────┐
                                               │ Total this order $415.00│
                                               └────────────────────────┘
   ┌─────────────────────────────────────────────────────────────┐
   │                         Memo Pad                             │
   │ Mr. Silver;                                                  │
   │   This sail was custom-designed to your exacting specifications.  We │
   │ take a great amount of pride in our work, and use only the best quality │
   │     <help:F1> <undo:Eso> <menu:F2> <print:F3> <search:F4>    │
   └─────────────────────────────────────────────────────────────┘

              <help:F1> <menu:F2> <eval:Alt-F10>
```

Figure 10.5

A sales order record is displayed in the OPEN ACCESS III general business program. The information was drawn from the database segment of the program.

Most programs in this category are very easy to use. A few, like those for project management and scheduling, are more difficult because they solve complex problems. After all, scheduling a 5000-task project among 20 overworked employees is a more complex undertaking than printing mailing labels for 2000 customers. (See Figure 10.6.)

Here are some of the common business applications that software programs have been written to handle:

Automated proposals/quotes	Name tags software
Bid analyses	Office productivity
Business plans/Forecasting	Personnel management
Decision support	Project management
Forecasting	Project scheduling
Forms design	Sales calculations
Mailing labels/lists	Tax calculations
Marketing	Time and billing
Mapping demographics	

Figure 10.6

This screen is from the ABRA 2000 Human Resources System, which is designed to manage personnel records. It displays the information for one employee and points to an error in the data.

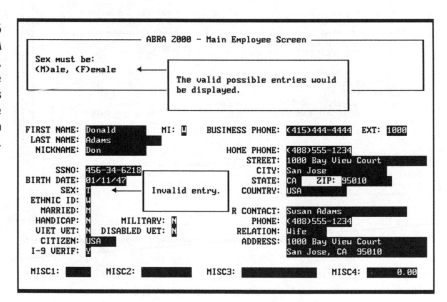

Educational Programs

Educational software is for students, teachers, and educational administrators. Students can find software to help them study foreign languages, reading, spelling, typing, and mathematics (see Figure 10.7).

Teachers can find software to help them mark and grade tests, record student grades, manage their classrooms and lesson plans, and develop

 **NOTE**

For teachers using Apple II computers, there are many A/S programs and templates made by teachers.

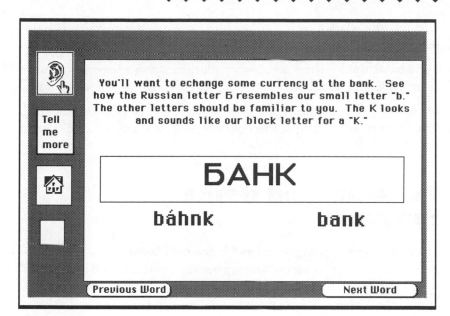

You'll want to echange some currency at the bank. See how the Russian letter Б resembles our small letter "b." The other letters should be familiar to you. The K looks and sounds like our block letter for a "K."

БАНК

báhnk   bank

Previous Word   Next Word

Figure 10.7
Computer-aided instruction in the Russian language now includes aural and visual feedback. With such specialized software, students can practice the language at their own pace.

Product at a Glance

Where in... is Carmen Sandiego? for DOS and Macintosh

Publisher:
Bröderbund Software

Suggested Retail Price:
$49.95-DOS/$49.95-Macintosh

DOS Requires:
80286 processor
DOS 3.1
640K RAM or more

Macintosh Requires:
68020 or better
System 6.0.5
2 MB RAM

Description:

Carmen Sandiego has led children and adults through diverse countries of this world and beyond. Some of the available programs are Where in Space is Carmen Sandiego?, Where in America's Past is Carmen Sandiego?, and Where in Europe is Carmen Sandiego? She has made us look into the past and think about the future, all the while solving some of the toughest heists in computer history, or should I say geography, or logic. A pioneer in educational and entertainment software, Bröderbund has always presented programs that stimulate thought and challenge the imagination and memory. Public broadcasting even has a Carmen Sandiego game show every afternoon.

computer-based training (CBT) in which the computer interacts with the learner (this software is called "authorware").

For administrators, there are programs for managing admissions offices, billing students, handling registration, and maintaining school records.

In addition, there are many software tutorials, that is, programs that will teach buyers how to use popular software programs such as WordPerfect, Lotus 1-2-3, or dBASE.

Personal and Home Programs

NOTE

Don't judge the usefulness of a program by its size. Some very small programs found in the Windows Accessories group can be very handy.

Software programs for personal and home use abound. This broad category includes programs for genealogy tracking, nutrition and health, personal and home finance, and legal, religious, and time-management applications. Many of these programs are available as freeware or shareware and often appear on computer club disks. Depending on the application, they range in size from small programs that are included in other software packages to full-sized programs. For example, the small program, *Calendar*, included with the Microsoft Windows package (Figure 10.8), is a very good example of a personal home program.

Here are some programs available in the personal and home area:

Address books	Home loans
Architecture (home design)	Legal software (do-it-yourself wills and rental agreements)
Award, certificate, banner design	Nutrition and health
Calendar and appointment scheduling	Personal finance and taxes
Desktop communications	Resume preparation
Genealogy tracking	Stamp collection tracking

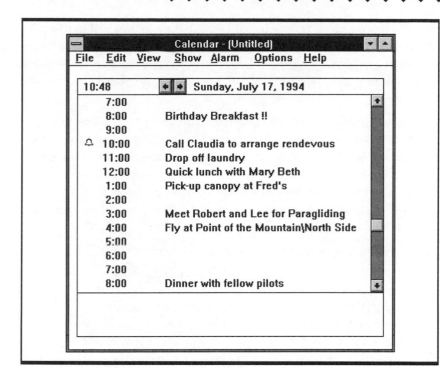

Figure 10.8

A calendar program that lets you schedule all your appointments days, weeks, and months in advance. It will even sound an alarm to let you know when it's time to do something.

Vertical Applications

The name "vertical applications" comes from the idea that these programs handle all of the needs of one particular business from top to bottom. It's used in the same sense as vertical and horizontal business markets. Although a good word processing program is "wide" enough to take care of all your writing needs, it wouldn't handle your record-keeping, billing, and inventory effectively. Vertical application programs derive from examining a business, say a medical office, and creating a program that covers everything such an office would need, from patient billing to reordering medicines to government paperwork.

Because there are so many specific businesses that need specific records to do specific jobs, there are hundreds of these programs available. These programs often include basic accounting and billing features that you'd find in a more general program, but because they are tailored to fit a particular industry, we call them "vertical applications." If you think you may need a vertical application, take a look at some before you purchase an accounting and billing program. You might not have to buy two programs.

In addition to industry-specific programs, this category also includes specialized tools and databases. For example, the architecture subcategory includes interior design tools, three-dimensional design and sketching programs, and databases of standard components and landscape materials. The health care subcategory includes programs and databases for medical diagnoses, medical image processing, and medical product information. The list, and the available software, goes on and on.

Here is a sampling of the wealth of programs available in this area:

Advertising
Airport operations
Art gallery management
Banking and finance
Beauty salon management
Campaign management
Cleaning/maintenance work
Clothing rental management
Construction
Copy services management
Courier management
Dental office management
Facilities management
Farming

Field service management
Flight planning

Florist management
Financial planning/analysis
Garden design and lawn care management
Hotel, motel management

Job shop estimating
Legal architecture
Library management
Liquid waste industries
Medical office management
Museum management
Photography
Printer shop management
Publishing
Real estate
Recording studios
Restaurants
Season ticket tracking
Storage facility management
Survey processing
Technical support management
Telephone management
Tour agencies
UPS and shipping management
Vehicle management
Water/Utility billings

How Do I Learn How to Do It?

How easy an A/S software program is to learn depends on the software design. The more the programmer understood the needs of a specific target audience, the easier the program is to learn. For example, if an attorney has been running her office for years without a computer, she will quickly learn how to run her office *with* a computer. She will do the same tasks with different tools. If she has been entering client hours on a paper ledger and figuring out the bill with a calculator, she will now enter the hourly rate and the number of hours for consultation into her computer. She does not have to learn about billing clients. She already knows how to do that.

Sometimes, however, one has to simultaneously learn how to use the software and how to run the business. So, a new physician starting up a first office with an A/S software package will have more to learn than will an experienced physician who has been running an office for years without a computer.

Much of the time, though, industry-specific programs are easier to learn because you don't have to spend time learning about the computer or mastering theoretical concepts such as database design or programming. Usually you can choose just what you want from an opening menu and immediately start entering data, printing a report, running calculations, or querying a database. In short, with these programs you can focus immediately on what it is you really want to do.

NOTE For the Macintosh, there's a lot of public domain software created on HyperCard stacks. Don't overlook this valuable and generally free source of Mac software. (HyperCard comes free with your Macintosh.)

NOTE A lot of software that was created several years ago may be difficult to run on the newer systems. This tends to be a problem with the public domain software more so than with the commercial programs.

Text versus Graphical Interface in Application-Specific Software

Because of the diversity of A/S programs, both text-based and graphics-based computer systems (interfaces) are widely used, depending on the application. Your choice will depend on what you need to see on the screen—text characters or graphic and icon-like pictures.

In general, scientific, engineering, mathematical, and most educational programs require graphics-based systems so you can see pictures, graphs, mechanical drawings, and equations on-screen.

Many accounting, general business, office management, industry-specific, and personal programs require only text-based systems. But it's a mixed bag. Many other programs that perform the same tasks will need a graphics-based system.

The program will specify on its packaging what type of system is required to run it. If it's designed to display graphs or other detailed images on the screen, it will most likely require a graphics-based system. But some graphic programs can run in text mode—if you're perfectly happy seeing only text characters, then a less-expensive, character-based system may do the job just as well.

What Do I Need to Know If I'm Going to Buy?

When looking at A/S software, you'll want to consider the following points:

- **Can it get the job done? Is it better than noncomputer methods?**
  Because A/S software is designed to accomplish a specific task, it is reasonable to want a program that does what you want the way you want it done. With some programs, it's necessary to rearrange the way you do things. If one software package requires changing the way you do things, and another accomplishes the same goal but uses methods more like the ones you usually use, get the software that works best in your established routine. Of course, software that provides some flexibility, especially for growth and change, is the best to buy.
  Also, you should ask yourself if the computer version is more effective and efficient than your noncomputer version. Let's

face it, a computer can do a lot of things very well, but if some other method works as well or even better for your specific needs, don't buy software that will not do the job as efficiently just for the sake of computerizing.

- **Does the package have good support?**
Application-specific software may or may not require support. For more expensive and complex software, you should expect help to get you up and running. In some cases, you can buy a service contract that will provide extended support for an additional fee. In general, the less you pay for the software, the more minimal the support.

Some software, such as a complex office management system, is going to require support. For example, what happens when the government changes tax rates and payroll deductions? Make sure that the supplier will be able to adjust the software to handle these changes.

- **Can the developers provide you with names and telephone numbers of people already using their packages and/or consultants?**
If you are to trust your business operation to a program, be sure to talk with people who've already used the package. Some people who have spent a good deal of time with A/S software can be hired as consultants. You should be able to get the name of a consultant either from the vendor or others who use the same software.

How to Find Application-Specific Software

Application-specific software can be a bit trickier to find than general purpose software. But difficult doesn't mean impossible! Here are some suggestions on searching for those special programs:

Computer/Software stores: These are excellent sources for A/S software in the areas of games, entertainment, accounting, general business, personnel management, and some educational categories.

However, with shelf space at a premium, most stores stock only the most popular A/S programs. For programs with a smaller potential audience—especially vertical applications—you'll need to search a bit further with some other approaches suggested below.

Computer magazines: Magazines serving the computer industry provide the latest information on both general purpose and A/S software. In these, you'll find both brief and in-depth software reviews, announcements about new software, advertisements by software developers, and advertisements from mail-order companies selling software. Most mail-order ads list software by subject area.

Trade publications/associations: If you are seeking software in a specific business area, such as law, medicine, engineering, dentistry, cosmetology, or plumbing, take a look at your favorite trade publications. You'll usually find ads for software aimed at businesses in your field. Ask members of your professional associations what they are using to run their businesses. The chances are good that someone will know someone who's using a program worth reviewing.

Product directories: These publications (also called Buyers' Guides) provide software listings and brief descriptions of each program. This makes them great sources for determining what A/S software is available. Typically, publishers of product directories do not sell the products they list, but catalog publishers do.

Mail-order catalogs: Like product directories, these catalogs contain program listings, descriptions, and indexes. You can use these to buy programs you've decided to purchase. They are not hard to find. If you order software from a mail-order house, subscribe to a computer magazine, or are in a professional association, you'll probably be on a lot of catalog mailing lists. This will earn you an amazing amount of junk mail that isn't junk at all, including very useful catalogs and product announcements.

A Final Note

No matter what your business or personal needs are, there's undoubtedly a computer program out there to ease your life. While software programmers have created hundreds of general purpose programs to do word processing or database manipulations, they have also created *thousands* of special-purpose programs to perform specific tasks for specific purposes. If your question is whether there is a software program that can help you do your job or handle some specific personal task, most likely the answer is a resounding "Yes."

Part Three

Getting the Right Equipment

Eleven

Inside Computers

· ·

emember, there's not a whole lot you need to know about a computer's internal components.

When you buy software, a program may state that it requires 2MB of RAM. You don't need to know how RAM works, but you do need to know that you must have 2MB of RAM in your computer. As you read this chapter, keep in mind that its purpose is to provide a general overview of how computers work so that you'll be better equipped to understand what will best satisfy your computing needs.

How Do Computers Work?

Basically, a computer is just a very fast calculating machine. Even when it manipulates words or graphic images, it does so by adding and subtracting numbers millions of times each second. It's an *electronic* device, which means that it operates on a very low-voltage current of electrons through a circuit of components called semiconductors. (If you've seen the inside of a transistor radio, you've seen what a circuit of semiconductors looks like.) At any given time, the voltage at any location within the circuit can be either on or off. If it's on, we assign it a value of 1. If it's off, we assign it a value of 0. With only two digits available, clearly we need a way to group the digits together to represent numbers larger than 1. The system used is called *binary* numbering.

Binary Numbers

Binary numbering is not hard to understand if you think in terms of using only two digits (0,1) instead of ten (0–9). Essentially, it works in the same way as our familiar decimal system, except that we run out of digits faster. Compare counting to 10 in the binary and decimal systems.

Binary	Decimal
1	1
10	2
11	3
100	4
101	5
110	6
111	7
1000	8
1001	9
1010	10

Both numbering systems work the same way. When we run out of digits, we shift one to the left, start at the beginning with 1 and place 0's in the empty spaces to the right. Remember, the reason we use binary numbers is that we need to rely on a system that operates on an electric current being either on (1) or off (0).

The most basic arrangement of binary numbers is in groups of eight digits. An eight-digit binary number has a decimal value between 0 and 255. So, to represent a number from 0 to 255, the binary system requires eight digits while the decimal system needs only three. To better understand this, we will look at some units of measurement used in computers (see Figure 11.1).

Figure 11.1

Eight bits make up a byte. Each byte contains values composed of binary numbers. This byte has a decimal value of 82.

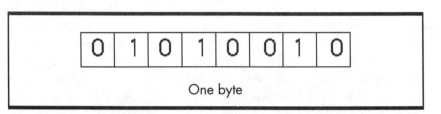

One byte

Some Units of Measurement

Like all specialized disciplines, computers have their own systems of measurement. Here are some of the measuring units used in the computer world:

- **Bit**: The electronic current can be on or off; a single 1 or 0 in the binary system is stored in a bit. The word "bit" is short for binary digit, which is the smallest unit of information handled by a computer.

- **Byte**: A collection of eight bits is a byte. A single byte can have a decimal value between 0 and 255. (In binary, this would be stated as between 00000000 and 11111111.) Figure 11.1 shows how information is stored in a byte.

- **Kilobytes**: A kilobyte is roughly one thousand bytes (actually 1024 or 2^{10} bytes). The measurement is used to define the size of computer files, computer memory, and diskette storage. Items measured in kilobytes usually are referred to as something like 300K, pronounced "300 kay."

- **Megabyte**: A megabyte is roughly one million bytes (actually 1,048,576 or 1024^{10} bytes). Most contemporary computers measure both RAM (Random Access Memory) and hard drive space in megabytes. It's abbreviated MB and is usually referred to as something like "100 meg."

- **8-bit, 16-bit, 32-bit**: These describe the sizes of the data and instruction packets various computers use. Usually the larger the number, the faster and more powerful the computer.

RAM & ROM

As stated in Chapter 2, the memory is the part of the computer where programs and data are stored electronically. The following lists describe the several different types of basic memory:

NOTE

In the not too distant future, we will be hearing about gigabytes of memory—billions of bytes.

- **RAM**: This stands for Random Access Memory. It's memory that changes constantly whenever you are actively working in a program. It's where both the program and the data you enter are stored temporarily for immediate access by the processor.

- **ROM**: This stands for Read-Only Memory. This is memory that is cast in stone. You cannot alter it; nor would you want to. It contains the information necessary to start up your computer and the basic instructions that operate it. It's a software program built into the computer hardware.

Usually, when *computer memory* is discussed, as in "How much memory does your computer have?" or "How much memory does it take to run a program?" the reference is to RAM. Physically, RAM is a bank of silicon switches called core storage. When the computer is turned off, everything in RAM is erased. You can save what is in RAM to a disk and reload it again when you restart your computer, but if you forget to save your work that is stored in RAM, it's gone for good.

Memory has become an increasingly important computer feature because software programs are becoming larger and require more RAM. Today, most popular software needs at least 640K of memory to run, and many graphic-based programs require memory that is measured in megabytes.

If you have a computer with an 80286, 80386, 80486, or Pentium microprocessor (IBM-compatible), the types of RAM you can have are as follows:

- **Conventional memory**: The first 640K of RAM is called conventional memory. DOS uses conventional memory as do any utilities and applications that are in your CONFIG.SYS and AUTOEXEC.BAT files. Conventional memory is where all your programs run. This 640K limitation of DOS was placed there by the original designers.

- **Expanded memory**: Expanded memory was the first attempt to deal with the 640K limit of conventional memory. Expanded memory is "paged" in and out of an address between 640K and 1MB. This memory is used by DOS programs but not by Windows. To use expanded memory you'll need a program called an expanded memory manager.

- **Extended memory**: This is memory above 1MB. Windows loves this kind of memory and, in fact, needs some in order to run at all. For extended memory to be shared, you need a memory manager. Microsoft Windows comes with such a manager in a file called HIMEM.SYS.

- **RAM cache**: RAM is also available in the form of 64K, 128K, and 256K caches. A RAM cache is a bank of super-fast (and expensive) chips on the computer's motherboard. If you are going back and forth between different views in graphics or desktop publishing, you can save a good deal of time with a RAM cache. This is especially true in a graphics environment such as Windows.

NOTE

If you have DOS 5 or 6, you already have an expanded memory manager called EMM386.EXE. Check your DOS manual for instructions on installation.

Greater memory will increase the number of programs that will run on your computer and make those programs run faster. When you load a typical software program, part of the program is brought into memory for very fast access while other parts remain on the disk storage device, available if needed. Programmers try to design programs so the parts you'll need most are in memory and the parts you'll use occasionally remain in disk storage.

Think of RAM as the kind of information that you store in your own mind. You can access your mind a lot faster than you can look up something in a book. In the same way, a program can get to the information in RAM faster than if it has to access the disk system to find it. What slows programs down is that it takes much longer to get something from storage than from RAM (see Figure 11.2).

If you have a lot of RAM, your program can use it as if it were a disk, storing parts of itself and temporary data files in memory. Getting information from memory is so much faster than getting it from a disk that your programs (particularly large, complex ones) will appear to be supercharged.

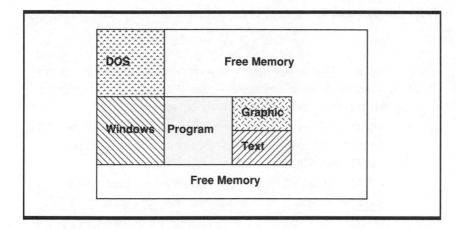

Figure 11.2
Your computer's memory can be filled with DOS, Windows, your programs, text, and graphics. The more memory you have, the more programs you can work with simultaneously. Note that some computers' memories are so small that they can handle very little.

What's Inside the Box?

Your computer may look like a maze of wires, slots, boards, circuits, chips, and boxes inside. However, if we break it down, there are just a few key components. The main board, called the motherboard, contains the microprocessor chip and supporting chips and circuits. A metal box holds the power supply that provides the electrical current for the microprocessor and drives. Floppy and hard drives are in a few more boxes. Several cards are in slots, and a bus connects all the parts.

With any luck at all, you'll never see your computer's innards. However, knowing what's inside it may help you understand how your computer works.

Microprocessors

The microprocessor is the brain of the computer. If a computer could think, the microprocessor is what would be doing the thinking. But since a computer can't think, what the microprocessor does is add and subtract billions of electrons.

A fascinating fact about the microprocessor is that it's one of the smallest things inside the computer. It's not much bigger than a fingertip and is

How Is It Done?

You may have wondered how in the world your computer can do word processing using numbers. Actually, there are four different tools that a computer uses to interpret binary values:

- **Instructions**: These are commands that tell the computer what to do. Programmers write both arithmetic and logical (true and false) instructions.
- **Addresses**: Inside computers there are areas where instructions and data are stored. For example, in a system with 1MB of memory, there are more than one million bytes available to store instructions and data. Each byte has an identifiable location called an "address."
- **Numeric data**: Numeric data constitute real numbers that can be manipulated mathematically.
- **Alphanumeric data**: This type of data is a code for the alphabet, special symbols such as the dollar sign, and the representation of numbers. In America a special code called ASCII (American Standard Code for Information Interchange) is used.

When you press the letter "A", the keyboard sends a 65 (01000001 in binary) into the computer. Your computer recognizes it as an alphanumeric code and not the decimal value 65. The code is then sent to a memory location (address) that is used for screen output, and the letter "A" appears on your screen.

enclosed in a plastic case about $1\frac{1}{4}$" square by $\frac{1}{4}$" high. It's also called the *Central Processing Unit (CPU)*, *the processor*, and sometimes just the chip.

This chip does all the processing and manipulating of data that we think of as computing. When we talk about what a computer can do with data, we are almost always talking about what this chip is capable of doing. Everything else in the box is there to support and get information from this one little chip.

Every microprocessor is made up of tens of thousands of transistors, diodes, and other components etched on tiny slivers of adulterated silicon. Although these chips are separated into "families," the chips are very much individuals. And they are the core element in determining what any computer can do.

Each microprocessor began with a basic design. Then someone made the chip faster and gave the new version a new name. Early chips worked mostly with 8-bit data packets. Then they were improved to work with data in 16-bit packets, and then 32-bit packets; each version became faster and more powerful than the one before.

Let's look at the three main families of microprocessors in use in microcomputers today. Like many things in the computer world, each chip is named with a number—the higher the number the newer the chip. The first numbers represent the family and the rest of the numbers represent the individual chip. For example, the 80386 chip belongs to the 80XXX family (where X could be any number), but most people call it by the numbers that make it unique. They'll say: "I use a 386." This means the speaker has a computer that runs on an 80386 microprocessor.

Here are the three main families of microprocessor chips:

- The MOS Technologies 65XXX family was used in very early computers from the 70s and 80s. This family includes the

How Do They Make It So Tiny?

You know that a computer processor is made up of electrical circuits. These circuits are made out of silicon, which conducts electricity only under certain circumstances (hence the term *semiconductor*). Imagine painting the layout of the full circuits on many walls. Then imagine photographing the walls and reducing the photos to microscopic size. Then place the film on wafer-thin sheets laid on top of each other, with circuits touching between the sheets if they need contact. Finally, seal it all up into a chip. That's the general idea.

8-bit 6510, the 65C02, and the 16-bit 65816. The Apple II family of computers so prevalent in primary and secondary schools has this type of chip.

- The Motorola 680X0 family is used in the Macintosh, Atari ST, and Mega, Amiga, and NeXT computers. This family includes the 16-bit 68000 and 68020, and the 32-bit 68030 and 68040. The 680X0 family of chips is capable of *multitasking*.

- The Intel 80X86 family is used in IBM-compatibles and the IBM PS/2 line of computers. This family includes the 8-bit 8088, the 16-bit 8086 and 80286, and the 32-bit 80386, 80486, and Pentium (80586). The 386 and 486 both come in two versions: the SX (slower and cheaper) and the DX (faster and more expensive). In the Intels, multitasking begins with the 80386 chip.

NOTE

Generally, each higher-numbered chip can run all the programs of any lower-number chip in the same family.

Sometimes you'll see a chip referred to as a 16/32-bit microprocessor; that means it processes at one level and communicates at another. The 386SX is a perfect example. It can work with memory 32 bits at a time, but can communicate with peripherals only 16 bits at a time. (The 386DX is faster because it does everything in 32-bit packets.)

Operating Systems

Every computer has an operating system. The operating system creates a file system and provides the tools for the user to interact with that file system. It also provides a way to run other programs and to control the disk drives, keyboard, video display, and any other outside device. (See Chapter 3 for a discussion of operating systems.)

Power Supply

The power supply gets its electricity from the wall socket and transforms it into a usable form for the computer. Basically, it transforms high-voltage alternating current (AC) into low-voltage direct current (DC) that a computer can use. If you open up the computer you'll see a metal box that says LEAVE THIS ALONE (or its general equivalent) in big letters and several different languages. This is the power supply. Don't mess with it.

The Motherboard

The motherboard ties everything together. The microprocessor, memory, and the supporting circuits are all on the motherboard. If you upgrade your computer from an 80286 to an 80386, the chances are good that you'll end up with a whole new motherboard instead of just a new chip. Different types of microprocessors require different motherboards, and even chips from the same family require different motherboards.

The motherboard is the board in the bottom of your computer. It has slots in it so that you can plug in other boards that enable peripherals to communicate with the microprocessor. Figure 11.3 shows a typical motherboard.

NOTE

Sometimes you can upgrade your computer by merely putting in a new motherboard. But in some cases you'll also need a new power supply, more memory, etc., so upgrading can end up costing more than a whole new computer!

Figure 11.3

This motherboard shows the microprocessors, circuitry, bus, and memory chips. Those odd-looking things in the upper left corner are actually the slots into which you plug in add-on boards.

The Bus

Think of a bus as a wire that connects everything together. Furthermore, any bus contains three buses: power, data, and ground. The power bus supplies power to all of the parts that need electricity. The data bus is a "telephone line" between the parts of the computer that need to send and receive data. And, finally, the ground bus is a ground wire that makes sure everything needing a ground gets one. Keep in mind that for most computers you will not have to select a bus. The buses are built in.

The Boards

Any device mounted on a printed-circuit board that plugs into one of the computer's expansion slots is informally called a *board* or *card*. These devices allow communication, either between a computer and the outside world, or between the motherboard and other components within the computer.

Here are some of the boards typically used in a computer:

- **Disk controller**: The disk controller controls communication between the motherboard and the disk drive. It tells the drive when to send data to the motherboard or to save information from the motherboard. Obviously mandatory.

- **Video**: The video board links the motherboard to the video display. It controls signals that are sent from the keyboard, mouse, light pen, or directly from the motherboard to the video monitor. Also required.

- **Mouse**: The mouse board can be either a dedicated board or a port. Most mice plug into the serial or parallel ports (other boards), but some have their own boards. Only required if your mouse requires it.

- **Modem**: Internal modems are discussed in Chapter 9, "Telecommunications." If you use an internal modem, it's simply a modem on a board you plug into a slot. The modem board is required only for an internal modem.

- **Scanner**: A scanner converts pictures into electronic codes. The scanner card is the interface between the scanner and the motherboard, and is only needed if you have a scanner.

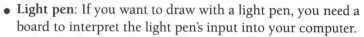

- **FAX card:** Instead of buying a FAX machine, you can get a card that works like a FAX for sending and receiving text and graphics. It does not scan documents; instead it takes documents created in your computer, such as a text file or a graphic, and sends it to other FAX machines. It turns material received from other FAX machines into computer files.

- **Light pen:** If you want to draw with a light pen, you need a board to interpret the light pen's input into your computer.

You're getting sleepy... sleeepy....

Ports

The ports on your computer may or may not be added as boards. On many IBM-compatible computers, the ports are on boards plugged into available slots. However, on the Macintosh, the ports (two serial ports and one mouse port) are built into the computer. Other computers have ports that come with the system and allow more ports to be added.

The two most important types of ports are as follows:

- **Serial port:** In this kind of port, data is sent sequentially, or serially, one bit at a time. This port is used for external modems, mice, and some printers. You should have at least one serial port on your computer; most come with two.

- **Parallel port:** In this kind of port, data is sent eight bits at a time, simultaneously; hence the term "parallel." A parallel port is faster than a serial port for transmitting data. It's often called the "printer port" since most printers require a parallel interface. On non-Macintosh computers there's usually a parallel port for a printer. The Macintosh uses serial interfaces for its printers.

NOTE
You can purchase devices that will convert a serial port into a parallel port. This can be handy if you have a Macintosh computer and a parallel printer.

BIOS

BIOS is an acronym for the computer's Basic Input Output System: this is a set of instructions located in ROM. When you first turn on the computer, this program is activated and begins the process of transferring information between the elements of the system, such as memory, disks, and the monitor.

In IBM-compatibles, the BIOS typically has three parts:

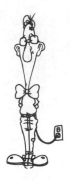

- A set of simple programs for communicating with all the hardware in the system.
- A program known as POST (Power-On Self Test) that examines the entire system to make sure everything is functioning properly.
- A program known as the "bootstrap loader" that contains just enough instructions to start the operating system loading. Because the bootstrap loader seems to bring the operating system up from nowhere, the computer is said to be "pulling itself up by its own bootstraps." Hence the term "booting the computer."

A bootstrap program gives your computer information about loading the operating system. The operating system tells the computer how to get information from the disk, but the computer has to load the operating system from the disk.

Loading an operating system rather than having it stored entirely in ROM chips allows the operating system to be updated easily and inexpensively by changing disks. All modern computers have a way of loading the operating system from a disk.

Speed

Anyone shopping for a computer has seen advertisements that describe particular models as 25MHz, 33MHz, and so forth. These numbers identify the *clock rate* of the main processor chip, which is a measure of the speed at which it can execute instructions. A microprocessor uses a clock circuit, generally a quartz crystal vibrating at a fixed speed (measured in Megahertz, millions of cycles per second), to synchronize the pulses of electricity with which it operates. Each instruction takes one or more cycles (pulses) of the clock.

Succeeding generations of chips have created faster clock rates. Whereas the 8086 ran at 4MHz, 80486 chips can run at 66MHz. 286 computers typically run at 8–10MHz and since no one's making new ones, that's where they'll stay. 386 machines run at 14–40MHz, and 486 machines at 25–66MHz. The 68XXX family of computers has comparable speed ranges, with the more expensive ones, of course, being faster.

Clock rate, however, is a theoretical measure of a chip's possible speed. A more accurate comparison of computer speed may be MIPS (millions of instructions per second), which measures whole instructions actually executed. The most recent crop of 80386 computers often have a MIPS indicator on the front panel to let you know how many millions of instructions your computer is grinding through each second.

The most important thing to know about speed, however, is that you may not need it. It depends on what you're going to do with the computer. Even slow computers can handle most word processing tasks quickly. It's true, however, that with complex graphics you do need speed.

Here are some general guidelines for evaluating your speed needs:

- Printers, modems, disk drives, and other peripherals work at their own pace. Megaspeed doesn't help much here, since even the slowest processors usually have to wait for the printer or modem to catch up to them.
- Word processing, small spreadsheets, and database applications run just fine on an 8–10MHz IBM-compatible or an 8MHz Macintosh.
- Graphics programs, desktop publishing, and large-scale spreadsheet/database projects do fine on a 14–16MHz processor, but you will probably want a 25–66MHz upgrade if you do very complicated graphics.

NOTE

Discussing **need** when it comes to computers is somewhat misleading. It's true that no one really **needs** a Jaguar just to tootle around town. And very few people actually **need** a 66MHz computer—but both are a whole lot of fun if you can afford them.

Just how fast computers will become is unclear at the moment. Some people think that there's a theoretical upper limit to the speed that silicon-based computer chips can achieve. But silicon replaced vacuum tubes only a short time ago and new technology may be lurking around the corner, even now, waiting to replace silicon.

Today, research labs are experimenting with exotic semiconductors, such as gallium arsenide (known as GaAs, pronounced "gas"), which promise faster performance than silicon. Also, researchers are working on computers that use light instead of electrical currents, which may mean that computers of much greater speed and efficiency might appear even before silicon has achieved its full potential.

The direction that computer technology is going is anyone's guess, but the safe bet is on computers becoming faster (and smaller) all the time.

Architecture and Expandability

Occasionally, you may hear someone describe a computer's "architecture" as either "open" or "closed." What do these terms mean, and how important is the distinction?

Broadly, *architecture* refers to the overall design of a computer, meaning how its parts work together. An *open* architecture is one in which you can add or change internal components, usually with the goal of improving performance; and a *closed* architecture is one in which you cannot. A manufacturer creates an open architecture by doing the following: 1) including *expansion slots* into which the user can insert new devices such as disk drive controllers, additional memory chips, math coprocessors, and any of the add-ons discussed under "Boards," and 2) not patenting the technical specifications for such add-ons, thus allowing other manufacturers to design similar add-ons without paying a licensing fee. The PC, introduced in 1981, was designed with an open architecture in order to allow other companies to improve upon the computer and increase its popularity. Perhaps it worked too well, as the open architecture allowed others to copy the whole machine, thus producing the cheaper "clones" that have replaced the IBM PC in the marketplace.

When Apple introduced the Macintosh in 1984, it kept the technical details proprietary and guarded them with patents. Anyone who designs add-on devices for the Mac must first pay a licensing fee. Besides the price (there are no low-cost alternatives to the Mac), the most important difference between Macs and PCs for the consumer is expandability.

With open architecture, you can adapt your computer to changing needs and take advantage of new technology by adding or replacing components without having to replace the whole system. For example, if you are running a word processor that fits within 640K of memory, your present needs can be met by a Macintosh Classic. If you needed to run a sophisticated spreadsheet program that required 4MB of memory, with the Mac, you'd have to have someone install additional memory for you. The newer models of Macintosh such as the IIci, however, have a more open architecture.

It's Running Too Slowly

If your program is running too slowly, there are a number of things that might be done to increase its speed.

- If your system has a lot of other programs in memory at the same time, as in a multitasking system such as Multi-Finder on the Macintosh, you can clear out some programs and provide more available RAM. Or, better yet, you can purchase more RAM for your system.

- If the program reads and writes to the disk a lot, you can install a RAM disk. This is not a hardware item; rather it fools RAM memory into thinking that one of the drives is in RAM. Since there are no mechanical movements, disk access is much faster.

- Maybe you're running out of hard disk space. Check to see if your hard disk is full.

- You may have to upgrade your computer with a new, faster chip.

A Final Note

Knowing how a computer works is important primarily for understanding what you need to run applications. Usually all you need to know is how much memory you need, the minimum microprocessor required, the amount of disk space you need, and whether you need any special peripheral such as a math coprocessor. However, the most important thing to consider when purchasing a computer is how well and easily it performs the tasks you require. Chapter 12 compares how well different computers do different tasks.

Twelve

Computer Systems

· ·

If all this talk about kilobytes, megahertz, and MIPS in Chapter 11 has your head spinning, just keep in mind that buying a computer system boils down to three basic questions: (1) How big? (as in "How much memory and disk storage?" as well as physical size), (2) How fast? (as in "How quickly can this machine get the job done?"), and (3) How much? (as in "…am I willing to spend?")

246

The final question has a simple answer, flowing out of the first two. The bigger, in terms of memory and disk storage, and faster the machine is, the more it will cost.

In this chapter we'll discuss some general guidelines to follow when purchasing a computer. Then we'll look at some examples of what's available, and try to give you some approximate price ranges for various computer capabilities.

However, as we've mentioned previously, we can only give you ballpark figures. The cost of a complete system depends on many factors, including what kind of monitor you purchase, what kind of printer you buy (if any), and of course, what software packages you want to use with your system.

Also, computer prices change all the time. Fortunately, the prices always tend to go down, though the prices of individual components—particularly memory—can fluctuate. So if you need up-to-date price information, you should check with your local dealer, or skim the ads in a few computer magazines.

Things to Think about before Buying

I can't tell you how many times someone has said to me "I'm thinking about buying a computer, but I can't decide whether I want a Mac or a PC. What do you think?" My response, which is generally not the one they want to hear, is always a resounding "It depends…."

The reason for this vague reply is that choosing a computer is not just a matter of deciding between "Brand A" and "Brand X." Rather, it's a matter of buying a machine that will do whatever it is you want it to do. In the following sections we'll discuss some of the things you might want to think about before you start shopping for brand names.

Evaluate Your Needs

Most people purchase a computer to *do* something, be it word processing, invoicing, project management, graphics—whatever. And as we've said before, it's the *software* that makes the computer do whatever it is that *you* want to do.

So, if at all possible, try to pick your favorite software packages *before* you buy the hardware to run it. In earlier chapters, we presented the capabilities and hardware requirements of various types of software packages. But we could not cover every product in every genre in depth.

If you need more information before you buy, you might want to check out the latest reviews of products in a computer magazine. Seek out a friend with computer-nerd tendencies. Ask questions of anyone who appears to have a clue about computers.

Ask a dealer to give you a hands-on demonstration. If time permits, perhaps you could even take a course in how to use a particular program, or buy or borrow a book on that program to get an in-depth look at just what the program can and cannot do.

Once you have some idea of the specific programs you'll want to use, you can find out what the hardware requirements are for each program—and then purchase the hardware accordingly.

Remember, too, that even though disk storage requirements are additive, RAM memory requirements are not. For instance, if you choose a database management system that requires 4MB of RAM, and a word processing system that requires 1MB of RAM, you don't need 5MB of RAM. Instead, you need only as much as the largest program requires—4MB in this example.

Think about the Physical Size

Although the physical size of a computer, in terms of how much desk space it requires and how much it weighs, has little to do with power and cost, it can be a consideration when buying one. There are three basic configurations to choose from, pictured in "generic" format in Figure 12.1.

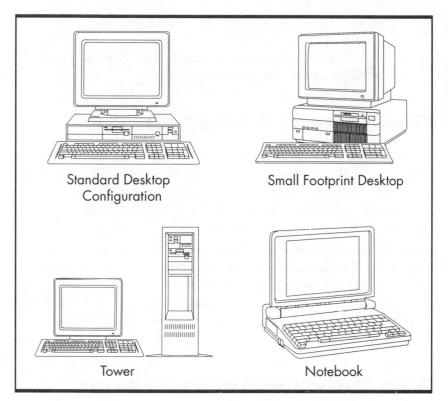

Figure 12.1
Basic computer configurations
include the desktop system,
small footprint desktop, tower,
and portable notebook sizes
pictured here (although not
shown to scale).

Standard Desktop
Configuration

Small Footprint Desktop

Tower

Notebook

- **Desktop**: The system unit goes on top of your desk, usually under the monitor. This puts the floppy drives within easy reach, although it does take up considerable space.

- **Footprint**: This is basically the same as a desktop computer except that it has a much smaller base (hence "footprint") and is slightly taller than a standard desktop computer.

- **Tower**: A tower configuration stands the computer on its end, and is designed so that you can set the computer on the floor rather than on your desk. (A minitower is a little shorter and wider than a standard tower, and can go either on the floor or your desktop.)

- **Notebook**: Usually, a notebook computer is small enough to fit in a briefcase ($8\frac{1}{2} \times 11$-inches) and can run on battery power. If you need to take the computer with you, a note-book computer is the way to go. Notebooks are sometimes called laptops, though the original laptops were much bigger and heavier than the later notebooks.

Think about Compatibility

If you're buying a computer for home use, and want to be able to share information with the microcomputers at the office, compatibility is a major consideration. For example, if your office is filled with PCs, and you buy a Mac for home use, you won't be able to take work home from the office and do it on your home computer.

In the PC world, there's also the constant problem of two sizes of floppy disks: $5\frac{1}{4}$-inch and $3\frac{1}{2}$-inch. If you're buying a PC, do yourself a favor and get one that has both $5\frac{1}{4}$-inch and $3\frac{1}{2}$-inch high-density floppy drives (in addition to the hard disk). That way you will never have to worry about getting data or a program on a disk that your system can't read.

Give Yourself Room to Grow

One of the more painful aspects of buying a computer is knowing that your state of the art computer will be a K-Mart special in 18 months or less.

As a result, many computer companies are touting future expandability as a big feature of their systems. So when faster processors become available, you won't have to pitch your whole system to get up to date. Instead, you can just remove the old chip, put in the new one, and your position on the cutting edge (or even the bleeding edge) of technology will be restored.

Likewise, if you buy a computer with 4MB of RAM that's *expandable* to 32MB of RAM, you don't have to bang your head against the wall when you later find that some of the more advanced operating systems insist on 8MB of RAM. Just have the kid at the computer store plug in some additional RAM and you're still in business.

It is a little tougher to add hard disk storage. For instance, if you buy a 40MB hard disk and later discover that you need 80MB (and you will), you can't just "add" another 40MB. You'll need to replace your old drive with a bigger one. Space on your hard disk is like space in your closets—it's not possible to have too much.

NOTE

You can expand your hard disk by using one of the disk compression utilities such as Stacker or Double-Space. These made more sense, however, in the days when hard disks were really expensive. They're less useful today when you can get a 200MB hard drive for about $200.

Special Considerations for Portable Computers

If you're thinking about buying a portable notebook computer, here are a few other matters to consider:

- **Screen readability**: The best notebooks offer displays that measure nearly 10-inches diagonally, and approximate the 4:3 ratio of width to height that larger desktop units offer. Backlit display, active matrix, and gas plasma technology help in dimly lit situations. Supertwist makes better use of reflected light, offering higher contrast and improved readability.

- **Quick charge battery with long life**: A notebook with a dead battery won't do you much good on the road. When considering the battery life of a notebook, don't forget to think about how long it takes to recharge the battery once it's dead. Most notebooks come with a lightweight transformer that lets you plug the computer into a wall socket so you're not always dependent on the battery.

- **Built-in mouse or mouse port**: Because most modern programs are designed with a mouse in mind, you'll certainly want to be able to add a mouse to your notebook. A small clip-on trackball mouse may be your best bet for working in close quarters—e.g., the coach section of a Boeing 727.

- **Standard keyboard configuration**: If you'll be using a standard size keyboard at home or in the office in addition to your notebook computer, make sure the keyboard layouts are similar on both systems. In particular, make sure the heavily used ⏎, Ctrl, Alt, and Shift keys are in the same places.

- **Connectivity with other machines**: Again, if you're planning to use a notebook computer in addition to a larger one, consider how easy it is to transfer data back and forth between

You're getting sleepy... sleeepy....

the two machines. You don't want to be dependent on transferring data on floppies if you can possibly avoid it. A high-speed parallel or serial port on both machines, coupled with a cable and a file transfer program such as LapLink, can make data transfer quite painless.

- **Internal fax/modem**: If you need to sign on to on-line services or send data back to the office while you're on the road, make sure you get an internal modem. Otherwise, you'll have to carry an external modem and the extra wires/cables that go with it.

- **Weight**: Needless to say, the less weight the better when it comes to portable computing. But a large part of a notebook's weight is the battery. And batteries that last longer tend to weigh more. So rather than focusing just on weight, think in terms of getting the most battery life per pound.

Where to Buy

When the question "Where should I buy a computer?" is asked, another question arises—that of services and support—i.e., how do you get the thing fixed if it breaks down?

Basically, there are three places to buy a computer:

- Computer dealers
- Discount warehouse and department stores
- Mail-order and classified advertisements

Some of the advantages and disadvantages of each place are discussed below.

Computer Dealers

Generally, computer dealers will offer a wide selection of hardware and software. Moreover, many dealers will let you test-drive a few systems and even some programs before you buy. Reputable dealers guarantee the products they sell. So, if repairs are needed, you can put the computer in the back seat of your car and take it to your local dealer rather than packing it up and shipping it back to the manufacturer.

For the novice, a dealer offers the peace of mind of dealing with someone who's in the business close at hand. On the other hand, let's face it. All the salespeople on the floor at your local dealer probably aren't computer scientists. So look for a dealer with at least one techie on hand, so that most questions can be handled on-site. This can save a lot of time and grief. Having a living, breathing person—who knows more about your system than you do—available for consultation can remove much of the anxiety of the first few weeks of ownership.

Discount and Department Stores

Department stores and discount warehouses also carry computers these days. Their prices are usually lower than those of specialized computer dealers, sometimes a lot lower. The computers they sell are ready-made packages, so you have to take them as-is. In other words, you can't take the Chinese restaurant approach: "I'll take this monitor with that keyboard and that processor with a different hard disk, etc."

And even though they can compete on price, they can rarely compete on support. The chances are good that if your machine ever needs service, you will have to send it to the manufacturer or find a local repair shop. Also, if questions arise and you need guidance, you can't expect department store or warehouse club salespeople to help.

On the other hand, if there are computer user groups in your vicinity, you may be able to get all the free advice and help you need just by joining that group. Look in the back section of your local computer magazines or ask your local guru about how to get in touch with a group. So, if you have a support system such as a user group, and you want to save a few bucks, a discount or department store might work fine for you.

Mail-Order Houses

Thousands of computer users purchase their systems through mail-order houses. Although the very thought of mail-ordering *anything* might give you the willies, mail ordering computers is very common.

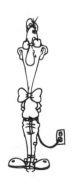

Mail-order is a huge and highly competitive part of the microcomputer industry, particularly in the PC world. Unlike retail stores that must support the considerable overhead of a storefront, sales personnel, and so forth, mail-order houses have relatively little overhead, so their prices can be very, very good.

On the convenience side of things, many mail-order houses will assemble your machine after you order it. So you can get not only the amount of memory and disk storage you want, you can specify the type of video card, the brand of monitor, or any other particularity. And, since mail-order houses are accustomed to building machines on-the-fly, you can get an exact price quote on what your "dream machine" will cost.

Look for a mail-order house that advertises in the big computer magazines. Any mail-order company that's been in business for several years has earned its reputation and success by delivering on its promises.

Classified Ads

If you're on a tight budget, and are approaching this whole computer purchase with trepidation, don't hesitate to consider buying a used computer. Computers have almost no moving parts. So, unlike cars and washing machines, they don't wear out with time. A used 386 computer is just as fast and as powerful as a brand-new one.

Of course, computers do date and you don't want to buy a used system that's way behind the times. But if you shop wisely, often you can find someone who's selling a used but fairly up-to-date machine. Some people sell their computers because they've never taken the time to learn to use them. And there are always people who need to sell perfectly good 386s so they can move up to 486s.

 NOTE

Shareware software is not copy-protected, so you don't need a license or serial number to be its rightful owner. If you use a shareware program regularly, however, you are supposed to send in the registration fee.

If you do buy a used machine, make sure to *clearly* resolve with the seller how you're going to handle the software that he or she may sell with the computer. Most copyrighted software is licensed for use on one machine only. And every software package includes a serial number giving one person the right to use that software and, in many cases, the right to free telephone support.

If you buy a used computer that comes with some software, be sure to also get the original manuals and disks that the software was sold with. The receipt of the sale should list all software packages that are included in the transaction. That way, you will become the rightful owner of the software, rather than the holder of a "bootleg" (illegal) copy of the program.

Name Brand Shopping

The "mainstream" world of microcomputers is divided into two camps—PCs and Macs. Each camp has its die-hard loyalists who would rather sunbathe in Antarctica than use one of those "other machines."

But to say PCs are "better than" Macs, or vice versa, is a bit like trying to compare the proverbial apples (no pun intended) and oranges. Choosing one or the other is largely a matter of personal taste. Before you make a decision, try to get some hands-on experience with both types of machines; then see which feels best to you.

When the time comes to actually shop, be aware that shopping for a PC is vastly different than shopping for a Mac, as you'll learn in the next two sections.

The World of PCs

In 1981, IBM released its first microcomputer, named the IBM PC. (The PC stands for *personal computer*.) Since that time, the term PC has come to include the huge class of computers that are sometimes called IBM-compatibles, or IBM clones.

A quick glance through the ads of a PC-oriented computer magazine will give you some idea of just how many brands of PC computers there are. Compaq, AST, Gateway 2000, NEC, Austin, Tri-Star, Zeos, Dell, Northgate, ALR, Toshiba, Standard, CompuAdd, just to name a few, all manufacture IBM-compatible computers. They can all run the same programs and do the same jobs (see Figures 12.2 and 12.3).

The reason there are so many companies offering IBM-compatible machines is that the PC has an *open architecture*. This means that any company can buy the appropriate parts required to produce a "PC" type of computer, assemble those parts into whatever combination they think makes up a good system, print their brand name on the cover, and market the machine however they wish.

It also means that you, the consumer, are given a mind-boggling array of options from which to choose. However, it all becomes much simpler once you become aware that, in the PC world, you're buying *capability* rather than a specific brand. As stated in Chapter 2, the main difference among the capabilities of different PCs is the microprocessor around which the system is built. Basically, the higher the number of the microprocessor, the faster the computer:

- **286**: Running on the 16-bit 80286 chip, a 286 will handle just about any nongraphical word processing, spreadsheet, database, graphics, or desktop publishing tasks. These sell for under $500 if you can find one. Don't look; they're outdated. You'll need the patience of a saint to run more modern programs on a 286.

- **386**: The 80386 system is the industry standard in the PC world. Most modern programs, particularly the newer graphical programs, are written specifically to take advantage of the 386 processor chips. The basic 386SX system will cost a little more than the 286, and the 386DX system will cost several

Figure 12.3
The AST Premium 486/33TE tower system is a powerful IBM-compatible. The 33MHz system supports six drive bays enabling up to two gigabytes (2 billion) of internal hard drive storage. (Photo courtesy of AST Research, Inc.)

hundred dollars more. These range in cost from $700–$1500. If you add a low-cost laser printer, that will cost another $600 or more. But you'll have a system you can use for desktop publishing, graphics, and/or major database work.

- **486**: The price of a 486, last year's "dream machine," has dropped like a stone. A complete 486DX system including a color monitor, 4MB RAM, and a 212MB hard drive can be found for under $2000.

- **Pentium or "586"**: The latest speed-demon chip is the Pentium from Intel. Using 64-bit data addressing, the Pentium system is the ultimate answer (at least *this* year) for processor-intensive programs such as Computer-Aided Drafting (CAD) and graphics applications. A Pentium system with the requisite trimmings—a 500MB hard drive, 256K RAM cache, etc.—will set you back $5000 or more.

Usually, there's a second number following the processor model number that indicates the computer's clock speed in megahertz. For example, a 386/20 system is based on the 80386 microprocessor and runs at a speed of 20MHz. A 486/33 is based on the 80486 and runs at 33MHz. The bigger those numbers, the more powerful, faster, and more expensive the machine.

So the bottom line is deciding how much you want to spend, and getting the "biggest numbers" that you can for that amount of money.

On the other hand, if your budget is flexible, and you just want to ensure that you're getting a PC that's up-to-date, able to run popular business software, and will handle newer memory-hungry versions of future software, here are some guidelines. You will need the following:

- At least an 80386 processor. Preferably an 80486 if you want to run high-end graphics-based software. Minimum clock speed of 33MHz.

- At least 4MB of RAM. If you think you will be content with the textual interface of DOS, this will do fine. If the graphical interface of Windows sounds easier to learn, plan on buying at least 8MB of RAM.

- At least a 200MB hard disk. Two-hundred million characters of storage sounds like a phenomenal amount, but you'll be surprised at how quickly you can use it up. Do get both $5\frac{1}{4}$-inch and $3\frac{1}{2}$-inch high-density floppy drives as well.

- At least a VGA display. If you are going to use Windows, get Super VGA (SVGA) and consider a video card with 1MB of added memory.

The Macintosh World

When Apple Corporation designed the Macintosh, they took a different approach than did IBM. Rather than following an open architecture, the Mac has a *proprietary (closed) architecture*. This means that other computer manufacturers cannot produce Mac "clones" without a license from Apple to do so. And, because Apple rarely grants such licenses, Mac "clones" are few and far between.

There are advantages and disadvantages to a proprietary architecture. One advantage, for both the consumer and the Apple Corporation, is that it makes buying a computer much simpler. Rather than buying a "Brand-X" 386/20, the Macintosh user just buys a Mac! There are different Macs to choose from, but they use names, like Centris and Quadra, to distinguish among the various models.

Another advantage of a proprietary architecture is that it gives Apple strict control over the quality and consistency of the user interface. Unlike the PC world, where different programs often sport entirely different interfaces, all Mac programs follow a standard graphical interface. Therefore, each time you learn a new Mac program, a good deal of what you've learned previously will be applicable to the new program.

Moreover, the graphical interface that the Mac offers is a great one—few people would disagree with that. User-friendliness and ease-of-use are the hallmark of Mac computing.

The disadvantage of the proprietary architecture of the Mac, at least to the consumer, is that it eliminates competition. Lack of competition from "clone manufacturers" gives Apple a free hand to price the Mac as they see fit. In fact, about the *only* complaint you ever hear about the Mac from Mac users is the cost of buying one.

Of course, the Mac is getting some competition these days. The graphical interface of Windows, now offered on PCs, is also a user-friendly interface that offers consistency of use among different programs. And as might be expected, the price of the Mac has been going down since the introduction of Windows for the PC.

The Mac Family

Currently the Mac is offered in six basic configurations, summarized below:

- **Classics:** The Mac classic series is based on the compact design of the original Macintosh introduced in 1984. The most recent classic, the Color Classic (see Figure 12.4), sports a 16MHz Motorola 68030 processor. With 4MB of memory (expandable to 10MB) and a 80MB hard disk, its suggested list price is $1389. This model is the first Classic available with a color monitor.

- **Performas**: These computers are designed for the mass end-user market and sold through retail stores like Sears or Wal-Mart. The lower-end Performa 200, with a suggested list price of $1150, offers the same features and ease of use as the Classic II: 16MHz Motorola 68030 processor, 2MB of memory, and a 40MB hard disk. The higher-end Performa 600 provides a faster 32MHz Motorola 68030 processor, 4MB of memory, and an 80MB hard disk. Its suggested list price is $1849. For an additional $500, the Performa 600 CD can be purchased with a built-in CD-ROM drive.

- **LC**: These modular Macintoshes follow the configuration of the PC Desktop computers, with a monitor and system unit offered as separate components. The Mac LC III (see Figure 12.5) offers the Motorola 68030 running at 25MHz and a color monitor. With 4MB of RAM (expandable to 36MB) and a 40MB hard disk, its suggested list price is $1249.

Figure 12.5
The modular Macintoshes separate the system unit from the monitor into two separate components, like the desktop's PC. This Macintosh LC III is shown with a full page view on the Portrait Display. (Courtesy of Apple Computer, Inc. Photo by John Greenleigh.)

- **PowerBook**: In 1992, Apple released a notebook-sized Mac dubbed the PowerBook. Models include the 145b, 160, and the 180. The latest addition to this line of Mac is the PowerBook 165c. This 7-pounder comes with a 33MHz 68030 processor, 4MB of RAM, and a 80MB hard disk. Its suggested list price is $2339–$2699 with a 120MB hard drive (see Figure 12.6).

- **PowerBook Duo**: A new line of Modular PowerBook models. The PowerBook Duo 210 and 230 weigh 4.2 lbs and use a 68030 processor. The PowerBook Duo 210 runs at 25MHz and the 230 runs at 33MHz. Both come with 4MB of RAM and an internal hard drive. When you want the added capabilities of a Desktop Mac, you just plug the PowerBook Duo into the Macintosh Duo. The Macintosh Duo supports several different monitors and has two bus slots to expand. You

Figure 12.6

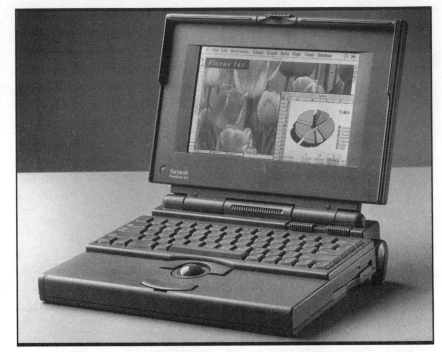

The PowerBook is Macintosh's notebook-sized computer. The latest Model, PowerBook 165c, weighs only 7 pounds. (Photo courtesy of Apple Computer, Inc. Photo by John Greenleigh.)

can also add a full-size keyboard to the Dock. If you do not need the expansion options, you can choose the mini Dock. This allows you to connect other peripherals to your Power-Book Duo (you must use a Dock to hook up any peripherals). A PowerBook Duo 210 with 4MB RAM and an 80MB hard drive with a mini Dock costs about $2088.

- **Centris**: This new family of Macintoshes includes midrange computers with fast performance. There are two brand-new additions, the Centris 610 and the Centris 650. The Centris 610 comes with a 20MHz 68040 processor, 4MB of RAM (expandable to 68MB), an optional CD-ROM drive, and lists at $1659. The Centris 650 comes with a 25MHz 68040 processor, 4MB of RAM (expandable to 132MB), and an expandable 80MB hard disk, and lists at $2139. There's a Centris 660AV that comes with a microphone, speakers, and an optional CD-ROM drive built into the case, and voice-recognition software as part of the system.

- **Quadra**: The top of the line in Macintosh computing is the
  Quadra family. The two latest models, the Quadra 800 (see
  Figure 12.7) and the Quadra 950, are both based on the Motorola 68040 processor, offer full color graphics, and have a
  "tower" configuration. The 800 stands only $14\frac{1}{2}$ inches
  high, runs at 33MHz, and comes with 8MB of RAM (expandable to 136MB) and a 230MB hard disk. The Quadra 950 offers the same configuration as the 800 but packs in 24-bit
  video, more expansion slots, and peripheral bays. Its suggested list price is $5188. Like the Centris 660AV, the Quadra
  840AV comes with expanded hardware and software capabilities ready to address the growing world of audio/visual
  computing.

Figure 12.7
The top-of-the-line Macintosh is the Quadra. This Quadra 800 comes with a "tower." (Photo courtesy of Apple Computer, Inc. Photo by John Greenleigh.)

When looking for a used Mac, keep in mind that many of the early original models have since been retired and are no longer actively manufactured. These include the Mac SE and SE/30, Mac II and IIcx, and the
original "luggable" Mac Portable.

Outside the Mainstream

Although the vast majority of microcomputers now on people's desks are PCs and Macs, these are not the only players in the market. If being in the mainstream is not a top priority, and you're looking to have some fun with your machine, don't overlook the Amiga and NeXT computers.

Amiga

Amiga computers are very high-performance machines able to create television-quality graphics and animation. They are often found in television studios and advertising agencies. Since the home-video camera became so popular, the Amiga has become a very popular low-cost animation and editing tool.

Commodore, the manufacturer of the Amiga, is promoting the machine as a multimedia computer, able to interface with CD players through its own program called *Amigavision*. A multimedia machine offers superior sound and graphics, and is particularly well-suited to developing computer-assisted instruction, high-quality computerized presentations, and animation.

NeXT

Although NeXT is no longer manufacturing hardware, a number of NeXT computers remain in use. The NeXT computer is a super high-powered machine offering phenomenal graphics and digitized sound. Although the power that the NeXT offers may be "overkill" for "everyday" business and personal computing (both in terms of capability and cost), you can't beat it for 3-D imaging, animation, voice recording, and similar power-hungry applications.

A Final Note

Choosing a computer isn't likely to be one of the more monumental decisions of your life. But making an informed decision is certainly better than taking a shot in the dark. The most common mistakes people make in this arena are these: (1) buying an underpowered machine (i.e., one that doesn't have enough memory and/or disk storage to do everything you want it to do) and (2) buying a used (or even a new) computer that is severely outdated.

The first mistake is relatively easy to fix if your system is expandable. You just part with a little more money, buy some more memory and/or disk storage, and you're back on your way.

The latter problem, buying outdated equipment, is more depressing. If you buy an older IBM PC, XT, or even a 286, or one of the earlier retired Mac models, you are likely to feel "snubbed" as you discover that more and more of the newer programs simply will not run on your equipment. Furthermore, because that equipment is outdated, you won't be able to unload it too easily.

On the other hand, you must also face up to the fact that *anything* you buy will eventually become outdated and far more quickly than seems quite decent.

Your best recourse, then, is simply to buy whatever equipment is current, "mainstream," and expandable for the future. That will keep you "current" for several years—which is quite respectable in the computer world.

Thirteen

Interacting with Your Computer

• •

nput and *Output* are abbreviated as I/O. To have a workable computer you need both. You have to get information *into* the computer and the computer has to get the results back *out* to you. That's what this chapter is about—the hardware devices that allow you and your computer to communicate. The computer "hears" you through its various input devices, such as the keyboard, and it "talks" back to you through various output devices, like the computer screen. Now let's look at all the common input devices and the most straightforward of output devices—the computer screen.

266

Getting the Data into the Computer

How do you "talk" to a computer to give it information with which to work? Since computers don't have ears, you need a device to turn the information you want the computer to know into an electronic form it can understand. Below are the most commonly used devices for doing this:

- Keyboard
- Mouse
- Trackball
- Joystick
- Light pen
- Tablet
- Scanner

All these devices have some contact with the motherboard inside your computer (discussed in Chapter 11, "Inside Computers"). Some of these input devices require a board in a slot inside your computer.

Keyboards

Using the computer keyboard is probably the main way you communicate with your computer (screaming and yelling doesn't count). The computer keyboard is essentially the same as a typewriter keyboard. Additional keys, however, provide access to functions that are available only on a computer. You can also get special keyboards for added functions. Although some keyboards have ten function keys (F1–F10), nowadays most keyboards, such as the one shown in Figure 13.1, have 12.

On an English-language keyboard, you can even find special keys for foreign language characters. For example, if you wanted to type the ñ (a specially accented "n" used in Spanish) on a Macintosh, you would press Option-n and then press the letter "n." On an IBM-compatible, you'd have to press the Alt key and hold it down while typing 164 on the numeric key pad. (Most word processors include extended character sets

Figure 13.1

The 101 keys on the Omnikey 101 computer keyboard allow you to do more than just type text. (Photo courtesy of Northgate Computer Systems, Inc.)

and symbols, but using them involves a number of additional keystrokes.)

Even for the most patient user, that's a lot of work to do to get one character. On a keyboard built especially for the Spanish language, however, the ñ would be made with a simpler key combination, such as Ctrl-n. A foreign language keyboard provides easy access to foreign characters—when you press the letter on the keyboard, it sends a code directly to the computer.

If you buy a foreign language keyboard, you will also get a guide that tells you which keys produce which characters and a code sheet that tells you what codes the various key combinations produce.

Mouse

Typically, a mouse is a palm-sized device, about the size of a bar of soap. On top of the mouse there are buttons for communicating with the computer. A "tail" or wire extends from the mouse to a connection on the back of the computer. Figure 13.2 shows a mouse made by Microsoft.

The mouse is designed to slide around on your desktop. Its motion sends a signal to your computer that moves a screen image variously called a *pointer* or *mouse cursor*. The pointer usually looks like an arrow or I-bar. Slide the mouse left and the pointer moves left. Move the mouse in circles and the pointer will move in loops on your screen.

Figure 13.2

While the mouse was originally identified with Macintosh computers, the rise of the graphical Windows interface has made it a must for IBM-compatible computers as well. Pictured here is Microsoft's latest mouse design. (Photo courtesy of Sheldon Dunn)

What makes the mouse especially useful is that it is a very quick way to move around on a screen. Move the desktop mouse half an inch and the screen cursor will leap four inches. Making the same movements with the arrow keys takes much longer. The mouse also issues instructions to the computer very quickly. Point to an available option with the cursor, click on the mouse, and the option has been chosen.

Mice are so widely used in graphics applications because they can do things that are difficult, if not impossible, to do with keyboard keys. For example, the way you move an image with a mouse is to put the pointer on the object you want to move, press the mouse button, and *drag* the image from one place on the screen to another. When you have the image where you want it, you release the mouse button and the image stays there. Similarly, the mouse is used to *grab* one corner of an image (say a square) and stretch it into another shape (say a rectangle). Both of these actions are so much more difficult to perform with a keyboard that most graphics programs *require* a mouse.

The buttons on the mouse are used to select items at which the mouse points. You position the mouse pointer on an object on the screen, for example, on a menu, a dialog box, or a tool in a paint program, and then you press the mouse button to "select" it. Mice are also used to load documents. One common way to load a stored document into a program is to put the pointer on the file name and to *double-click* on the name—that is, you press a mouse button *twice* in rapid succession.

The number of buttons your mouse has depends on the manufacturer. The number of buttons ranges from one on the Macintosh mouse to three on some PC mice. The Microsoft mouse, a widely used mouse on PCs, has two buttons, which is probably the most you'll ever need. The Microsoft mouse is also the most compatible, which means that most programs can use it. So make sure that if you buy a non-Microsoft mouse, it's compatible with your computer.

Many new models of computers have built-in mouse support. (This support is a *dedicated* port just for the mouse. It leaves the serial port free for other add-ons, like an external modem.) This means you can take the computer end of the mouse cord, plug it into the back of the computer, and you can use it with applicable programs without needing any special hardware.

For computers without built-in mouse support, there are two other choices:

The "bus" mouse: This mouse comes with a board that you plug into an expansion slot of the "bus" inside the computer. The board

NOTE

Boards, buses, ports, and expansion slots are discussed in Chapter 11, "Inside Computers."

A Note on Mouse Compatibility

In fact, it's not the mouse itself that may be incompatible, but the mouse driver. The driver is the program that lets the mouse and various programs communicate with each other. If you buy a mouse from a major supplier such as Microsoft or Logitech, you can be sure that the mouse driver will be able to communicate with almost any program. Plus, if new programs come out that the driver can't talk to, the major companies will be able to provide you with a driver that *will* work.

This is not necessarily true if you buy an off-brand mouse and driver from Moe's Mouse Supply.

comes with a connection for the mouse plug. (And you load the mouse software too.)

The serial mouse: You plug the mouse cord into one of the normal serial ports of the computer, load the software, and run the mouse from there. (If there are no empty expansion slots, this is the only choice you have.)

Trackball

Naturally, after the mouse became popular, people began thinking of ways to improve it. One such improvement is called the trackball. It looks like a large mouse lying on its back, as you can see in Figure 13.3.

The trackball does the same things a mouse does. There're a zillion different designs for trackballs and the degree of comfort-in-use varies wildly—so be sure you try before you buy. Some people find trackballs easier and faster to use than a rolling mouse, particularly since they don't take up as much space on your desktop.

Figure 13.3
A Laptop computer with a LogiTech trackball mounted. (Photo courtesy of Sheldon Dunn)

Trackballs are really popular with users of portable computers. If you're working in a plane or a car, very often you don't have a flat surface to use a mouse.

Joysticks and Yokes

Joysticks were developed primarily for games in which quick forward/backward and left/right movements are required. If you want to, you can use them to turn your PC into an effective arcade game center. Typically, they come with a flexible stick for movement and a button for firing weapons.

The yoke, a variation on the joystick, is designed to interface with aircraft simulators. The yoke plugs into a game port (the joystick port) in your computer and does the same things, except that it looks like an airplane yoke instead of a joystick. You can even buy pedals to go with the yoke to simulate actual flying conditions.

Light Pen

Basically, the light pen is a pen-like device with a light on one end and a wire connected to the computer on the other end (see Figure 13.4). At one time, it was thought that the light pen would be as popular as the mouse has become. The idea behind the light pen is that you can touch the screen with the pen and "smart" circuitry inside the system recognizes the light pen's location. Thus, the pen can be used for drawing on the screen, selecting items, marking a checklist, and a variety of other applications.

Light pen circuitry was built into the original IBM PC and still exists in most of today's clones. But the mouse has set the standard as the main alternative input device.

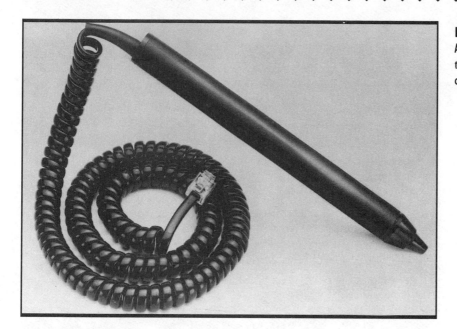

Figure 13.4
A light pen is an input device that looks like a pen. (Photo courtesy of FTG Data Systems.)

Tablet

Another way to pass information to a computer is via a drawing tablet. This is a pressure-sensitive tablet that has thousands of tiny monitors under its surface. These monitors transmit information to the screen. This method allows artists and designers to draw on the computer's screen while working on a familiar form (see Figure 13.5).

When you draw on a tablet, it communicates the location to the computer, which then interprets your drawing according to its software. The tablet's most popular use is for tracing existing information.

Some companies have tablets that work like clipboards. You can write information on the tablet and that information—your writing—is translated into text or images by the computer.

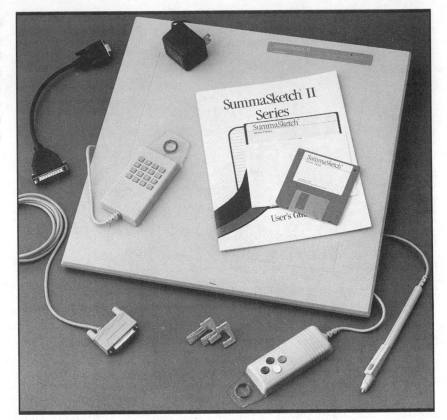

Scanner

A scanner is a different type of input device than the ones we've discussed so far. It's not an alternative keyboard, nor is it an alternative to the mouse. It's more like a copier machine that can take pictures for your computer, or a copier that can read text (see Figure 13.6).

Scanners can work either as a graphics scanner or a text reader. Most scanners are capable of both, although there are some hardware scanners specifically designed to read text.

A *graphics scanner* works like a copier. You place original art face down in the scanner, operate some scanning software on your computer, and the image is imported into the computer. Once it's in the computer, you

Figure 13.6

A full-page scanner is easy to use and gives remarkable results with drawings, photographs, and other images. The ES-300C from Epson produces up to 16 million colors and 256 shades of gray with a 300 x 300 resolution, which is the same resolution as a typical laser printer. (Photo courtesy of Epson America, Inc.)

can manipulate the image in a painting or drawing program, or incorporate it into your desktop publishing or presentation package. A low-end full-page scanner starts at about $600.

There are also small hand-held scanners available. They can copy an image only about 4 inches wide by 14 inches long, but they are widely used as an inexpensive alternative to the larger scanners. At prices that begin around $160, they represent a significant savings. They work differently than full-page scanners. Rather than placing the image on the scanning surface, you move the scanner over the picture. Typically, these scanners hook up to a board inside the computer and the software that comes with them creates the image you're copying on the screen (see Figure 13.7).

If you work with computer graphics or desktop publishing, a scanner (at least a small one) is likely to be essential if you ever need to capture pictures that exist only on paper for computer use.

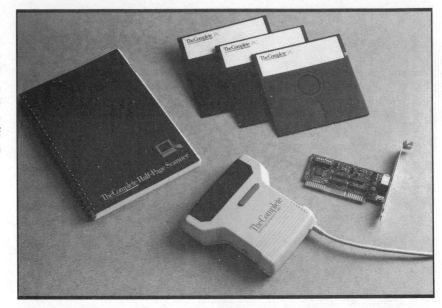

A *text scanner* reads text characters into the computer instead of pictures. So, instead of placing graphics in the scanner, you lay down a page of text. Then, special Optical Character Reader (OCR) software interprets the text letter-by-letter and feeds the text characters to the computer.

This can be very useful if you have a lot of text that you don't want to re-type to put it into the computer. The text scanner can input the pages, and then you can edit the text on-screen just as you would with any other word processed documents.

Although a scanner and OCR software are relatively expensive and slow, if you have large amounts of text that must be rewritten, it can save a good deal of time and money over hiring a typist.

Getting the Data Out: Displays

Once you have information in your computer, you need a way to see what you have. In this section, we'll cover how the computer communicates with us—through its screen. The terms "monitor," "CRT" (Cathode-Ray Tube), and "display" always refer to the computer screen.

If you buy a Macintosh with a built-in screen, you needn't concern yourself with a monitor at all. On the other hand, for most IBM-compatibles, you must get the correct video display card for the monitor you purchase. Also, you need the right driver so your software can work with your video display card.

NOTE

The closer the display can approximate the printed results, the less work and fine tuning you will have to do.

There are a number of decisions you need to make when buying a monitor. So let's examine what's available.

Monochrome

Monochrome is the computer term for a one-color monitor. A monochrome monitor is usually one color and black: green and black, amber and black, "paper" white and black, and so forth.

A monochrome display generally is cheaper and sharper than a color display. Because a color monitor uses three colors to produce white text on a black background, characters on a color system are fuzzier than on a monochrome setup. Also, monochrome monitors flicker less than color systems, and over the long haul are easier on the eyes.

Grayscale is the term for monochrome systems that use shades of gray to emulate color. Grayscale is the effect you get by turning down the color knob on your TV set. Instead of seeing combinations of red, blue, and

Quality Control

Know the old expression: Ask a stupid question, get a stupid answer?

Computerese for this process is GIGO. It means *Garbage in, Garbage out.* So if the answer you get doesn't seem to have much to do with the question you asked, take another look at the information you gave to the computer.

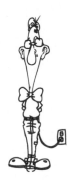

green in different shades and intensities, you see grays. A grayscale monitor is ideal for working in desktop publishing, design, and graphics. However, except for laptop/notebook portables, monochrome screens have been almost completely replaced by color displays. You'll have to do some sleuthing to find a new monochrome monitor (used ones can be found, however).

Color

Most people getting a computer today buy a color monitor. People are switching to color monitors for the same reason they flocked to color TVs. The color is now good enough and the price is low enough that black-and-white has no appeal by comparison. Besides, nowadays, most software programs and all games are designed to run in color.

Screen Basics

Two pieces of hardware determine what you will see on-screen. These are:

The monitor: This is the thing that looks like a TV. It has to be physically able to create the colors and resolutions you want.

The display adapter card: This is the circuitry inside the computer (typically on a board) that runs the monitor. Its job is to take the video instructions from whatever program is running, translate those instructions into a signal the monitor can understand, and then send that signal to the monitor. If you want a green dot above and a black dot below, the display card tells the monitor so. Also called *graphics cards*, these cards transmit the resolution of the screen images and the colors available to the monitor. The monitor must have the hardware capability to display the colors and resolution. The cards can also come with added RAM for more colors. The RAM is separate and does not delete anything from your conventional, extended, or expanded RAM.

So, to create screen images, you buy two pieces of hardware—the monitor and the display adapter card inside the computer that interfaces with the monitor. The card and monitor must be able to work together. The whole system, monitor and adapter, are referred to by various initials, defined below:

MDA: This is the original IBM Monochrome Display Adapter. It displays text only on a monochrome monitor.

HGA: Hercules Graphics Adapter. Provides both text and graphics on monochrome monitors.

CGA: Color Graphics Adapter. This was the first graphics standard for the PC. It was like the early color TVs. Lousy color and lousy resolution.

EGA: The Enhanced Graphics Adapter followed CGA with more colors, higher graphics resolution, and better looking text. Replaced very quickly by VGA.

VGA: The Video Graphics Array card is the current minimum standard. VGA provides thousands of colors at many resolutions and has the best color text display of any PC graphics adapter.

MCGA: MultiColor Graphics Array is a subset of the VGA standard included on some PS/2 systems. Most of the popular MCGA modes (including an impressive grayscale mode) are included with the Super VGA displays.

SVGA: Super VGA is a loose standard that provides the same text display as VGA but better colors and resolution. It's rapidly becoming the standard for graphics.

XGA: Short for eXtended Graphics Array. This is a display from IBM that increases resolution and color. It shows no sign of becoming popular, largely because of its very high price.

8514/A: A very high-end standard for graphics professionals with deep pockets. Excellent color and resolution.

Resolution

The smallest unit of a screen's display is called a *pixel*, which is a single dot out of thousands. Resolution is the measure of how many pixels (and how many colors) you can have on the screen at the same time. Standard resolutions available are:

640 x 480: The standard VGA graphics display. This means the display is 640 pixels wide by 480 pixels high.

800 x 600: This is the usual SVGA graphics display.

1024 x 768: This is the upper limit for SVGA. This resolution has more than twice as many pixels as the standard VGA display so everything on the monitor is sharper but a lot smaller. This may require a larger than standard monitor to be usable.

1280 x 1024: This resolution is only available with 8514/A and XGA graphics displays. You'll need a big monitor to run this without serious eyestrain.

All of these video cards come with software that you need to load on your computer to make them work. Other graphics standards will undoubtedly be popping up soon. At the moment, and for some time to come, Super VGA is your best bet.

Special-Use Monitors

There are special types of computer monitors available for special circumstances. Not every user needs a standard 80-character by 25-line monitor, and some applications clearly need more.

In the odd and interesting category of special-use monitors there are these:

Full-page displays: This is a tall monitor. It is used primarily for desktop publishing applications in which it helps to see an entire page in "life size." It is more expensive than a standard monitor, but for desktop publishing and graphics, the price is often worth it.

Two-page displays: These monitors are the dual-page version of the full-page display. Usually they are big enough to fit two full pages side-by-side. Again, this type of monitor is expensive, but it is ideally suited for desktop publishing and graphics applications.

Multiple monitors: It's possible to hook up more than one monitor to a computer. Most PCs can have both a color and monochrome monitor hooked up, and the Macintosh can have several monitors running at one time. This allows you to transfer windows, documents, or icons from monitor to monitor with ease; a special *control panel* makes it all possible. The usefulness of multiple monitors lies in being able to see and use more than one document or program at a time. Whether multiple monitors will work depends on the software that's running. Some PC software recognizes two screens immediately and will take advantage of both; some will not.

Presentation Screens

To end this section on output devices in a "big way," note that there are also specific, "super displays" used primarily for computer presentations. When giving a presentation, rather than have everyone huddle around one tiny PC screen, you can hook up your PC or laptop output to a mammoth-sized screen. Then everyone in the boardroom can see your presentation. These are also excellent for self-running demonstrations and controlled presentations.

Presentation systems range from very large and expensive monitors to specific devices, known as projection panels, that are designed to show a computer's display on a movie screen. The latter devices simply lie on top of an overhead projector. Light shines through them and projects your pie charts and bar graphs onto the screen.

They work by hooking up the projection system to your PC's video output. The computer (most likely a laptop) then faces you as you face your audience. A duplicate of what you see on the screen is projected overhead and behind you. That way you can see what you're doing and so can everyone else.

This type of projection system is the reason a lot of laptop PCs come with VGA display systems. The VGA graphics look horrid on the tiny LCD (liquid crystal display) screen on the laptop. But when you hook up a large monitor or overhead projection system, the colors become very bright and sharp.

NOTE

Special software, such as Aldus Persuasion, is available to create a presentation that will be shown on a projection system.

Some Buying Guidelines

The difficulty of buying I/O devices depends on whether you purchase an entire system or put together separate components. If you buy a low-end Macintosh system, the only I/O decision you'll have to make will be what type of keyboard you want—extended, regular, or new ergonomic. On the other hand, if you put an IBM-compatible together by purchasing the components, you may have to make decisions about everything from a mouse to the interface card for your monitor—unless you buy a bundled (already made up) system. One bundled system was recently advertised with a VGA color monitor, 16-bit VGA card, a 101-key enhanced keyboard, and a mouse as part of a package that included a 486DX 33MHz

CPU, 4MB of RAM, an 80MB hard disk, along with DOS 6.0 and Windows 3.1 for $1199. That's a very good deal indeed.

Prices for I/O components can vary enormously. For example, one advertised Super VGA 20-inch monitor was advertised at $1150, and another Super VGA color 14-inch monitor was advertised at $249. Both are Super VGA monitors, but there is a $900 cost difference. Why is there a $900 difference? Answer: Each is a Super VGA monitor, but one is six inches wider than the other.

In another instance, the difference in price between a Super VGA and a regular VGA monitor was only $30. In this case, the higher resolution and better color from the Super VGA are worth an extra $30.

Keep in mind the following considerations when buying one of the various components discussed in this chapter.

Keyboards: On a Macintosh, the choice is between the regular, extended, and new ergonomic keyboards. The extended keyboard has IBM-type function keys so that if you run IBM software on your Mac, you can use the function keys required for a lot of IBM-compatible software. The ergonomic keyboard has all the features of the extended keyboard plus it can be arranged at different angles to minimize the risk of hand injuries. The price difference from the regular to extended keyboard is about $30. To upgrade from the extended to the ergonomic keyboard will mean a price increase of about $60.

For PC users, you can upgrade to an enhanced 101-key keyboard for about $39. (The enhanced keyboard is usually bundled with new PC systems.) You'll need to decide if you want your function keys on the top of the keyboard or on the left side. Touch typists will be happier with the function keys on the left.

Mouse & Trackball: For Macintosh and Amiga users, the mouse is part of the package, so you won't have to worry about the kind of mouse to buy. With a PC, there is a wide range of choices. If a mouse is not bundled with the system, you can buy a Microsoft mouse for about $89. Serial mice complete with software, mouse pad, and adapter have been advertised for as little as $18. Make sure the mouse you buy is compatible with your software. If you are not sure about compatibility, get a Microsoft or Microsoft-compatible mouse.

You're getting sleepy... sleeepy....

The same considerations apply to buying a trackball. But trackballs cost more, ranging from about $70–$125. If you are going to use the trackball as a replacement for a mouse, make sure that it is Microsoft-compatible. If used for games, check to see if it is compatible with your game software.

Joystick & Yoke: There's a wide range of joysticks, and the prices range from $19–$39. The purchasing decision is probably best made in consultation with a person who plays games. The yokes available for flight simulation software begin at about $99.

Scanners: Full-page black and white scanners start at about $800 and color ones start at about $1500. The hand-held scanners begin at about $130. There is a wide range in the quality of hardware and software in this area, so before you buy, go to a computer store, get a demonstration, and try it yourself. This is especially important for hand-held scanners because they're more difficult to manipulate.

Monitors & Video Boards: Monitors can cost from $250 to well over $2000. Don't buy the cheapest and don't buy the most expensive unless you have a rational reason for doing so. Take a look at a monitor running the programs you're going to use. Don't get anything less than VGA.

Along with getting the right monitor, get the best graphics card you can afford. The added RAM on these cards is not that expensive, and by saving a few dollars initially, you can wind up with a lot less display power. For example, a video card with 512K of RAM is advertised at $59. Another card with 256K of RAM is advertised at $49. So for only $10, you can double the amount of RAM on your video card.

If you plan to use drawing programs or do desktop publishing, get a video card with an accelerator chip and at least 1MB of memory. You'll be glad you did.

NOTE
The computer does not care whether it gets its input from a keyboard or joystick. Buy the input device that fits your needs.

A Final Note

Usually you don't think much about the I/O devices on your computer until something breaks or you want to upgrade (two events that often occur simultaneously). By taking a little time at the outset, however, you can save both money and time getting what you need now, and you won't have to upgrade for a long time.

In Chapter 14, we'll discuss where to permanently store everything you will create on your computer. Output is only temporarily stored (displayed) on your monitor; disk storage is more permanent. Your screen can handle only one screenful of data at a time, but disk systems can handle thousands and even millions of screens of processed information and raw data. Getting the right disk storage is as important as getting the right I/O devices.

Fourteen

Storing Your Work

• •

Because RAM is directly connected to your processor, it's an ideal storage place for information. It's fast, and the processor can move things around very quickly in RAM. There's just one problem. Whenever you turn off the power, everything in RAM disappears. Words you wrote, numbers you entered, pages you formatted...gone...like wiping off a blackboard.

Clearly, what you need is a place to store a *permanent* copy of your work—something like a file cabinet where you can store a letter out of the way but still available when you need to refer to it.

This chapter is about the computer's file cabinets—the electronic devices that allow you to store (and easily retrieve) your work. They're called disk drives.

285

What Are the Main Storage Devices?

To understand document storage in personal computers, there are three things you need to know about:

1. **Floppy disks**: A floppy disk (also called a diskette or just a floppy) is a thin sheet of plastic (mylar) inside a protective covering. The plastic is coated with a magnetic oxide. Data is encoded on the oxide layer.

   You can slide a floppy into the computer's floppy drive, copy a document or program onto it, and then pull it out and store the information "saved" on it. Floppy disks come in two sizes: $5\frac{1}{4}$-inch square (inside a paper or plastic sleeve and somewhat flexible or "floppy") and roughly $3\frac{1}{2}$-inch square (covered with hard plastic).

2. **Floppy drives**: A floppy drive is an electronic device that can read and write information onto floppy disks. Typically, floppy drives are packaged as part of the computer and they also come in two sizes, depending on which size of disk they can read.

3. **Hard drives**: A hard drive (also called a hard disk) is an electronic device that can read and write information (data) on its own metal or glass recording surface. Hard drives are very fast and can hold hundreds of megabytes of information. They have become today's main microcomputer storage device.

Different types of disks and drives hold different amounts of information. In the early days of personal computing, an Apple II $5\frac{1}{4}$-inch disk held about 145K of information. Today's standard $5\frac{1}{4}$-inch disk holds about 1200K (1.2MB) of information. Hard disk drives holding 500MB are not uncommon. To use an analogy, some disks can hold as much as a file drawer, others as much as a file cabinet, and a hard disk can store the contents of a whole roomful of file cabinets.

For a personal computer system you need two floppy drives as well as a hard drive.

How a Computer Stores Information

Normally, in a personal computer, information is stored on either the thin plastic of a removable disk or on the rigid disks of a hard drive. A disk drive writes information to and reads information from these storage locations.

How does the computer do that? Disks and drives are analogous to cassettes and tape recorders. The recorder can both record and play music, but the music itself is stored on the cassette. Similarly, the drive is the electronic device that does the storing, but the disk is the medium on which the information is stored.

As you may recall from Chapter 11, "Inside Computers," all information in a computer has been reduced to two digits—0 or 1; the digits correspond to an electric current that's either off or on. The computer forms letters and numbers from those two digits according to their grouping. So when a read/write head moves over a disk, whether it's a hard disk or a floppy disk, all that it does is reorganize the orientation of magnetic particles—pointing them one way to represent 1 and the opposite way to represent 0.

That's all there is to it. When the computer rereads those 1's and 0's in the same order that it put them down, it's right back where it was when it saved the digits, and it knows how to turn them back into the same letters, graphics, and numbers that you saw on your screen. Presto! You have the same document you saved earlier.

Mechanically, what's happening inside the drive is that the disk itself is spinning and the read/write head is sitting in one place. In fact, most modern drives have two heads; one on the top and one on the bottom. Both are working at the same time. Not only does that make the read/write process twice as fast, it also doubles the amount of information that can be written to the same disk (see Figure 14.1).

Figure 14.1
Double-sided disk drives and
hard drives have heads that
read the top and bottom of
disk platters.

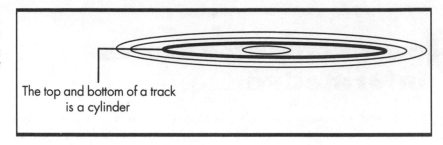

The top and bottom of a track
is a cylinder

Computer disks (hard or floppy) start out the same way as phonograph records, with the initial recording in the outer grooves and subsequent recordings in the inner grooves. Programs are arranged sequentially from outer to inner. When you delete a file, you create a "hole" between the files. Or you might replace the first draft of a document with a longer second draft, and your new file may be placed somewhere else because the space used for your first-draft isn't adequate anymore. Soon, you may have "holes" all over—wasting lots of space.

NOTE

There are no actual "holes" where files have been deleted on disks. Instead there are areas that are flagged as available for added data to be stored. The old data is still there.

Recognizing this space problem, engineers made the electronics that control disk drives a bit smarter. Now, one part of the file can be placed in one hole, the next part in another hole, and so on, using *address links* that tell the computer where to find the next piece of the file. (Utility programs, such as SpeedDisk in *Norton Utilities* or the Defrag program in DOS 6, can rearrange the data on your disk to get rid of the "holes" so that your drive will read and write faster.)

Floppy Drives and Disks

Floppy drives and floppy disks used to be the primary storage tools for microcomputers. The drives did the work, and the disks were used to hold both the programs to be run and the data results that the programs created.

The dual floppy-drive system served well until the mid-1980s when two things happened. First, the price of hard drives dropped drastically (from thousands of dollars down to hundreds). Then programmers started taking advantage of the extra space on hard drives by developing much larger and more complex programs. Programs such as word processors and spreadsheets were developed that could do lots of amazing things they couldn't do before, but they couldn't fit on a floppy disk.

Thus, the hard disk became the microcomputer's primary storage device.

Today floppy drives and floppy disks are used mainly for:

Software distributing: Software you buy for your computer will come on one or more floppy disks. You transfer the programs to your computer's hard drive, which is faster and a more reliable storage place.

Transporting files: Floppy drives are also used to copy data files from one computer to another. You can work on something at your office, copy the file to a disk, and then take it home to finish it.

Creating backups: You'll hear a lot about the need to create frequent "backups" (duplicate copies) of everything on your computer's hard disk. Typically, this is done by copying all your work to floppies. Then if something goes wrong with your hard disk, you'll have an emergency copy of everything important. There are lots of good backup programs available including one that comes with DOS 6.

Because floppy drives cost only about $60, nowadays manufacturers include both $5\frac{1}{4}$-inch and $3\frac{1}{2}$-inch drives on most computers. (If your PC comes with only a single floppy drive, you can add a second drive so that you have at least one $5\frac{1}{4}$-inch drive and one $3\frac{1}{2}$-inch drive.)

Disk Sizes and Formats

When you buy disks, you need to be sure to get both the right physical size ($5\frac{1}{4}$ or $3\frac{1}{2}$) and the right capacity (high-density or low-density). If you have a high-density floppy drive it can format (and read) high-density or low-density floppies. A low-density drive can only format (and read) low-density floppies.

When you buy new floppies, you can tell their densities from the abbreviations on the label:

DS/DD: This stands for "Double-Sided, Double-Density." It means that the disk has been verified on both sides by the manufacturer, and that, when formatted, a $5\frac{1}{4}$-inch disk will hold 360K and a $3\frac{1}{2}$-inch disk will hold 720K of data (for PCs). These disks are also referred to as "low-density."

NOTE

Don't buy a computer with low-density floppy drives. Low-density drives (particularly the $5\frac{1}{4}$-inch) don't hold enough information and more and more software is being supplied only on high-density floppies.

DS/HD: This stands for "Double-Sided, High-Density." "DS" means that the disk has been verified on both sides by the manufacturer. "HD" means the 5¼-inch disk has a capacity of 1.2MB and the 3½-inch disk holds 1.4MB of data when formatted (for PCs).

Macintosh computers use 3½-inch disks only. They are formatted in three sizes: single-sided disks hold 400K; double-sided disks hold 800K; and high-density disks hold 1.4MB.

Floppy Disks Decoded

If your disks are new, the manufacturer's labels will tell you if the disk is high density or low density. But if the disk has been relabelled or it's a generic-type without a label, there's still an easy way to tell the disk size:

- 5¼-inch double-density disks (360K) will have a reinforcing ring around the hole in the middle of the disk. It'll be a contrasting color or maybe a slightly darker color than the rest of the disk. A high-density 5¼-inch disk (1.2MB) will not have this ring.

- 3½-inch double-density disks (720K) will have a single hole in the plastic housing (looking from the label side, it's in the upper right corner). High-density 3½-inch disks (1.4MB) will have an additional hole in the opposite corner (from the label side, it's the upper left corner).

If you have a high-density 5¼-inch drive and want to format a low density floppy, you have to remember to use the DOS command FORMAT *drive*: /f:360 (*drive* being either your A or B drive). For 3¼-inch disks, the equivalent command is FORMAT *drive*:/f:720. If you don't want to be bothered, use File Manager in Windows or Safe Format in *Norton Utilities*. They both make it very hard to go wrong.

With a Macintosh you initialize a disk and the process is done automatically.

Backups: Advice Nobody Takes Until It's Too Late

If everything on your computer could disappear tomorrow and you wouldn't bat an eye, then don't worry about backups. Otherwise, you must do them regularly. This means that you must copy your work to floppies or to a special tape drive. (A tape backup uses a cartridge tape to store the contents of the backup. The tape backup drive can be installed in the same way as a floppy drive.) If you do not make a backup, one of the following events will almost certainly happen:

- Your hard disk will crash, taking your 400-page novel with it.
- You will accidentally erase your tax records for the last five years.
- Your roommate will attach your floppy to the refrigerator using a magnet.
- Your kid and the dog will use an imporant disk as a frisbee, and you'll never see it again (or at least you'll wish you hadn't).

However, I know from experience that no one listens to this advice until important files or programs are lost. So go ahead and lose an important file that you have not backed up. Then, after an appropriate period of mourning, resolve to back up your files. Mean it.

Until then, I know you won't listen, because no one ever does. (Am I starting to sound like your father?)

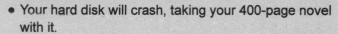

Once you've formatted a disk it will run on all similar machines. For example, a disk formatted on a Macintosh will run on any other Mac and a disk formatted on an IBM will run on any IBM-compatible computer, but it can be read only by a Macintosh with a special drive. That's part of what makes computers "compatible" and allows you to move programs and documents from one computer to another.

If you're smart and not compulsively frugal, you'll buy preformatted disks. They cost a bit more, but will save you the excruciating boredom of the formatting process.

Hard Drives

Currently, hard drives (or disks) are the main microcomputer storage device. They're fast, reliable, hold lots of information, and are relatively cheap. Nearly every personal computer sold these days has a hard disk, and most of the best-selling application programs require them. You may recall from earlier chapters that some of these programs take up to 20–30MB of disk space.

Hard drives come in all sizes and price ranges. You can find a low-end 80MB hard drive for less than $200 and (a more logical choice) a 120MB hard disk for about $30 more. A 250MB drive costs under $300 and those around 350MB or so cost about $350–$400. Hard drive prices will probably continue to go down and the storage capacity will probably continue to go up.

How a Hard Drive Works

A hard drive works in essentially the same way that a floppy drive does, with a few important differences. Both media store information as magnetic patterns in a layer of iron oxide that coats the disk surface, and both use one or more read/write heads to translate the patterns into electronic pulses (1's and 0's) for the computer.

However, in a hard drive, the coated surfaces are (as the name implies) rigid. They are sealed in an air-filtered compartment and there are two or more surfaces, called *platters* (see Figure 14.2). This sealed compartment provides an ideal environment for storing and exchanging data and allows manufacturers to design hard disks to much more precise tolerances, which in turn means greater speed, storage capacity, and reliability.

Both the hard drive and the floppy drives interact with the computer (motherboard) through a disk controller that is either built into the

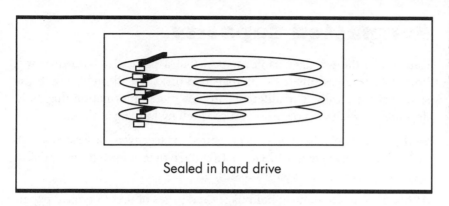

Figure 14.2

A hard drive is something like a stack of double-sided floppy disks, but it's sealed in a box. Hard drives are much faster than floppy drives.

Sealed in hard drive

motherboard or is in an expansion board in a slot. The controller allows the data to be transferred from the disk drive to the microprocessor and RAM.

There are two reasons that the hard drive can store so much information: The first is the speed of the rapidly spinning disks, and the second is the tiny distance between the disks and the read/write heads.

1. Because the disks are rigid, it's possible to spin them at speeds up to 6,000 rpm (revolutions per minute). This is 20 times faster than a floppy drive's speed, and it's possible only with a rigid disk. When you spin a flexible floppy disk that fast, it becomes unstable and starts to flutter—which is not the best condition for storing information reliably.

2. The second reason for a hard drive's great storage capacity is the close proximity of the read/write heads to the disk itself. The heads float only microns above the surface of the disk, which is too narrow an area for even a microscopic particle of smoke to pass through.

How to Evaluate a Hard Drive

Clearly, the hard disk is one of the most valuable components of any computer you may buy. When you are comparing different models, make sure the one you select has a hard disk that meets both your present and anticipated needs. Only three items on the "spec sheet" are significant. They are the capacity, the speed, and sometimes, the controller.

Formatted Capacity

Capacity is the *amount* of information that a particular hard disk will hold. What makes this tricky is that hard disks are all pretty much the same size physically. The difference in how much information they hold depends on what's inside. And you can't tell by looking at them.

So the capacity of a hard drive is measured in *megabytes,* described as MB or M. Each megabyte is 1,024K, or 1,048,576 bytes of program, or document, or anything else you want stored.

Although a megabyte may hold pages and pages of text (a typical paperback book uses only 600K or .6MB of hard disk space), it's important to know that you will need many megabytes of hard disk storage to run an efficient computer system.

Speed

Hard drive speed is measured in milliseconds, abbreviated *ms*. What's being measured is the average access time, or the time it takes information to be read from any given spot on the disk. The smaller the ms number, the faster the drive.

Anything above 40ms is very slow. 20ms is OK, though you can go even lower for more money. If you do desktop publishing, graphics, or any type of application that reads and writes to the hard disk a lot, paying for more speed will be well worth the time you will save.

Controller

The controller is the little-known but important second half of a hard drive. It sits inside the computer and is responsible for controlling the actions of the hard drive and connecting the computer's internal circuitry with the hard drive mechanism.

There are many controller types, most of which will probably be chosen by your dealer or whomever installs your hard drive. The type of controller and drive must match. Standard encoding schemes and interfaces on controllers are as follows:

- **IDE**: Integrated Drive Electronics. This is the type of drive found on almost all PCs today. The controller on an IDE drive is part of the IDE drive and not a separate card.
- **SCSI**: Small Computer Systems Interface (pronounced "scuzzy"). This is the standard type found on the Macintosh and optionally on PCs. It is widely held to be the controller of the future.

Older types of encoding schemes are the:

- **MFM**: Modified Frequency Modulation
- **RLL**: Run Length Limited (newer, faster encoding scheme)
- **ESDI**: Enhanced Small Device Interface

The only place you're likely to see these last three is on fairly elderly machines.

Making a RAM Drive

A RAM drive is a *simulated* disk drive that resides in RAM. This may sound like a strange arrangement because, as you will recall, when the computer is turned off, whatever is in RAM will be lost. There are, however, many uses for RAM drives. We will briefly explain what these are, and how to set up a RAM drive on your system.

Use a RAM drive when you have several files that must be opened and closed frequently. When your computer reads data from either a hard or floppy drive, it takes time for the mechanical parts of the drive to read and write data. With a RAM drive, part of RAM thinks that it is a disk drive, and, with no mechanical parts to turn, your system can read and write data instantaneously.

On a Macintosh, a RAM drive is set up just like any other application. You simply run it. On IBM-compatibles, you can set it up by adding a line to the CONFIG.SYS program that automatically runs when you turn on your computer. A file called RAMDRIVE.SYS comes with Microsoft Windows. The command line:

    device=C:\WINDOWS\RAMDRIVE.SYS 256 /E

creates a RAM drive of 256K in extended memory.

NOTE
When using a RAM drive, save your work to a mechanical drive occasionally so you won't lose your work if your system crashes.

Once you have your RAM drive set up, it acts just like any other drive. If you have a system with two floppy drives and a hard drive, they are most likely referred to as Drives A, B, and C. When you add the RAM drive, it will be treated as Drive D. Figure 14.3 shows a directory tree window with the RAM drive selected. Note the different symbols shown for the floppy, hard, and RAM drives.

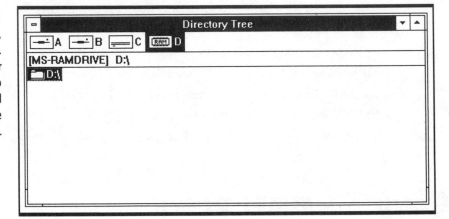

The main drawback to a RAM drive is, of course, that everything on the RAM drive will be erased when you turn off the computer. Therefore, you **must** remember to save anything you want to keep to a hard or floppy disk before turning off the machine. Also, RAM drives use large amounts of RAM that would otherwise be used by applications. So, if you have a big application or have several applications running simultaneously, your RAM drive may get in the way. However, barring those drawbacks, the RAM drive can speed up disk file access considerably.

Other Storage Devices

There are other long-term storage devices for computers. They're not a substitute for floppy and hard drives—more an adjunct for special uses.

CD-ROM

Unlike a hard disk, CD-ROM (pronounced see dee RAHM) is a read-only storage device. You can only access information on the CD-ROM disk; you can't write new information to it or erase what's there. It's very like a compact disc for a CD player. CD-ROMs are very useful for software and other files that are bulky in the extreme, such as graphics programs, fonts, sound files, medical and legal references, or the entire Oxford English Dictionary.

Feed Me

To use CD-ROM you need a CD-ROM drive, which is almost the same thing as a compact disc player. The drive can be internal—it's installed inside your computer and looks rather like another floppy drive. Or it can be external, hooking into your computer via an expansion card. Special software is then required to access and use the information on the CD-ROM. Usually, you can access the drive as if it were just another hard drive.

All CD-ROM players can handle disks with up to 600–700MB of data. CD-ROM players come in two speeds: slow and slower. The speed is based on the number of milliseconds it takes to access data. Considering that a modern hard disk will have an access time of 12–25ms, the fastest CD-ROM, at just over 200ms, is poky indeed. But if you want to have the address of every business in the U.S. or the complete works of Shakespeare or 750 fonts easily available to use on your computer, nothing but a CD-ROM will do. For more information on CD-ROM, see Chapter 15.

Optical Disks

The optical disk is a type of CD-ROM. It's a CD-ROM you can both read from and write to.

One type of optical disk is accessed by a WORM drive. The acronym WORM stands for Write Once/Read Many. You can write to a WORM optical disk—but only once. It's like indelible ink. It cannot be erased or overwritten. Once the information is there, you can read it back as many times as you like. When the disk is full, you simply buy another one and start over.

The true optical disk (like a CD-ROM you can write, read, erase, and write to again) requires a magneto-optical drive in order to run. It's really a miracle of modern technical engineering, and could someday replace the floppy and hard drives as a computer's permanent storage medium.

Tape Systems

Tape systems are used on personal computers primarily as a form of *backup*, just in case something goes wrong with your computer.

A special, high-quality tape cartridge is used to store up to 250MB of hard disk information. The cartridge fits into a tape backup unit, which can be external to the computer or internal. An internal tape backup with 120MB of storage costs under $150. You can increase that to 250MB for about $50 more.

By running special software, you can back up your hard drive to the tape. True, it may take the same amount of time as a standard floppy disk backup. But the tape backup operation is continuous, and it can be done at a preset hour (depending on the software). The user can start the backup and go off and do something else. The advantage of tape backups is that people are much more likely to *do* them because of their relative ease.

Removable Drives

Removable drives are the fastest way to get long term storage. The most common of these are *Bernoulli* drives. A Bernoulli drive attaches to your computer and provides very high-speed backup and storage. A 90MB capacity drive will cost just over $500. You insert and remove the disks in the drive just like floppies.

Removable hard drives, real ones, do exist. The first removable hard drives were of the "disk pack" type. The entire disk and spindle mechanism (and sometimes the drive motor) were completely removable. One can be pushed in or pulled out almost as if it were a squat, fat video cassette.

Later advances streamlined the size of removable drives. Syquest offers a removable hard disk that's mainly a hard disk platter in a clear plastic case. The internal version with an 88MB capacity will cost about the same as a Bernoulli.

Buying Guidelines

As a general rule when buying a storage system, the greater the storage capacity and the faster the data accession, the greater the cost. When you buy a floppy drive, get the highest capacity drive that is available. Buy both a $5\frac{1}{4}$-inch and a $3\frac{1}{2}$-inch floppy drive for greater versatility in managing data among computers. New floppy drives cost about $60 for IBM-compatibles.

Anyone who does a lot of computer work will tell you that you can't have enough hard drive capacity. Realistically, most users can get by with 80–120MB, paying between $180–$250. If you are doing work with a lot of different programs, especially graphics or database programs, buy something in the 170–250MB range for between $225 and $300.

Users who need a lot of graphic images or fonts should consider a CD-ROM drive. A CD-ROM can provide a wide range of needed materials on a single disk.

A Final Note

Floppy drives transfer information to $5\frac{1}{4}$ inch or $3\frac{1}{2}$- inch disks, which are thin pieces of magnetized plastic inside a protective covering. Floppy disks are used for distributing software, transporting information between computers, and storing duplicate copies of all your programs and documents.

Hard drives, however, are the main storage devices on today's personal computers. Because hard drives can store hundreds of times as much information as disks can, they are used to hold all the computer's programs and documents for easy access.

Fifteen

Multimedia: Just Bells and Whistles?

• •

ultimedia may not be just bells and whistles anymore. It is quickly becoming a worthwhile, productive addition to the personal computer world that really *isn't* just for fun. Although it certainly can be!

When you hear the term multimedia, think of having the ability to add talking pictures to your sales presentation, use interactive forms for adding data to your parts list, send digital photos of flood damage to your insurance adjustor without processing the film, or research a day in the life of a fruit fly right from your keyboard.

There are two ways to get started with multimedia. Upgrade a system that has enough of the basics to support multimedia or take the easy route and purchase a "Multimedia System" outright. The second choice takes a lot of the mind-boggling guesswork out of buying a computer and its peripherals and may be the best route.

What Do I Need to Get Started?

Whether your computer is a PC or a Mac, the basic multimedia requirements are the same. You'll need a lot of RAM. It's theoretically possible to run some of the programs on machines with as little as 4MB of memory, but they'll be so unendurably slow that you'll constantly be wishing for more RAM. Don't waste your time: With either type of machine, you'll need 8MB of RAM or more.

Next, you'll need lots of hard drive space. Even if you are going to be using only a CD-ROM to access information from a reference, the information is transferred to your hard disk before you get to see it. So make room. Graphics and sound clips take up much more space than text files. A fifteen-second video clip can take up 20MB of hard disk space, just in the 8-bit video mode. Many of the video capture packages come with file compression software, but even these compressed video files are huge. The photographs saved from a digital camera can be 200K in size, and photographs from a Kodak Photo CD can range in size from 93K to 1.5MB in size.

NOTE
An oddity of some video capture systems is that they won't work if you have **more** than 12MB of RAM, because of memory addressing limitations.

Beyond RAM and hard disk space, you'll need a CD-ROM and a sound card. Speakers and a microphone are optional: with them you can command your computer with your own voice and record your own sounds. A camera (digital or your trusty old 35mm) and a scanner are also nice additions to a multimedia system, but are not absolutely necessary.

CD-ROMs

The greatest advantage of CD-ROMs is that they can hold large quantities of data, whether it is straight text, formatted documents, movie clips, photographs, sound bites, or whatever. The standard capacity of CD-ROMs is about 650MB of digital data. That's enough space for about 100 color photographs or slides on one disk. All the works of William Shakespeare fit on one disk. Entire encyclopedias, the Oxford English Dictionary, and the entire Adobe Type Library are all available on CD-ROM. There are so many new CDs on the market these days that maybe the next available CD-ROM will be a catalog of what's available on CD-ROM!

The programs that use the most advanced graphics and sound enhancements are being shipped on CD-ROM instead of floppy disks because more screens and sound bites can be shipped with the program. But there are several considerations to remember before buying a CD-ROM player.

If you expect to use the digital photo technology, you need to have a CD-ROM that can read Kodak Photo CDs. Make sure your CD-ROM is compatible with Kodak's Photo CD and is multisession (ask your salesperson before you buy). Multisession is a specification that allows a CD-ROM to be "mastered" in separate sessions and then read properly. This mastering allows for maximum storage capacity on the CD.

If you are using a CD-ROM–based educational software package (see Figure 15.1) or other entertainment software package, you may not find the speed of a CD-ROM player to be a critical issue, because many programs are designed to transfer data to the hard disk ahead of the time the data are needed. But, if you are using a video package or some virtual reality application, the speed at which the CD player accesses the data on the CD-ROM will be much more important. You should not consider a CD-ROM player with an access speed slower (higher) than 350-400ms (microseconds) or a transfer rate of less than 300KBps (kilobytes per second) unless you don't mind waiting.

A CD-ROM player can be either internal or external. My personal preference is for an external player, simply because I can then use it on any of several systems, and even travel with it to a remote site. But if you have only one system and do not intend to share your toys with others, an internal drive can save space on your desktop.

On a PC, you also have to consider whether you have any empty slots and any available IRQs (interrupts) and base addresses for the player. You will need an interface card to connect a CD-ROM to your system, whether the

Figure 15.1

Where in Space is Carmen Sandiego, a multimedia educational program. (Photo courtesy of Brøderbund Software, Inc.)

CD-ROM is internal or external. If you already have a sound card or other multimedia device installed, you may already have a built-in interface for a CD-ROM. Check the specifications of that interface to ensure that it will handle the CD-ROM of your choice.

If you intend to use an external CD-ROM player with a PC, you have two options. You need an interface to let you use the SCSI (Small Computer Systems Interface, pronounced "scuzzy") player with your computer. You can install a SCSI interface card in your computer (if you have a slot to put it in), or you can use a parallel-to-SCSI device, which lets you plug the CD player into the converter that is plugged into your parallel printer port. Just about every IBM system in the world has a parallel port, but you don't always have a slot available, especially in laptops.

Internal CD-ROM players also require a SCSI interface device, but you may already have an interface available to you through Windows 3.1, eliminating the need to use another slot (and another IRQ) in your system.

For Macintosh users, external players are just plugged into the SCSI port or at the end of an existing SCSI daisy chain, using the drivers included with the player to indicate the type of player to your Mac. Internals work like externals except you have to have a place in your Mac to put the internal drive. This can be a problem in Macs made before the 1990s, and has contributed to the popularity of external players in the Mac world.

And just a last quick note about CDs: You can play your music CDs in your computer's CD-ROM player.

Sound Cards

Sound cards add a new dimension to the business or home-based computer. Your sales presentation can include an audible explanation of why sales soared in the last quarter. You can attach audible reminders to some fields of your database data entry form to ensure that data entry is more accurate.

Although this technology is rather new, sound cards come equipped with a variety of features, so shop around for those options you need the most. Consider including a microphone with your purchase if one doesn't come with the card. Consider voice recognition, a feature that enables your computer to respond to your voice commands rather than just your keystrokes.

Generally, sound cards enable you to record, edit, and play back mono or stereo sounds. You may wish to take advantage of your stereo sounds with stereo speakers.

Sound clips are used in the Windows environment by some Windows applications, some DOS-based software, custom applications, games and entertainment, and educational programs. Most of the comparable software on the Macintosh platform can also take advantage of the built-in sound capabilities.

Software publishers have been enhancing their software packages by adding stereo sound effects that can make it feel like you are in a movie theater watching a Star Wars film. To take advantage of these new sounds you may want to get a sound card and stereo speakers for your system. Programs like Brøderbund Software's Living Books series use sound to teach children to read and encourage them as they improve their reading skills. "Just Grandma and Me" (see Figure 15.2) comes with English, Spanish, and Japanese vocabularies, all on one CD-ROM. The program is *interactive*—it provides audible feedback in the form of a verbal explanation or definition when you click on an object or word.

Other options available to you in multimedia include full-motion video and still-frame photography.

Figure 15.2
Brøderbund Software's Just
Grandma and Me. (Photo
courtesy of Brøderbund
Software, Inc.)

Digital Video Options

Digital video options are a fast growing section of the multimedia computer market. Several years ago, there were simple black-and-white cameras used with their proprietary interface boards to produce grainy images. Now we have full-motion color video viewing and capturing capability coupled with multiple input capabilities and stereo sound input and output (see Figure 15.3).

One package that includes a lot of extras is Microsoft's Video for Windows (VfW), which comes conveniently bundled with popular video capture boards. With it you can pick individual frames of a movie to clip—maybe before you lost your footing on that big wave in Hawaii—or capture a scene from a product demonstration. Then edit the clip using the tools found in VfW or another package such as Macromind Action!.

NOTE

Make sure that you use a disk optimizing program before you capture to disk. If the video clip cannot be saved in one continuous space on your hard drive, frames of the full-motion video will be dropped while the heads of the drive move to the next available space.

Figure 15.3

A frame captured from a home video using Video for Windows. (Photo courtesy of Sheldon Dunn.)

Digital Cameras

Digital cameras, which use a standard serial port on your computer, let you snap a picture, save it on your computer, and include it in your next letter home. Or let your insurance agent take a picture of the damage done to your fender by that dump truck and immediately send the picture to the claims office.

Or, if you prefer to use your favorite 35mm camera, the pictures (or slides) can be put on a CD-ROM so you can view, edit, or print them from any computer equipped with a CD-ROM player. Several cameras are now on the market.

The pictures on a CD-ROM can then be touched up or otherwise manipulated to produce an image that you can use in practically any type of document—word processing, spreadsheet, database, graphic, or whatever.

The FotoMan Plus from Logitech (see Figure 15.4), the makers of the ScanMan and other pointer devices, lets you take up to 32 black-and-white pictures that you can then save on your computer. The FotoMan uses a serial port on your computer, and every system comes with at least one serial port. Use the FotoTouch software included with the camera to shave off that beard you've had since 1975, or remove the reflection of the

flash from a glass surface. The pictures can be saved in any of the standard graphics file formats including TIFF and BMP.

A Final Note

The multimedia world has made the transition from the high-tech studio to the desktop computer system. Compaq ships several models of their desktop systems with sound chips on the motherboard. Apple's two new multimedia models, the Centris 660AV and the Quadra 840AV, have stereo speakers and a microphone built into their computer cases, and a voice recognition system.

Although your options for full-motion video, still-frame photography, voice recognition and response systems, and other applications definitely give you a lot to consider, hardware developers are quickly coming to your rescue with prepackaged all-in-one systems.

Sixteen

Printing Your Results

♦ ♦ ♦ ♦ ♦ ♦ ♦ ♦ ♦ ♦ ♦ ♦ ♦ ♦ ♦ ♦ ♦ ♦ ♦ ♦

Virtually all personal computer applications produce printed output. No matter how important electronic mail and telecommunications become, paper continues to be a convenient medium for circulating information. So no matter what you're doing with your computer, you'll need a printer or access to one.

Printers are available in a wide range of capabilities and prices. They range from those than can only print text in a single typeface to ones that can print text and images in color. The output ranges from low-resolution dots to type-set quality text and images. To help you evaluate which model will best meet your needs, this chapter discusses the major printer types and their characteristics.

Some printers work by printing a lot of little dots on paper to form words and images; others work by striking a formed character against an inked ribbon (just as typewriters do). Some print only text, others print almost any image you can envision. Some make very good pictures, others very fuzzy ones.

What Kinds of Printers Are There?

The three main types of computer printers are listed below:

- Dot-matrix
- Ink jet
- Laser

There are other specialized printers that are useful in certain circumstances. These include the following:

- Color printers
- High-speed printers
- Label printers
- Plotters

Fortunately, you don't have to worry much about computer-printer compatibility. Generally, any type of printer can be used with any computer. There are a few exceptions, however, so you should double-check to make sure your printer and computer are compatible.

One fact you do need to keep in mind is that a printer is probably the hardest working piece of mechanical equipment your computer has. It's the only one that does hard labor. Although most computer components work with electronic currents or shifting magnetic particles, the printer moves its mechanical parts all the time. So the availability of replacement parts is an important consideration when purchasing a printer.

Dot-Matrix

Dot-matrix printers are still widely used for PCs because they offer a balance between acceptable price and acceptable printouts. As you might surmise from the name, these printers work by placing dots of ink on a page. The more dots in a particular area, the sharper the print will be.

Older dot-matrix printers are very noisy and don't provide good output. If you decide on a dot-matrix printer, consider a 24-pin printer. The older 9-pin printers provide truly lousy results and are way too noisy to live with. It's possible to still buy a 9-pin, but not recommended.

To get a nice looking result at a sound level that doesn't induce psychosis, get a 24-pin printer that provides both *draft* and *letter quality* (or *near letter quality*, abbreviated as *NLQ*) output (see Figure 16.1). The more capable 24-pin printers range from $200 to $400, though they can go higher with added features.

Dot-matrix printers work by driving tiny pins into an inked ribbon to place dots of ink on paper. If you look closely at the print head of a dot-matrix printer, you will see that it is composed of a line of tiny vertical wires. Ordinarily, these wires (or pins) are flush with the face of the print head. Each pin has a solenoid coil. When electricity flows though the solenoid, the pin is driven forward, pressing a ribbon against the paper,

Figure 16.1

The LQ-200 is a typical 24-pin dot-matrix printer. It has seven built-in letter quality fonts. (Photo courtesy of Epson America, Inc.)

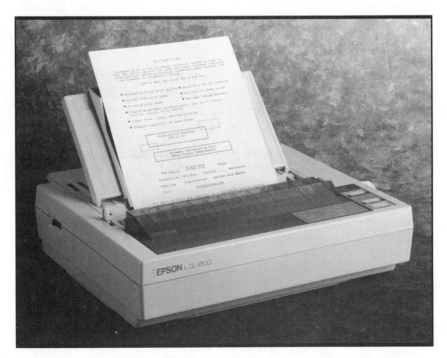

resulting in a black dot on the paper. When all the pins are actuated at once, they form a vertical line. By carefully synchronizing the firing of the pins, the printer forms letters and other images.

Dot-matrix printers come in two widths, narrow and wide. The narrow one accepts normal $8^1/_2$-inch by 11-inch paper. The wide printer accepts paper 14-inches wide, which works for accounting sheets and wide spreadsheets. The narrow ones are called 80-character printers because they will print up to 80 pica characters from the left to right margins. The wide ones will print up to 132 characters.

Typically these work with what's known as *fanfold paper*. You buy this paper by the box. It holds something like 2500 sheets joined together with sprocketed holes on each side so it can be fed through the printer's *tractor feed*. Basically, the tractor feed is two wheels with knobs on them. The wheels go around and the knobs pull the sprocketed paper through the printer. (They also keep the paper straight.) Figure 16.2 illustrates a typical printer using fanfold paper.

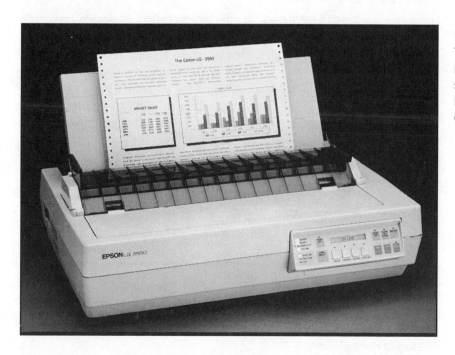

Figure 16.2
The tractor-fed paper is identified by holes along its sides as shown in this Epson LQ-2500 printer. (Photo courtesy of Epson America, Inc.)

Most of these printers also allow you to remove the fanfold paper and print a single sheet. It works just like a typewriter then, and comes in handy if you want to print on an envelope or a piece of letterhead stationery. (This is called *friction feed.*) Most dot-matrix printers allow you to print documents in several modes. (See Figure 16.3.) These include the following:

Draft: Printing is done at the fastest rate and poorest quality. Typically used to get a quick "rough" draft of what you're working on, sometimes to see what the page looks like.

Normal: Printing is done at the regular speed and quality.

Double-strike: Each dot making up the letter is struck twice. This takes twice as long as normal but it makes letters look darker and more substantial.

Near letter quality: This mode is offered by most 24-pin printers. The letters are double-struck at a slight offset to closely resemble typewritten text. It is usually the slowest print speed, but it produces the sharpest letters.

Nearly all dot-matrix printers also offer what's called *condensed* type. Remember 80-character versus 132-character widths? Well, condensed type allows you to print 132 smaller characters on a normal 8½-inch page. The good printers do it by printing clear characters about half as wide and nearly as tall as normal characters. That means you end up with a 52-line page of very readable small characters. Other printers try to accomplish the same thing by cramming normal characters together and overlapping them. It works, but it's not very readable.

The newer printers offer several typefaces (e.g., Times Roman, Courier) and most type styles (bold, italics, underline) in almost any point size. Because these printers work with dots, they also print graphics images such as pictures, lines, and light-gray screens.

Figure 16.3

Dot-matrix output is clear and readable, and there are many instances in which it is the best choice.

```
This is a sample of printing on a DOT MATRIX printer.
(draft quality)


This is a sample of printing on a DOT MATRIX printer.
(letter quality)
```

There are dozens of manufacturers of dot-matrix printers, but Epson, Panasonic, C. Itoh, Star, and IBM are some of the most widely selling brands. Epson and IBM set the standard for dot-matrix printer operation. Most printers will emulate one or the other of these printer types.

Ink Jet

Ink jet printers provide a big step up in output quality from dot-matrix printers. They can produce text in many fonts and graphics just like dot-matrix printers, but they use a completely different technology to get a sharper image. They are also available in portable models that are very popular with laptop users.

Rather than drive tiny pins against a cloth ribbon, ink jet printers squirt tiny beads of ink at the paper. The ink droplets are so fine that these printers can place 90,000 dots in a square inch of paper, each positioned perfectly.

Ink jet printers represent the lowest-price entry to the desktop publishing and graphics fields. They are popular with users who don't want to buy a laser printer but want higher quality output than they could get from a dot-matrix printer.

With ink jets, you can print designed pages instead of just text and pictures. Able to print any typeface, type style, or graphics image, ink jet printers are often advertised as *laser-quality* printers because they produce the same resolution as laser printers. (See Figure 16.4.)

Ink jets can print one to four pages of text per minute, which is faster than a daisy-wheel or a dot-matrix printer running at "Near Letter Quality." However, like all printers, they slow down quite a bit when printing graphic images or a wide variety of typefaces at one time.

The ink jets come with one or two standard typefaces in the machine. Most permit you to switch to a sharp condensed type. Newer models allow you to print in both normal $8^1/_2$-inch by 11-inch *portrait* mode or sideways in *landscape* mode (an 11-inch-wide, $8^1/_2$-inch-long page).

Other typefaces can be created with software instructions from the computer and with plug-in cartridges containing additional typefaces. The cartridges cost $40–$100. They can help you print pages that look typeset.

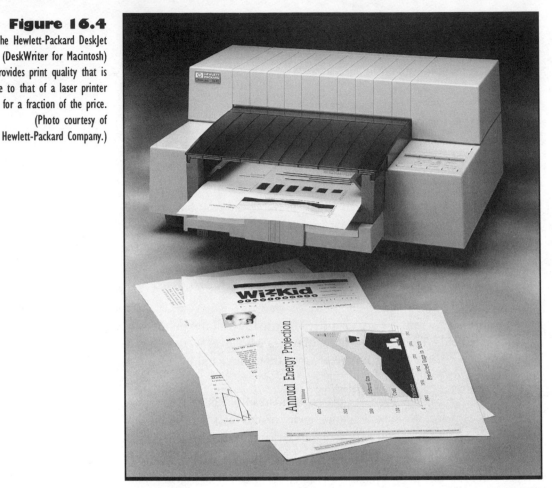

Figure 16.4

The Hewlett-Packard DeskJet (DeskWriter for Macintosh) provides print quality that is close to that of a laser printer for a fraction of the price. (Photo courtesy of Hewlett-Packard Company.)

Ink jets are completely silent in operation, except for a slight click as the print head moves from side to side. They work with single sheets of $8\frac{1}{2}$-inch by 11-inch paper, normally stacked in a tray and fed automatically to the printer one sheet at a time, just like a photocopy machine.

Instead of using a ribbon (as the daisy-wheel and dot-matrix printers do), they use ink stored in a plug-in cartridge that costs about $19. How long the cartridge lasts depends on whether you're printing all text, text and graphics, or all graphics. About 300 double-spaced pages of text will deplete one cartridge.

Hewlett-Packard and Canon are the leading manufacturers of ink jet printers. They both have ink jet printers for $300–$350. Apple Computer sells its StyleWriter, a compact ink jet, for about $395.

Laser

Laser printers have all the good features of ink jet printers and operate twice as fast. Naturally, they dominate the top end of the printer market (see Figure 16.5).

These printers produce printed output that goes far beyond letter quality and moves into the *near-typeset* category. Laser printers can provide text of most typefaces and sizes, and they print the sharpest of all graphic images. They're widely used to prepare computer-generated publications of all types, from books to magazines to corporate reports.

The cost of laser printers is largely determined by the number of fonts they have, whether they have PostScript (a page description language), their amount of RAM, their resolution, and the speed of their output. They start at about $600, but the average cost is about $1000.

Figure 16.5
The HP LaserJet III from Hewlett-Packard offers improved print quality, typeface scaling, and vector graphics. (Photo courtesy of Hewlett-Packard Company.)

Feed Me

There are two main laser-printer languages, PostScript and PCL. Most high-end desktop publishing and graphic software packages are compatible with PostScript for Macintosh and IBM machines. A PostScript cartridge costs about $375 for a non-PostScript laser printer, and PostScript printers themselves have been reduced in price. Today, a PostScript laser printer sells for as little as $1000.

The advantage of the PostScript language over PCL is the wide range of fonts available and the transferability of PostScript files.

Color Printers

There are a few color dot-matrix printers, including the Star Micronix NX-1000 Rainbow, the Apple ImageWriter II, and the Epson LQ-860. Generally, these printers can produce up to eight colors by reprinting a line over and over with different colored ribbons. Naturally, this is time-consuming and the results are, well, lousy.

Color ink jet printers can give you relatively inexpensive access to color printing. The color ink jets are a lot more expensive than black-and-white, but only a fraction of the price of a color laser printer. They represent the most practical choice for home or small office users. Instead of spraying just black ink onto the page, these printers also spray cyan (blue), yellow, and magenta inks. The inks can mix into a very wide palette of colors. These printers can create outstanding transparencies for color presentations.

Hewlett Packard, Canon, and IBM manufacture the most popular of these printers. The price ranges from a low of $700 for the HP DeskJet 550C to $2500 for the IBM Postscript Color JetPrinter. Replacement ink cartridges are about $30.

True color laser printers are available starting at about $5000 and going up to the stratosphere. They can produce nearly photographic quality printouts.

High-Speed Printers

There are also super high-speed printers available that use multiple print heads and print multiple lines at a time. Amazing speeds have been achieved this way—up to 720 characters printed per second (cps). Pages pop out in seconds. Hewlett Packard makes a 17-page per minute laser printer that sells for about $3500. But most other high-speed printers are $5000 or more, so they're not often seen in homes—or even home offices.

Label Printers

Both laser and dot-matrix printers can print labels for envelopes and packages. However, on a dot-matrix printer it is troublesome and time-consuming to remove the regular fanfold paper and change the sprockets to fit the labels, then print the labels, and then reverse the whole process to reinstall the regular paper. Likewise, on a laser printer, getting the special label paper and the software to line up just right can be equally time-consuming. And none of it makes any sense when you just want to print one label for a package.

Recently, a new kind of printer has emerged in response to the difficulty most standard printers have printing envelopes. Seiko has created a printer and software that prints labels only, either directly from the screen, a mailing list file, or the program's built-in database. These sell for about $180; a roll of labels costs about $13. If you have a mail-order business, send newsletters, or work with any other type of application for which you have to switch regularly from labels to paper, a label printer can be very handy and cost-effective. They don't take up much desk space, as is shown in Figure 16.6.

NOTE With the right software, you can print an invoice and then print the label separately on a label printer.

Plotters

Plotters are a special kind of printer. A plotter uses pens to draw very detailed designs on paper. Used for blueprints and engineering drawings, they are a favorite of specialized designers such as interior decorators, engineers, and architects.

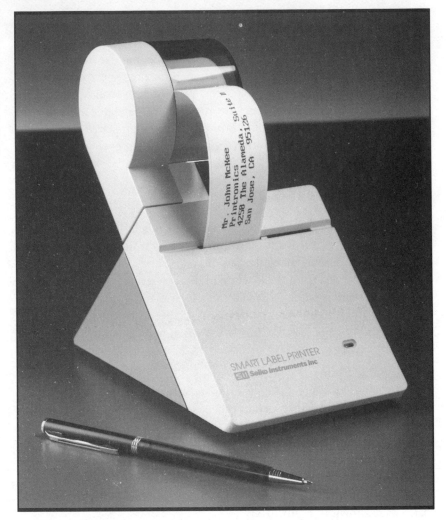

Figure 16.6

Seiko Instruments USA's Smart Label Printer prints letter-quality labels for envelopes, files, bar coding, and other label applications. Note the size of the printer relative to the pen. (Photo courtesy of Seiko Instruments, Inc.)

A few plotters work by moving the paper back and forth while the pen moves side to side inside a print head, but most desk plotters move the pen and hold the paper stationary.

A professional-quality floor-standing plotter can cost several thousand dollars, but desk plotters list at between $1000 and $2000. Plotters are rated by inches per second (ips), which refers to the number of inches the pen moves over the paper. Speeds up to 12 ips are common for desk plotters. If you are looking at plotters, make sure the one you purchase is compatible with the Hewlett-Packard HPGL file format, which is the established standard.

Plotters work with six to eight colored pens, and you must make sure that you'll always be able to restock your supply of pens. If the plotter uses Hewlett-Packard compatible pens, this won't be a problem. Finally, adjustable pen pressure and automatic pen capping and return are also essential options.

How to Evaluate a Printer

In this section, let's consider the main criteria you should use to decide which printer is right for you.

Printers are judged by the following:

- Print quality
- Speed
- Noise level
- Cost

Cost is last on this list because, strangely enough, it may be less important than other factors. If a printer is inexpensive but so slow that it causes you to miss deadlines, or it prints so badly that nobody can read its output, then, clearly, no matter how little you pay, the printer is no bargain.

If the final product of your computer work is destined for public consumption, an inappropriate printer can hurt. Just remember that if you have a less powerful computer system and a superb printout, you're more likely to get your point across than if you have a superb computer and lousy printouts.

Print Quality

The quality of a printer refers to how sharp the letters and images are when printed on paper. This is undoubtedly the single most important issue when rating a printer's capabilities.

Laser printers produce the sharpest prints, with ink-jet printers coming in a close second. They are the most versatile in producing any image on paper.

The 24-pin dot matrix printers produce quite acceptable graphic images and text characters of any size and style, which is why they are still very popular with home and small office users.

Nine-pin dot matrix printers produce readable text and graphics but even their best work is not exactly beautiful. It's a false economy to buy one when you can get an good 24-pin printer for only a little more.

One term you'll hear often when evaluating print quality is *dots per inch* (dpi). Usually, this rating tells you more about print quality than anything else, although not always.

Lasers and ink jets typically print at 300 dpi, which means they have 300 dots in a single line an inch long, or 90,000 dots per square inch. Such a high concentration of dots creates sharp text and graphics. The HP Laser-Jet 4 series produces a resolution of 600 dpi. In contrast, a dot-matrix printer delivering 72 dpi prints only 5184 dots per square inch, which gives you a much less defined picture.

You may hear about 24-pin dot-matrix printers that claim a resolution of 360 dots per inch (dpi), a figure seemingly beyond the capability of most laser printers. This figure is misleading because the pins used in the print head are far larger than $1/360$-inch in diameter. The 360 dpi is only a horizontal measurement rather than the 300 x 300 (square) resolution of laser printers.

Print quality of all printers has improved greatly over the years. Printer sales is a competitive field and printers that do a poor job tend to drop quickly from the market. Inferior printers are still offered in close-out sales. But be wary of a printer offered for what seems to be too good a price. It might be a great deal, but you must look carefully at what the printer can produce. You must also make sure that printer drivers and other printing supplies are readily available.

Speed

Printer speed refers to how fast the printer delivers finished pages. This can be a major issue if you're printing a 500-page manuscript or you need to turn out your work quickly.

The speed of a printer is measured in one of two ways: either in terms of pages produced per minute (ppm) or characters printed per second (cps).

The reason for two measurements is that some printers print one character at a time and others print full lines or partial pages at one time.

Without a doubt, laser printers are the fastest. They can turn out 4 to 11 pages per minute, with some expensive units rated at up to 50 ppm.

Generally, ink-jet printers produce about 2 pages a minute, although the latest version of the DeskJet printer from Hewlett-Packard can manage 4, which is about the same as a low-cost laser printer.

Dot-matrix printers also print about 2 pages a minute, roughly 96 cps for *normal* printouts.

But these ratings, too, can be misleading.

As you may recall, dot-matrix printers can print in several modes, from draft to normal to *near letter quality*, each of which improves the sharpness but slows the speed. So the real speed depends on *how* you'll print most of your documents.

For example, you'll often see a line like "192cps Draft, 64cps NLQ" in ads for dot-matrix printers. This means it prints about 3 pages a minute in draft mode and two-thirds of a page in the best mode. If you see only one number (192cps), you can assume it refers to draft mode. If you want to print your materials at a higher quality, the printer may be too slow.

You're getting sleepy... sleeepy....

The page-per-minute ratings present similar complexities. If you're printing multiple copies of identical pages, the printer should meet or exceed the given rating. But if you're printing consecutive pages of a manuscript, the printer will slow down. Also, printing graphics throws the credibility of all ratings out the door. I've waited as long as 20 minutes for a page full of graphics to emerge.

So take these ratings with a grain of salt. They are useful only for comparison. A 240 cps printer will work faster than a 192 cps, and an 8 ppm printer will be faster than a 4 ppm.

Noise Level

Noise level is an important consideration for any printer in your home or office. Dot-matrix printers range from pretty noisy to welcome-to-the-boiler-factory. There are two ways to deal with printer noise. You can put the printer in a closet or an adjacent room. Or buy a sound-buffering box to completely enclose it. You can find these boxes in catalogs and computer stores.

Ink jet printers make almost no sound except for a slight tapping as the print head moves from side to side on the page.

Most laser printers make virtually no sound. The whir of a laser printer while printing is only a little louder than a cooling fan. Some have a louder hum, but it's not usually distracting.

Cost

Although cost may not be the most important factor in printer selection, often it is the one that makes the decision for you. It's no coincidence that the printer that does the most—the laser—is also the most expensive.

Printer Memory

Programs send data to the printer faster than the printer can print it. Printers require enough memory so data from the software can be stored until printed. However, some printers are sold with only 512K of RAM. In fact, PCL laser printers are often shipped with a bare minimum of RAM to keep the cost down. If your laser printer has only 512K, or even 1MB of RAM, you may discover that there isn't enough memory for some printing tasks.

If you print only text, and use just the fonts in the printer, 512K is enough. But that amount of memory will print only about half a page of graphics. The second half of the page is then loaded into the printer's memory and printed on a second page. If you want to print a *whole* page of graphics on *one* page, or if you want to use downloadable fonts, you'll need at least one additional megabyte of RAM at a cost of about $90.

PCL (Printer Control Language—see "Printer Languages") laser printers cost between $640 and $3000. PostScript lasers typically run $1000 to $2500. As stated earlier, the price of a laser printer is determined largely by the amount of RAM, speed, number of fonts, and special capabilities it has.

24-pin dot matrixes sell for between $200–$500 and are currently dropping in price as well as noise level.

Ink jet printers start at about $400 new. Used ones run about $200. Frequently, an ink jet user will move up to a laser printer and sell the ink jet at a bargain price.

Printer Supplies

When looking at printers, you not only have to consider the initial purchase price but also the price-per-page of using the printer. Here's a summary of the items needed to keep printers running, and some informed guesses on their cost:

- **Dot matrix**: 2500-sheet box of fanfold paper ($18) or 500-sheet ream of single-sheet paper ($3–$4). Some use cheap reel-to-reel ribbons ($2–$4); most use a ribbon cartridge in the $4–$15 range.
- **Ink jet**: Ream of single-sheet paper ($3–$4); ink cartridges ($19); color ink cartridges ($30); font cartridges ($40–$60).
- **Laser**: Ream of single-sheet paper ($3–$4); toner ($80 new or $45 for refill).

These prices vary from store to store. The key issue regarding supplies is to make sure that the printer you choose uses standard paper and has easy-to-find replacement supplies. A printer for which you can't buy ribbons, toner, or ink cartridges has a very short useful lifetime.

You can buy most of these supplies through catalogs that usually will give you a slightly better price than your neighborhood computer store. A final issue to consider is the number of pages you get per laser toner cartridge. This cartridge costs about $80 new, and an ink jet cartridge costs only $20. However, a laser toner is good for about 3000 pages and an ink-jet cartridge only for 300 pages. So you pay 2.6 cents per page with a laser, but 6.6 cents per page with an ink jet.

NOTE

Throwing out empty toner cartridges feels wasteful and it is. In the back of many computer magazines you'll find companies that "recharge" them at a fraction of the cost of a new one. You can save money and feel virtuous at the same time!

Before you buy any printer, be sure to do some comparison shopping. You can save a lot of money. This is especially true for laser printers.

How Printers and Computers Communicate

Now let's look at the hardware and software links that tie the computer and the printer together. These are as follows:

- Parallel/Serial connectors (the cable between the computer and printer)
- Printer languages (how the computer "talks" to the printer)
- Device drivers (how programs "talk" to the printer).

Parallel & Serial Printers

Often, printers are categorized by the cable connecting them to the computer. You may have heard the terms "parallel printer" or "serial printer." These refer to the names of the connectors on each end of the cable leading from the back of the computer to the back or bottom of the printer.

Most computers, other than the Macintosh, have plugs for both parallel and serial connectors. (Macs are set up only for serial connections.) On many computers you can choose to hook up either a serial or parallel printer.

NOTE

Some software, especially for IBM-compatibles, does not provide the option of using a serial port for printer output. Such software should be avoided if you have a serial printer.

Most printers are parallel printers, which means they use the Centronics parallel interface that emerged very early in the microcomputer age. The name comes from the fact that a parallel interface sends eight bits of information to the printer at a time, so the bits are parallel with each other as they travel through the cable.

The serial printer gets its name from the data currents that travel one bit at a time, in serial fashion, through the pins and into the wires of the cable.

Today, serial interfaces are used mainly by Apple computers and printers. The Apple LaserWriter, StyleWriter (ink jet), ImageWriter (dot-matrix), and several third-party printers designed for use with the Mac and other Apple computers have serial interfaces. (The HP DeskWriter by Hewlett-Packard, for example, has an AppleTalk interface that connects easily to the Macintosh.)

Another issue to consider is distance. Parallel printers have a limited distance range. If the printer is more than 20 feet away from the computer, you will need a serial connector, because the signal in a parallel cable starts to get lost over longer distances. Serial cables handle distances a lot better.

Printer Languages

The two best-known languages are the PCL and PostScript languages that evolved with laser printers. Hewlett-Packard established PCL (which stands for Printer Control Language) with its LaserJet series. A few years later, when Apple released the Apple LaserWriter, it also introduced Adobe's page description language called PostScript. This is a language much like the Pascal program language, except that it's specially designed to describe a page to the printer. (Of course, you can use a PCL or Post-Script language printer without having to learn the programming language.)

In each PostScript printer, there is a computer that translates the Post-Script program into images. That's right. PostScript laser printers have their own computers built right inside. The real value of PostScript is that it's a device-independent language. As long as the printer understands PostScript, you can use any computer from a Commodore 64 to an IBM-compatible with an 80486 microprocessor to send PostScript output to the printer. You'll get the same results.

Fonts

The evolution of laser printers led to an explosion in the variety of typefaces and type styles available today on nearly all printers. This is the

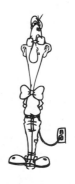

computer area generally known as "working with *fonts*." Fonts are collections of complete uppercase and lowercase alphabets, numbers, and other symbols that share common characteristics. The meaning of "font" is so close to the meaning of "typeface" that the two words are used synonymously. Figure 16.7 shows some different laser fonts.

Figure 16.7

These fonts were created on an Apple LaserWriter Plus, one of the older PostScript laser printers.

Bookman
Avant Garde
Palatino
Zapf Chancery

Fonts can come in specific sizes or they can be scalable to different sizes. PostScript printers come with a standard collection of fonts, including Times Roman, Courier, Helvetica, and Symbol. Because these fonts are what is known as *outline fonts*, they can be scaled to virtually any size. An outline font is only a description of a font in mathematical terms. To create larger or smaller versions of the fonts, the computer chip inside the printer simply performs some basic math. This enables printers that ordinarily come with a very narrow selection of fonts (such as the PCL laser) to print in a wide variety of typefaces. Generally, these typefaces are not as attractive as PostScript and other kinds of outline fonts because they print at a set resolution far below the resolution that ink jet and laser printers are capable of producing. However, some of the newer PCL laser printers have a built-in resolution enhancement to improve the quality of the typefaces.

PCL laser printers have another way to use fonts. Each can be fitted with a ROM cartridge that supplies the necessary information to create fonts. A font cartridge might contain three or four individual typefaces in a variety of sizes and styles.

A third way to use fonts with PCL laser printers is through what is called *downloadable* fonts. Bitstream Fontware is the primary supplier of these fonts. When you purchase a Bitstream font, you will store a collection of outline fonts on the hard disk in your computer. The software that comes with the fonts can scale the fonts to any size you request. The larger a font, the more space it will take up on your hard drive and in the memory of the printer.

Adobe Type Manager is another excellent set of fonts that can be used with PCL and PostScript printers. For about $60 per disk, you can buy several downloadable fonts for PCL and PostScript printers.

Graphics

PostScript printouts have the reputation of being the sharpest of all prints, but you don't necessarily need a PostScript printer for sharp quality. Some PCL printers also have vector graphics used for creating pictures without the "dotty" characteristics of bitmapped graphics. The page description language draws the graphics using formulas for making lines and curves. Thus, the graphics follow a path or are "vectored" rather than created by the rougher placement used for bitmapped graphics.

Printer Drivers

The printer driver is the last important feature to be aware of in computer-printer communication. Different types of printers require different drivers. For example, you'll need a different driver for an ink-jet, dot-matrix, or laser printer. Also, you need different types of drivers for different models of printers within a single category.

Basically, a printer driver is a program that makes sure the information sent by the computer to the printer arrives in a form the printer can understand. Software packages that require special printer drivers will come with those drivers. Macintosh computers come with software that supports Apple ImageWriters, StyleWriters, and various LaserWriters. Special driver installers also come with certain software such as Microsoft Windows. Likewise, when you purchase a printer, it will come with a driver that is understood by different computers or the specific computer for which it was designed.

NOTE

Make sure when you purchase a printer that the correct printer driver for your computer is already installed. Special driver installers also come with software such as Microsoft Windows.

Buying Guidelines

Some years ago, a somewhat autocratic friend of mine went to buy a computer system. He carried a page he wanted to reproduce on a computer printer. He knew next to nothing about computers, but he knew what he wanted. Salespeople of every stripe tried to convince him that he could not produce a page anywhere near the quality he wanted. They were subjected to his wrath. Finally, he came to a store that had a Macintosh set up for desktop publishing complete with a laser printer. In a few minutes the sales clerk created a page to his liking. He bought the system.

When buying a printer, you should do the same thing. If you want spreadsheets, databases, newsletters, labels, or multiple form invoices printed, take along a sample of what you want and ask for a demonstration. If you don't get what you want, keep looking.

If you want to do professional desktop publishing, you will need a laser printer. Low-cost lasers are now widely available. You should have no trouble finding one for under $800. Be sure to check their ability to do what you want, including graphics and different fonts.

Ink jet printers are also fine for high-quality, low-cost printing, and can save you a couple of hundred dollars over laser printers. As laser printers approach $500, however, the savings for ink jet printers lessen. Unless, of course, you really need to print in color. Then an ink jet printer makes low-cost sense.

If you want a reliable printer that produces mainly text, a 24-pin dot-matrix printer can save you several hundred dollars over the cost of a laser printer. For multi-part forms, a 9-pin dot-matrix printer is the best.

You should follow the example of my autocratic friend and shop around and see what works for you. Once you see something that offers what you want, compare it with other printers in the same class or check the next class up to see if the price difference is small. Remember, you can have great looking output if you have the right printer, but the best computer in the world can't do much with an inferior printer.

A Final Note

Printers perform a valuable service by providing a *hard copy* of your computer work. It's a lot easier to show off your results on a piece of paper than it is to carry the computer around.

Dot-matrix printers are popular because they produce good results and are fairly inexpensive.

Ink jet printers produce sharp, high-resolution pages of almost any typeface or graphic image. They do near laser quality work for less cost than a laser printer and are available in portable models.

Laser printers are the top of the line in printed output. They're faster, sharper, and quieter than other printers. Each year their prices go down. So what was out of reach of many buyers a few years ago may end up being the most bang for your printer buck.

Which one is right for you depends on what your needs are in terms of text, graphics printing, and your pocketbook. Only one thing is certain— you do need a printer. No computer system is complete without one.

Appendix

Your First Day with Your New Computer

N ow that you've decided on the computer setup you want, let's discuss that all-important first day with your new baby. What you do in this critical time can greatly enhance your future pleasure as well as forestall possible risks to your (sizeable) investment.

First we'll discuss what to do before you even leave the store. Even if you're buying your computer through the mail, read this section before sending in your order.

Before You Leave the Store

While you're still in the store, you should do a quick inventory to make sure that everything you purchased is actually present. For the things that you can't see without opening up the box, check the receipt and/or packing list to make sure everything is present and accounted for:

- the computer box and its electrical cord
- a hard disk of the type and size you ordered
- the amount of RAM you bought
- floppy disk drives
- keyboard and cable
- monitor and cable
- printer and cable
- mouse or trackball
- any add-ons you ordered such as a sound card or modem
- disks and documentation for DOS and any other software you ordered preinstalled on the hard disk
- your warranties and documentation for everything

If you're buying a more-or-less generic PC clone, the store should have assembled the parts and then done a "burn-in" before you came in to pick up the machine. This means they started the computer and ran it for two or more days to make sure everything in the box (the memory, the CPU, the power supply) is working. Like most electronic devices, if it's going to fail it's likely to do so at the very beginning.

If your computer came to the dealer ready-made, the testing should have been done at the factory.

You should ask the guru at the store to label the various ports on the back of the machine for you. You'll probably have two serial ports, one parallel (printer) port (on IBM-compatible systems), the keyboard port, and perhaps a mouse port. If you know which one's which before you start plugging things in at home, your job will be much easier.

While you're at the store, get a few basics just to get started. You can buy more supplies later, after you know how much you need and where to find the cheapest prices, but for now make sure you have the following:

- a surge protector. All it takes is one random surge of electricity to turn your beautiful piece of high-tech joy into low-tech junk. The best surge protectors allow you to plug in all your peripherals too. If you have very unreliable power in your area, you may want to look into an uninterruptible power supply (UPS), which is more expensive but more reliable.

- a box of 10 floppy disks. Get them in the size that fits in your A: drive (on an IBM-compatible). For a Mac, of course, there's only one size: $3\frac{1}{2}$-inch.

- a floppy disk file box in which to keep your software disks.

- a mouse pad. Your mouse won't work very well without one (the ball slips and slides on the average desktop). You don't need a pad for a trackball.

- enough printer paper to get started. Later you can buy a case of paper at a warehouse store, but for now you just want enough for the first day or two.

- an extra printer ribbon for your dot matrix printer or an extra ink cartridge for your ink jet printer. Don't bother getting an extra toner cartridge for your laser printer. The one supplied will last for thousands of pages.

Driving Home

The store should have packed everything up so that it's very safe to transport. In fact, you should insist that all the major pieces of your system be boxed up in the cartons provided by the manufacturer. That way you can do almost anything short of bouncing the boxes off the pavement without doing any harm to the contents.

Extremes of temperature, however, *can damage your computer*. Don't leave the boxes in the car for a prolonged period if it's either a very hot or very cold day. If the boxes do happen to get very chilled, bring everything indoors and let it warm up to near room temperature before trying to get it to run.

Setting Up

Before you start pawing around in the boxes, take a good look at the spot you've chosen for your computer. It's important to bear in mind that this is where you're going to be spending a lot of hours. It must be a place that is comfortable for both you *and* the computer. From the computer's point of view, consider the following:

- Is there adequate room for ventilation? The computer box and monitor require air circulation. Not a tremendous amount, but you can't just back them snugly into a bookcase. Besides, you may need to get at the back of the computer box to plug in and unplug stuff.

- Is there a grounded electrical outlet nearby? It helps to be close to an outlet to minimize the tangle of cords and cables strewn across the floor. A grounded outlet (the kind that accepts three-pronged plugs) is needed to protect your computer from stray electricity. It has the added benefit of protecting *you* from harm also.

- Is there a phone jack nearby for your modem?

From *your* point of view, consider the following:

- Space. Allow room to spread out. You'll need room for your mouse, the printer, books, papers, disks, and all the other miscellaneous gorp that collects in a workspace.

- The keyboard position. It's OK for the monitor to be at desk height—but not the keyboard. Most desks are about 29–30 inches high, while the ideal keyboard height is about three inches lower than that. If you can't lower the keyboard, think about raising your chair.

- Lighting. The ideal lighting for a computer is only slightly brighter than that required for a romantic dinner. A window behind you will produce glare on the screen. A window in front of you will make you squint (most unattractive!). Put the computer near a window only if you have easily adjustable curtains or blinds.

Hooking Up

NOTE

You should keep all the boxes and packing materials, at least during the warranty period. If you have to send anything back for service it will be a lot easier to ship if you have the original box and Styrofoam.

NOTE

Turn the computer off before plugging anything into the computer box or unplugging anything from the computer box. You may get away with it a hundred times, but you may also damage something expensive.

Now that you've picked the perfect spot, you can start opening up the boxes. Usually you'll have one for the monitor, one for the computer box, one for the keyboard, and maybe another one or two for software and other accessories.

Unpack the computer box first since everything else has to plug into it. You can put it on your desk or under it—just make sure that you can easily reach the floppy drives and the switches. Leave a gap between the desk and the wall so you can run the cords and cables easily.

Plug the power cord into the computer box and the other end into the surge protector. Don't plug the surge protector into the wall yet.

On a typical PC the power cords will have a normal, three-pronged plug on one end and a female plug on the other end that connects to a male receptacle on the device itself. Monitors and printers are sometimes constructed in the same way.

The signal cables are the heavy cords that provide the communication between devices. There's a signal cable between the monitor and the computer, between the printer and the computer, and between an external modem and the computer. The receiving points on the computer are called *ports*.

If the store labeled the ports for you, you'll be spared the trial-and-error approach.

Plug the monitor cable into the video port and the other end into the monitor (it may be permanently attached at the monitor end). Plug the monitor's power cord into the surge protector.

Plug the keyboard into the keyboard port or, on a Mac, one of the ADB (Apple Desktop Bus) ports. Plug your mouse (or trackball) into the mouse port if you have one or into the first serial port (may be labeled as COM1). On a Mac the mouse also plugs into an ADB port.

Leave the printer and any other external device out of the equation for the time being.

Now we're ready for the first test.

Port Basics

The back of your PC has lots of interesting places in which to plug things. These places are called ports. The two types of general purpose ports are *serial* and *parallel*.

Serial ports (also called COM ports and even RS-232 ports by some tiresome people) are used for modems, some types of mice, plotters, and (rarely) printers. They come in two different sizes, just to complicate things a bit more. One has 25 pins and the other has nine pins. These are pins that stick out and are hence called "male" connectors.

Parallel ports (aka printer ports) on the back of the printer have 25 receiving pins and are called "female" connectors.

Ready, Set, Go!

Now it's time to fire it up! But before you do, check that

- the computer and monitor are both switched off (or if they're plugged into a surge protector, that the surge protector is switched off).
- the monitor, keyboard, and mouse are plugged in securely. For cables that have little screws at one end, tighten the screws down to make a secure connection.
- the floppy disk drives are empty.

Now you can plug the computer power cord into a grounded receptacle, or if you have a surge protector, plug *it* into a grounded receptacle.

Turn the computer's power switch on. Turn the monitor's power switch on (or flip the master switch on the surge protector).

Things should start to happen immediately and within a minute your computer should be through its start-up routine. What you see on the monitor at this point depends on what software has already been installed. It may be the DOS prompt (C:>), or some other program such as

NOTE

If your power switch is labeled with a circle and a vertical line, the circle means "off" and the vertical line means "on."

Windows or the DOS Shell, or the Happy Face on your Mac followed by the opened desktop. It doesn't matter because you can always navigate in or out of whatever's there. Now that everything's working you can connect the printer and any other stuff you bought.

Connecting the Printer

Once you have the computer running, you can start to connect the printer and other peripherals you may have bought. First turn off the computer.

Position the printer so you can reach its controls and so there's room for the paper to feed in and out. Unless you are printing more or less constantly, you'll want to be able to turn the printer on and off independently from the rest of your system.

Most printers connected to IBM-compatibles will use the wide 25-pin female port (or parallel port) on the computer. In the unlikely event that you have two of these ports, plug the printer cable into the one marked LPT1. Not marked? Try the one that looks like it's the first one. If you're wrong, there's no harm done. The bigger end of the printer cable plugs into the port on the printer.

On a Macintosh, the printer cable is plugged into the printer port, which is identified with the image of a printer above the port. Another way in which the Mac makes things easier.

NOTE

Do yourself a favor: once you have everything plugged in and working, mark the cables and ports. Get little sticky tabs and put "Printer LPT1" on the cable for the printer and so on.

You can also plug in your external modem at this point. You'll need to connect the modem to a serial port on the computer (if you have a mouse in COM1, use COM2 for the modem), to a phone line, and to an electrical outlet. The Macintosh systems identify the serial port best used for modems with an image of a telephone handset above the port.

If your modem is internal (inside the computer box) you'll only need to plug a phone line into the connector on the back of the computer.

On the other hand, you may want to wait a day or two before tackling the modem. It's not all that tricky, but it does add a layer of complexity just when you're trying to get your bearings.

Are You Covered?

Be sure that your new computer is covered by your homeowner's or renter's insurance. Some policies have strict limits on the amount of coverage for a computer. Find out what they are. You may not be at the limit now, but in a year or two after you add a CD-ROM and a fax board and who knows what else, you could be up there.

Also, if you use the computer for business purposes, you may have to buy a special rider for your policy. Check with your insurance agent.

A Final Note

Take your time exploring your computer and its potential. Experiment. See what works and what doesn't. If you can, take a few notes as you go along so you can avoid making the same mistakes more than two or three times.

Don't worry about damaging the computer. It's virtually impossible to wreak havoc with only a keyboard and a mouse as weapons. You will, of course, make some mistakes but you can also have a lot of fun while accumulating skills that can only be of help in today's world.

Glossary

Definition of Terms

• •

Every discipline has its own vocabulary of weird-sounding words and acronyms and the computer biz is no exception. Even worse, sometimes one of these strange words is used to define some even stranger *other* word! So, to make it easier to use this glossary, if a computer term is used as part of the definition of another computer term, it's typeset in small capitals. The small capitals tell you that the term can be found in the glossary.

8-bit, 16-bit, 32-bit, 64-bit Sizes of the DATA and instruction packets various computers use. As a rule, the bigger the number, the faster and more powerful the computer.

286, 386, 486 Abbreviations for the Intel 80X86 family of MICROPROCESSOR chips used in IBM-compatibles and the IBM PS/2 line of computers.

Address The place inside a computer where INSTRUCTIONs and DATA are stored. For example, in a system with one MEGABYTE of memory, over one million addresses are available to store instructions and data.

Alphanumeric DATA containing letters of the alphabet, special symbols like the dollar sign, and/or numbers. For example, *P.O. Box 3384* is alphanumeric data.

Application Any PROGRAM that accomplishes a specific task such as word processing, DATABASE management, accounting, payroll, drawing, and so forth. (*Secondary meaning:* In the Windows world, a "program" is called an application.)

Application-Specific (A/S) SOFTWARE that is designed to perform a specialized task—be it running a particular kind of business, handling payroll, or scheduling appointments.

Applications generator A tool designed to help you develop custom APPLICATIONs with minimal programming.

Architecture The overall design of a computer. An architecture may be open or closed. An architecture that you can add or replace components in is called "open." If you can't add or change components, the architecture is "closed."

Archive A compressed version of a PROGRAM or FILE, which conserves storage space and can save time and money when you're transmitting DATA over telephone lines.

ASCII   An acronym for American Standard Code Information Interchange. It is the standardized means of representing letters and numbers in computers. ASCII text is normal-looking letters and numbers.

Background printing   (Also called "spooling" or "print spooling.") With background printing, the computer prints your DOCUMENT at the same time that you continue doing other tasks on the computer.

Backup   A duplicate copy of everything (or at least everything important) on your HARD DISK, for use in case something goes wrong with the hard disk or computer. Typically, hard disk backups are stored on FLOPPY DISKS, TAPES, or removable DRIVES.

Baud (bits per second or bps)   The number of BITS that can be sent or received every second. Dividing the baud rate by 10 provides a more realistic transmission rate: the number of characters per second (cps). Therefore, 2400 bps equals about 240 cps. Technically, baud and bps are not the same thing, but no one cares.

Binary number   A number containing only the digits 0 and 1. Binary numbers are used on computers because they best represent electric current, which is either on (1) or off (0).

BIOS   Acronym for Basic Input Output System (pronounced *BYE-ohss*). The BIOS is a set of instructions located in READ-ONLY MEMORY (ROM) that identifies the components of the computer so the computer can use them (i.e., type of HARD DRIVE, DISK DRIVE, KEYBOARD, and MONITOR).

Bit   The contraction for "binary digit," the smallest unit of information available to the computer, representing a single 1 or 0 within a BINARY NUMBER. Physically, a bit can be thought of as a single pulse (on or off) in an electronic current.

Bitmap   A group of tiny dots that form a GRAPHIC or picture. Bitmapped graphics are easier to use in creating pictures, but they typically do not print as smoothly as VECTOR GRAPHICS.

Boot up   The process of starting up the computer's OPERATING SYSTEM. Booting up is accomplished by a "bootstrap PROGRAM" that contains just enough instructions to start the operating system loading. The term comes from the phrase "pulling yourself up by your own bootstraps."

bps   Abbreviation for BITs per second (sometimes called BAUD).

Bulletin Board   A kind of computer mailbox that enables you to send and receive messages, request help and information, retrieve FILEs and PROGRAMs, and communicate electronically with other people using your computer, MODEM, and telephone line. Usually, bulletin boards are run by people called SYSOPs.

Bus   A wire that connects various parts of your computer. Each bus actually contains three buses: the power bus supplies power to all of the parts that need electricity; the DATA bus links the parts of the computer that send and receive data; and the ground bus makes sure that everything needing a ground gets one.

Byte   Equal to 8 bits, it's roughly the amount of space required to store a single character (letter, number, or symbol) on a DISK or in MEMORY. For example, the word *cat* requires three bytes of storage.

CAD   Acronym for Computer Aided Design (pronounced *kad*). CAD PROGRAMs are the high-end programs used by engineers and draftsmen to diagram and/or design all the drafting details required to build things ranging from houses to airplanes to electrical circuits for high-speed trains.

CD-ROM   A read-only storage DEVICE (pronounced *see dee RAHM*). Similar to the compact disk player, a CD-ROM lets you access information such as FONT FILES, GRAPHICS, and reference information, but you can't write new information or erase what's on a disk.

Central Processing Unit (CPU)   (Also called the MICROPROCESSOR, PROCESSOR, or CHIP.) The "brain" of the computer, the CPU performs the calculations that result in computer output.

CGA   Acronym for Color/Graphics Adapter. CGA was the first GRAPHICS standard for the PC (personal computer), providing the PC with color text and the ability to do graphics with a limited number of colors and a limited RESOLUTION.

Chat mode   A feature of TELECOMMUNICATIONS SOFTWARE that allows you to communicate with another user or the SYSOP who runs a BULLETIN BOARD. You type your end of the conversation on your KEYBOARD and read the replies on your computer screen.

Chip   (Also called the MICROPROCESSOR, PROCESSOR, or CPU.) A chip performs the calculations that result in computer output.

Clip art   Ready-to-use pictures that have already been created by professional artists and stored on FLOPPY DISKs or CD-ROM, or run through a SCANNER.

Closed architecture   A type of computer design that prevents the expansion or modification of internal components.

Command   INSTRUCTIONs or directions (entered by the user through a DEVICE) that tell the computer or a PROGRAM what to do.

Compatibles   (Also called "IBM clones.") Computers that are very similar to the microcomputers IBM produces and that use the same FILE FORMATs. The only important difference is that compatibles are cheaper than IBM machines.

Computer   A general-purpose electronic machine designed to help people get a job done. Computers are great for quickly doing the paperwork, calculations, record-keeping, trial-and-error experimentation, communications, information-gathering, and myriad other managerial tasks involved in getting a job done.

Computerphobia   An irrational fear of computers based on misinformation and exacerbated by bad experiences with computer "experts." Unlike the fear of spiders, computerphobia can be overcome given a little time, patience, and this book.

Connectivity   The ability of a portable computer to connect with and to quickly pass information between the portable and, say, an office desktop machine.

Conventional memory   The first 640K of RANDOM ACCESS MEMORY.

CP/M   Abbreviation for Control Program for Microcomputers. Immensely popular during the earliest days of microcomputing, CP/M was a no-frills, text-based OPERATING SYSTEM designed to run on machines with little MEMORY and minimal DISK storage.

cps   Abbreviation for characters per second. A way to measure the speed of a printer.

CPU   Abbreviation for CENTRAL PROCESSING UNIT.

Cut and Paste   A feature of many computer programs that lets you select any block of DATA in a DOCUMENT and move or copy that block to a new place in the document or to a different document.

Data   Information contained in a computer FILE.

Data processing   Number crunching (slang). The computer performs many numeric (data) calculations to produce output.

Data type   The information processed by a DATABASE MANAGEMENT SYSTEM. Typical DATA types are alphanumeric, numeric, date, and memo.

Data validation   The process of checking for errors as the user is entering or changing information in a DATABASE.

Database   An organized collection of information (DATA) stored in a computer FILE.

You're getting sleepy... sleeepy....

Database management system (DBMS)   A PROGRAM that allows you to enter information into a computer DATABASE, edit it, find it, sort it, search it, and view it or print it in whatever FORMAT suits your needs.

DBMS   Abbreviation for DATABASE MANAGEMENT SYSTEM.

Defragment   The process of rearranging separated pieces of FILEs onto contiguous areas of the HARD DISK, thus making the reading and writing of files smoother and faster.

Density   Refers to how densely information is stored on a FLOPPY DISK. High-density disks store more information than low-density disks.

Desktop publishing (DTP)   The combining of text, pictures, charts, graphs, and tables produced by other PROGRAMs into fully designed pages. Desktop publishing programs provide all the tools required to design and typeset anything from a newsletter to a novel.

Device   Any piece of equipment used with a computer. For example, the MONITOR, KEYBOARD, printer, and MOUSE are all devices of one computer system. Same as PERIPHERAL.

Device independence   The ability of a computer program to work regardless of the brand of the devices to which it is attached. For example, POSTSCRIPT is a device-independent computer language that facilitates communication between computers and PostScript printers. As long as the printer "understands" the PostScript language, it doesn't matter to what kind of computer or PROGRAM it is connected.

Digital camera   A camera that produces digital output rather than the traditional film medium. Output can be edited with photo retouching or finishing software to create a desired effect. Process or print only the shots that suit your needs. Store the images in your graphics library for future use in your documents and presentations.

Digitizer   A DEVICE that transfers video pictures into computer-readable form.

Directory   A designated (named) area on a DISK that is used to organize FILEs, much like a file drawer in a file cabinet is used to organize manila file folders.

Disaster Recovery   A UTILITY PROGRAM that helps you find and reinstate accidentally deleted FILEs that are still on the DISK.

Disk   A flat, circular surface used to hold computer DATA. An abbreviated term used collectively to represent HARD DISK, FIXED DISK, HARD DRIVE, DISKETTE, and FLOPPY DISK. The context in which "disk" is used will enable you to understand its meaning.

Disk drive   An electronic mechanism in the computer where PROGRAMs and DATA are stored and accessed.

Disk drive controller   The EXPANSION CARD that, when used with cables, connects the DISK DRIVEs to the computer.

Diskette   (Also called FLOPPY DISK.) The small, removable DISK used to hold computer DATA. Diskettes are available in $5\frac{1}{4}$-inch and $3\frac{1}{2}$-inch high- and low-density sizes.

Document   A DATA FILE that you create or edit with a word processing or desktop publishing program. (*Secondary meaning:* In the Windows world, any open window is correctly called a document, even Paintbrush GRAPHICS, or SPREADSHEET worksheets.)

DOS   Acronym for Disk Operating System (pronounced *dawss*). The name of the most widely used OPERATING SYSTEM for IBM PCs and compatible computers.

Dot-matrix printer   A relatively low-cost printer that uses a mechanical head and inked ribbon to put dots of ink on the page. Dot-matrix printers are less expensive and produce lower quality output than INK JET and LASER PRINTERs.

Downloadable font A scalable FONT that is stored on your computer's HARD DISK and loaded into the printer when needed.

Drive Another name for a DISK DRIVE.

Driver A small PROGRAM used by the computer to control each DEVICE in a computer system.

DTP Abbreviation for DESKTOP PUBLISHING.

Dumb terminal A terminal or PC that relies totally on a remote computer for prompts and DATA storage. Common dumb terminal types are the VT-100 and VT-52.

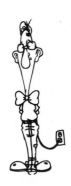

Duplex The ability of your PROGRAM and computer HARDWARE to simultaneously send and receive information. Half-duplex means that two computers can communicate with each other, but only one can communicate at any given time. Full-duplex means that both computers can send and receive information simultaneously.

Editing The process of making changes and corrections to a DOCUMENT or FILE.

EGA Abbreviation for Enhanced Graphics Adapter. A short-lived GRAPHICS display standard that followed CGA with more colors, higher graphics RESOLUTION, and better looking text.

EISA Acronym for Extended Industry Standard Architecture (pronounced *EASE-uh*). A BUS technology standard for IBM-compatibles developed by 9 non-IBM manufacturers. EISA supports the latest technology 32-BIT boards as well as 8- and 16-bit boards made as early as 1981.

Encapsulated PostScript (EPS or EPSF) The standard for GRAPHICS with POSTSCRIPT code. Sometimes EPS files contain PROGRAMs that draw pictures when printed, but they cannot be seen on the computer screen.

EPS Abbreviation for ENCAPSULATED POSTSCRIPT.

Expanded memory MEMORY added beyond the 640K of CONVENTIONAL MEMORY. When buying expanded memory, you must also purchase an expanded memory manager program.

Expansion card A circuit board used to connect an add-on to the computer. Expansion cards are inserted in EXPANSION SLOTS.

Expansion slot A slot inside your computer where you can insert new EXPANSION CARDS such as DISK DRIVE CONTROLLERS, additional MEMORY CHIPS, MATH COPROCESSORS and other add-ons.

Extended memory General-purpose MEMORY added to the 640K of CONVENTIONAL MEMORY. For example, a 1MB system would have 640K of conventional memory and 256K of extended memory. When buying extended memory, you must also purchase an extended memory manager program.

FAX card An expansion card that works like a FAX machine, sending and receiving text and GRAPHICS. Instead of scanning DOCUMENTs, however, a FAX card sends documents stored in your computer to other FAX machines. Likewise, FAX cards typically convert material received from other FAX machines into computer FILEs.

Field A column in a DATABASE TABLE that represents a specific type of information, such as Last Name, First Name, Address, City, State, Zip, and so forth.

File Like a file in a file cabinet, a computer file stores specific information or a particular PROGRAM.

File format The structure of the DATA used to record an image or FILE onto a DISK. The specific file format used is of particular significance in GRAPHICS PROGRAMS, for which many different file formats exist.

File group Same as DIRECTORY.

File name The specific name given to a FILE on a computer.

Finder   A special APPLICATION used on a Macintosh computer to organize and manage your DOCUMENTs and to start other applications. You use the Finder every time you power up your Mac, and whenever you move from one application to another.

Flat-file   A type of DATABASE manager, or file manager, that permits you to access only one database TABLE at a time.

Floppy disk   A removable DISK used to store information. Generally, floppy disks are used to copy information to or from the HARD DRIVE. They typically store less than two million characters of DATA.

Font   A typeface, such as Courier, Helvetica, or Times. Fonts are collections of complete uppercase and lowercase alphabets, numbers, and other symbols that share common design characteristics.

Form   In a DATABASE MANAGEMENT SYSTEM, a form is any display of information on the screen.

Format   To prepare a DISK for use by the computer using the OPERATING SYSTEM. Also, the general characteristics of a DOCUMENT, including its layout, FONT and font size, and STYLE.

Function key   Any of the keys on the KEYBOARD that are labeled with the letter "F" and a number. Function keys are generally along the top or on the left side of the keyboard. Many PROGRAMS assign specific tasks to some or all of the function keys. For example, in many programs you can press the F1 key to access ON-LINE HELP.

Gigabyte   About a billion BYTEs, or approximately 333,333 pages of text.

GIGO   Acronym for Garbage In Garbage Out. Refers to the fact that unlike computers in science fiction, real computers simply store and permit you to retrieve information as-is. Hence, if you put bad information into the computer, you'll get the same bad information back when you retrieve it.

Graphical User Interface (GUI) A computer PROGRAM or OPERATING SYSTEM that displays information to you in graphical, or pictorial, format. Most people consider graphical interfaces easier to learn and use than TEXT-BASED INTERFACEs. Windows is an example of a graphical user interface.

Graphics Anything that involves pictures on the computer, including graphs, charts, cartoons, logos, mastheads, drawings, and digitized photographs.

GUI Acronym for GRAPHICAL USER INTERFACE. (Pronounced *gooey*.)

Hard disk Same as HARD DRIVE.

Hard drive A built-in storage device that uses a hard metal recording surface (hence the name "hard drive"). Hard drives are very fast and capable of holding hundreds of MEGABYTEs of information for later access.

Hardware The part of the computer that you can see and touch—the machinery.

Host mode A feature of TELECOMMUNICATIONS SOFTWARE that allows your computer to answer modem calls from other computers.

I/O Acronym for Input and Output (pronounced *eye OH*). When working with a computer, you must put input into it, and you get output back from it.

Import/Export The process of importing data from, and exporting data to, other FILE FORMATs. You may need to use import/export features if you share text or graphics with someone who uses a different word processor than yours.

Index A special FILE that allows a DATABASE management PROGRAM to locate a particular RECORD quickly, rather than having to search through every record one by one to find the one you want.

Ink jet printer   A type of printer that squirts tiny droplets of ink onto paper. Ink jet printers can produce high-quality GRAPHICS and text in many fonts.

Instruction   A COMMAND that tells the computer what to do.

Interface   The method a PROGRAM uses to interact with you. The two main types of interface are text-based and graphical. (*Secondary meaning*: the HARDWARE used to send instructions from the computer to a PERIPHERAL such as a printer.)

ISA   Acronym for Industry Standard Architecture (pronounced *ICE- uh*). A BUS technology standard used in IBM-compatibles for communicating 8 or 16 BITS at a time between EXPANSION CARDs and the computer.

K   Abbreviation for KILOBYTE.

KB   Abbreviation for KILOBYTE.

Keyboard   The typewriter-like input device for the computer. Beyond the normal keys found on a typewriter, a computer keyboard includes a number of other keys such as function keys, a numeric keypad, and cursor movement keys.

Key field   A FIELD that uniquely identifies a RECORD in a DATABASE. For example, a Customer ID might be the key field for a Customer or Order record.

Kilobyte (K or KB)   A kilobyte is about 1,000 BYTEs (actually 1,024). Typically, kilobytes are used to measure the size of computer FILEs, computer MEMORY, and DISKETTE storage size.

LAN   Acronym for Local Area Network. LANs are used to connect many computers together so they can share FILEs and other resources such as LASER PRINTERs.

Landscape   A sideways paper orientation. A landscaped image is wider than it is tall.

Laser printer   A printer that uses a dry toner melted on a sheet of paper to produce a high quality output for both text and GRAPHICS.

Light pen   A pen-like input DEVICE with a light on one end and a wire connected to the computer on the other end. Light pens are used for drawing on the screen, selecting items, marking a checklist, and a variety of other functions.

Macro   A set of prerecorded keystrokes or COMMANDs you can play back at any time, without entering the keystrokes separately.

Mail Merge   A feature of many word processing and DATABASE PROGRAMs that lets you merge a form letter with a name-and-address list so the letter can be sent to hundreds or thousands of people.

Math Coprocessor   A specialized CHIP that speeds the processing of certain mathematical functions on your computer.

MB   Abbreviation for MEGABYTE.

MCA   Abbreviation for MICRO CHANNEL ARCHITECTURE.

Meg   Abbreviation for MEGABYTE.

Megabyte (MB, Mb, or Meg)   A megabyte is about one-million BYTEs. Typically, computer HARD DISK storage and MEMORY are measured in megabytes.

Megahertz (MHz)   A Megahertz is a million cycles per second. The speed of the computer's quartz crystal clock is measured in MHz, and faster clock speeds usually indicate a faster CPU.

Memory   (Also called RANDOM ACCESS MEMORY or RAM.) The fast, electronic secondary storage used for computer PROGRAMs and DATA. Memory contents are lost when you turn off the computer.

Menu   A set of choices, much like a menu in a restaurant. Selecting an option from a menu carries out some COMMAND or instruction in the PROGRAM.

MHz   Abbreviation for MEGAHERTZ.

Micro Channel Architecture   A BUS technology standard used with the IBM PS/2 computer line, which was designed to include many machines based on the 32-BIT 80386 CPU.

Microprocessor   (Also called CENTRAL PROCESSING UNIT.) The CHIP that controls the computer is called the microprocessor.

MIPS   Acronym for Millions of Instructions Per Second. A method that compares the relative speeds of various computer CHIPs by measuring the number of whole computer instructions that are actually executed each second.

Modem   Contraction for "MODulator and DEModulator." A modem is a device that transforms computer information into sound impulses that can be transmitted over telephone lines. Modem speeds are rated by BITs per second.

Monitor   The television-like DEVICE connected to the computer. It is used to display the FILES, PROGRAMs, COMMANDs, and any other DATA in your computer's MEMORY.

Monochrome   The computer term for a one-color MONITOR. It usually displays one color, such as green or amber, for text and/or GRAPHICS, and black for the background.

Motherboard   The board in the bottom of your computer that ties the system together. The MICROPROCESSOR, MEMORY, and the supporting circuits are all on the motherboard.

Mouse   An input device used to point to and select text and/or GRAPHICS on the screen. Most mice are palm-sized, have one or more buttons on top to communicate with the computer, and a wire or "tail" that extends from the mouse to a connection on the back of the computer. (The plural is "mice.")

ms   An abbreviation for milliseconds (thousandths of a second). The average time needed to read information from any given spot on the HARD DISK is typically measured in ms.

Multimedia   The incorporation of graphics, sound, animation, and text into your computer output.

Multitasking   The ability to run more than one PROGRAM at a time. Windows and OS/2 are examples of multitasking operating environments.

Normalization   In DATABASE terminology, normalization is the technique of breaking information into separate TABLEs and defining KEY FIELDs that relate the tables.

Network   A system of interconnected computers that share FILEs and other resources such as LASER PRINTERs. A LAN is a type of network.

Null modem   A special cable used to send DATA between two computers that are close together. When two computers are connected by a null modem, whatever is sent from one computer's SERIAL PORT is instantly received at the other computer's serial port.

OCR   Abbreviation for Optical Character Reader or Optical Character Recognition. OCR SCANNERs and SOFTWARE provide a quick way to input a large amount of text into a computer without entering the text manually. The OCR scans the text, interprets it letter by letter, and then feeds it to the computer. The resulting text can then be edited on-screen just as if a typist had manually entered it.

On-line Help   A PROGRAM's built-in help system, which helps users learn how to use specific features. *Context-sensitive help* provides help with whatever feature you are using at the moment. *Index help* lets you look up a feature on an alphabetical list, just as you'd look up information in a book's index.

Open architecture A type of computer ARCHITECTURE that allows you to adapt your computer to changing needs and take advantage of new technology by adding or replacing components without having to replace the entire system.

Operating System (OS) The main SOFTWARE that determines how you interact with your computer. The OS starts up your computer, performs various housekeeping tasks, communicates with PERIPHERAL DEVICES such as DISK DRIVEs, the MONITOR, and the KEYBOARD, determines which PROGRAMs you can (and cannot) use, and provides the chief INTERFACE (either text-based or graphical) between you and the computer.

Optical Disk A CD-ROM type disk that can be written to, read, and erased as often as necessary. An optical disk is accessed in a magneto-optical drive.

OS Abbreviation for OPERATING SYSTEM.

OS/2 Abbreviation for OPERATING SYSTEM 2. The operating system developed by Microsoft for IBM's PS/2 line of computers. Initially plagued with problems, OS/2 may become a rival for Microsoft Windows, with its promise of complete CONNECTIVITY among all types of computers, a graphical user INTERFACE, and the ability to run both DOS and WINDOWS.

Parallel port A Centronics INTERFACE port (or "printer port") used by most printers to communicate with the computer. Parallel ports transmit and receive all 8 BITS of DATA side by side, and use just one type of transmission PROTOCOL.

Parallel printer A printer that connects to a PARALLEL PORT. Most printers except those used by the Macintosh are parallel printers.

Parallel processing See MULTITASKING.

Parity The addition of a BIT to each character transmitted over a MODEM in order to detect transmission errors. To determine the value for a parity bit, the communications SOFTWARE adds up the number of one-bits in the character that is being transmitted or received, and then sets the parity bit to 0 or 1, depending on whether the transmission is using even or odd parity.

PCL   Abbreviation for Printer Control Language. A printer language developed by Hewlett-Packard to give the company's line of LaserJet printers the capability of creating varied GRAPHICS and near-typeset quality text of all sizes.

Pentium   The latest chip in the 80X86 family of processors. Successor to the 80486. The Pentium offers 64-bit data addressing and is therefore very fast. It's also very expensive and very hot (in the sense of temperature). Developers are scrambling to come up with hardware that can take advantage of the Pentium's capabilities.

Peripheral   Any piece of equipment used with a computer. For example, the MONITOR, KEYBOARD, printer, and MOUSE are all peripherals of one computer system. Same as DEVICE.

Pin   The end of a wire used to send or receive an electronic signal. Also refers to the wires used to print text on a DOT-MATRIX PRINTER.

Plotter   A special kind of printer that uses pens to draw very detailed designs on paper. Plotters are used most often by interior decorators, designers, engineers, and architects.

Port   A special opening in the computer for plugging in cables for various DEVICEs such as a printer, KEYBOARD, or MOUSE. Ports may be located on separate boards or they may be built-in to the computer.

Portrait   A paper orientation used to print an image that is taller than it is wide. (The opposite of LANDSCAPE.)

POST   Acronym for Power On Self Test. A startup PROGRAM that examines the entire computer system to make sure everything is functioning properly.

PostScript A mathematical page description language used on many LASER PRINTERs and typesetters. PostScript can scale any FONT or GRAPHIC to any size and works with computers and printers from many different manufacturers.

ppm Abbreviation for Pages Per Minute. A way to measure the speed of a printer.

Presentation graphics Graphs or text charts created from DATA that are entered manually or taken from a DATABASE, SPREADSHEET, or word processing PROGRAM.

Printer memory The MEMORY in a printer, which is used to store the text, FONTs, and GRAPHICS sent by the computer. Most LASER PRINTERs need at least 1.5 MEGABYTEs of printer memory in order to print multiple fonts and GRAPHICS.

Processor The MICROPROCESSOR CHIP that controls the computer.

Program (Also called SOFTWARE.) A set of COMMANDs or instructions that direct the actions a computer can take. Programs have been written to start up your computer, balance your checkbook, predict the weather, send humans to the moon, and almost anything in between that you can imagine.

Protocol The method computers use to transmit information to one another in an understandable way. The most commonly used protocols are 2400-n-8-1 (2400 BPS, no PARITY, 8 DATA BITs, One-STOP BIT) and 2400-e-7-1 (2400 bps, even parity, 7 data bits, one-stop bit).

QBE Abbreviation for Query-by-Example.

Query A database management technique for asking questions of your DATABASE, thereby isolating specific records for printing reports, displaying DATA on-screen, storing data for later use, and so forth.

Query-by-Example (QBE) A method of querying in which the PROGRAM shows you the names of the FIELDs in the TABLE or DATABASE about which you're asking questions. Then you can provide the program with an example of the kind of information you're seeking.

RAM   Acronym for RANDOM ACCESS MEMORY.

RAM drive   A portion of RAM that you can use as if it were a real DISK DRIVE. Because computer MEMORY has no moving parts, information can be stored and read from a RAM drive very quickly. However, because RAM storage is lost when the computer loses power, you must eventually copy DATA from the RAM drive onto a real disk if you want to save that data permanently.

Random Access Memory   Same as MEMORY.

RDBMS   Abbreviation for RELATIONAL DATABASE MANAGEMENT SYSTEM.

Read-Only Memory (ROM)   A special form of computer MEMORY that cannot and should not be altered by a computer user. ROM is a computer PROGRAM built into the computer HARDWARE, which typically contains information necessary to start up and operate the computer.

Record   A row in a DATABASE TABLE that is made up of all the FIELDs and provides complete information about a single item in that table. For example, the record for a customer in a database table might consist of the fields of Last Name, First Name, Address, City, State, Zip, and so forth, for one person.

Relational Database Management System (RDBMS)   A type of DATABASE MANAGEMENT SYSTEM that can manage multiple TABLES of information simultaneously, relating one table to another through the use of KEY FIELDs.

Release   See also VERSION. The public "unveiling" of a computer PROGRAM. Each SOFTWARE release is typically given a release number to differentiate it from past and future versions of the same program.

Report   Printed output from a computer PROGRAM such as a DATABASE MANAGEMENT SYSTEM.

Report generator   A feature of many DATABASE MANAGEMENT SYSTEMs that makes it easier to design, generate, and print sophisticated reports from your database.

Resolution   Refers to how close together the pixels (dots of light) are on a computer MONITOR or the dots of ink are on a printer. The higher the resolution, the sharper the screen or printed image appears.

RISC   Acronym for Reduced Instruction Set Computer. A new type of MICROPROCESSOR CHIP that uses fewer instructions and provides superior performance over most microprocessors in use today.

ROM   Acronym for READ-ONLY MEMORY.

Scanned images   Images produced by running a SCANNER over a picture that's on paper. Scanned images are stored in electronic form in the computer and can be used later in a GRAPHICS or DESKTOP PUBLISHING PROGRAM.

Scanner   An input DEVICE used to convert text or pictures into electronic codes that are stored on your computer's HARD DISK.

SCSI   Pronounced "scuzzy." An acronym for Small Computer System Interface. It's an interface standard for small computer devices that ensures compatibility between components. SCSI is the standard interface for a Macintosh and an optional interface for the PC.

Search and Replace   A feature in word processing and other PROGRAMS that enables you to find a given word, phrase, or code and replace it with another specified word, phrase, or code.

Serial port   A port used for external MODEMS, mice (see MOUSE), and most Apple printers. Serial ports transmit and receive BITS of DATA one after another and may use a variety of transmission PROTOCOLS.

Serial printer   A printer that connects to a SERIAL PORT. Most printers used on the Macintosh are serial printers.

Software   Same as PROGRAM.

Sound card   An EXPANSION CARD for the PC that provides high quality sound input and output such as voice recognition, microphone, and sound recording and editing capabilities.

Spooling   Same as BACKGROUND PRINTING.

Spreadsheet   A PROGRAM that manipulates numbers, text, and formulas in a row-and-column format. Spreadsheets are widely used to analyze various "what if" scenarios and to display and print pictorial graphs of mathematical calculations and statistical summaries.

SQL   Acronym for Structured Query Language (pronounced *SEE-quel*). SQL is a standardized QUERY language for searching a DATABASE. Although used mainly on larger mainframes and minicomputers, SQL is also available in some personal computer DATABASE MANAGEMENT SYSTEMS.

Start bit   A BIT used in TELECOMMUNICATIONS to signal that a BYTE or character is about to be sent to the receiving computer.

String   Computerese for groups of characters or words. For example, *Hello there* is a string.

Stop bit   A BIT used in TELECOMMUNICATIONS to signal that the BYTE or character is now completed, and the receiving computer should prepare itself to receive the next START BIT. Stop bits are not actually BITs, but are rather a specified time interval between characters.

Style   A predefined, consistent, typographical appearance for text such as topic headings, body text, lists, and so forth. After defining the styles you want, you simply apply them to the appropriate text as needed. If you change your mind about the way the text looks, you can change the style and *all* text

FORMATted with that style will automatically change to the new appearance you choose.

Style Sheet A feature of many word processing and DESKTOP PUBLISHING PROGRAMS that lets you define a STYLE for each element of your document. Style sheets help you to create a consistent look for your DOCUMENTs.

Sysop The person who operates a computer BULLETIN BOARD. (Pronounced SIS-op.)

System 7.1 The latest version of the Macintosh OPERATING SYSTEM, featuring balloon help, multitasking, a smoother user INTERFACE, color and 3-D shading, a much-improved FINDER, an easier-to-use system folder, True Type (displays and prints smooth text at any size), and exchange of "live" DATA between APPLICATIONs.

Table A FORMAT consisting of rows and columns of DATA. Tables are commonly used in DATABASE MANAGEMENT and SPREADSHEET PROGRAMs.

Tape A magnetic storage medium used to hold a copy of the DATA on a HARD disk.

Tape drive An electronic mechanism in or connected to the computer, which controls the TAPE used to back up the DATA on the HARD DRIVE.

Telecommunications The use of a MODEM and telephone lines to link your computer with another computer so you can communicate with someone else (via computer) or transmit DATA between computers.

Text-based interface A computer PROGRAM or OPERATING SYSTEM that displays text on the screen in response to commands consisting of alphabetic characters, numbers, and symbols.

TIFF Acronym for Tagged Image File Format. A GRAPHICS FILE FORMAT that stores BITMAPped images in various RESOLUTIONs, shades of gray, or colors.

Trackball An input DEVICE that works like a MOUSE, except that the roller is on top instead of on the bottom. You roll the ball with your fingertips or palm and press buttons on either side of the ball with your thumb. It doesn't need as much desktop space as the mouse.

UNIX (Abbreviation for (UNiplexed) Information and Computing System.) UNIX is a large OPERATING SYSTEM that is both MULTITASKING (capable of running several PROGRAMS at the same time) and multiuser (several people, each with their own KEYBOARD and MONITOR, can use the same computer at the same time). Traditionally, UNIX has been used on larger computers but is becoming increasingly available on microcomputers.

Utilities PROGRAMS that fill the gap between the basic functions of the OPERATING SYSTEM and the more specific work done by APPLICATION programs. Utilities are available for BACKUP, DISASTER RECOVERY, FILE and text search, HARD DISK optimizing, DESKTOP organizing, MACROS, VIRUS protection, and so forth.

Vector graphics Graphic images created with mathematical formulas that provide smoother corners and edges than BITMAP GRAPHICS.

Version A PROGRAM is typically given a version number to differentiate it from past and future versions of the same program. (See also RELEASE.)

Vertical application A PROGRAM that handles virtually all the needs of a particular business.

VGA Abbreviation for Video Graphics Array. The current GRAPHICS standard on PCs, VGA provides thousands of colors at many RESOLUTIONS, and has the best color text display of any PC graphics adapter.

Virus An insidious little PROGRAM designed either to display a bizarre message on your screen or to harm your FILEs. Viruses, which are created by high-tech nasties, can lurk inside shareware programs loaded via computer BULLETIN BOARDs. Special antivirus programs are available to seek out and destroy these viral varmints.

Window   A feature of many PROGRAMs and some OPERATING SYSTEMs that divides the screen into separate areas, each of which opens into different parts of one or more running programs. You can move, size, open, and close windows easily.

Windows   An extremely popular operating environment. Developed by Microsoft Corporation for IBM-compatibles, it features MULTITASKING, WINDOWS, and a GRAPHICAL USER INTERFACE.

Worksheet   The DOCUMENT that you work with in a SPREADSHEET PROGRAM.

Workstation   A high-end computer for engineering, design, and GRAPHICS APPLICATIONS. Most workstations have a very fast CENTRAL PROCESSING UNIT, an oversized high-RESOLUTION screen (usually in color), a huge amount of MEMORY, a UNIX-like OPERATING SYSTEM, and a price tag with five digits to the left of the decimal point.

WORM   Acronym for Write Once/Read Many, a type of OPTICAL DISK that can be written to only once, but read as often as needed. When the disk is full, you simply buy another and start over.

X-Windows   A GRAPHICAL USER INTERFACE for UNIX.

XENIX   A scaled-down version of UNIX that runs on personal computers.

XGA   A superduper color GRAPHICS standard that's expensive and not widely available.

Zoom   A feature of some word processing and many GRAPHICS and DESKTOP PUBLISHING PROGRAMs that lets you zoom in and EDIT a small portion of your picture as if you were working with it under a high-powered magnifying glass, or zoom out to get a bird's eye view.

INDEX

◆ ◆

Note: Page numbers in **bold** refer to primary discussions of a topic. Page numbers in *italics* refer to figures.

Numbers

X

POCKET-SIZED PC EXPERTISE.

550 pp. ISBN: 756-8.

T*he PC User's* es-sen'-tial, ac-ces'sible *Pocket Dictionary* is the most complete, most readable computer dictionary available today. With over 2,000 plain-language entries, this inexpensive handbook offers exceptional coverage of computer industry terms at a remarkably affordable price.

In this handy reference you'll find plenty of explanatory tables and figures, practical tips, notes, and warnings, and in-depth entries on the most essential terms. You'll also appreciate the extensive cross-referencing, designed to make it easy for you to find the answers you need.

Presented in easy-to-use alphabetical order, *The PC User's* es-sen'-tial, ac-ces'-si-ble *Pocket Dictionary* covers every conceivable computer-related topic. Ideal for home, office, and school use, it's the only computer dictionary you need!

SYBEX. Help Yourself.

2021 Challenger Drive
Alameda, CA 94501
1-510-523-8233
1-800-227-2346

SYBEX

Your Guide to DOS Dominance.

MAKE A GOOD COMPUTER EVEN BETTER.

350pp. ISBN: 1301-X.

The *PC Upgrade Guide for Everybody* is the no-hassle, do-it-yourself PC upgrade guide for everyone. If you know the difference between a screwdriver and a pair of pliers, this book is for you.

Inside you'll find step-by-step instructions for installing hardware to make your computer even more fun and productive. Add memory chips, CD-ROM drives and more to your PC.

You'll also learn how to diagnose minor PC problems and decide whether to repair or replace faulty components —without schlepping your PC to the shop and paying big bucks.

SYBEX. Help Yourself.

2021 Challenger Drive
Alameda, CA 94501
1-800-227-2346

WINDOWS HAS NEVER BEEN CLEARER.

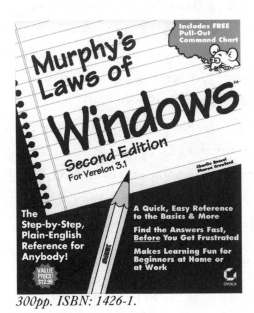

300pp. ISBN: 1426-1.

E ven though Windows has done so much to make computers easier to use, you can still run into trouble. That's why you need *Murphy's Laws of Windows*.

Whether you're new to computers or just new to Windows, you'll get a gold mine of problem-solving information you can use. You'll learn how to avoid problems with Windows, correct Windows mistakes, and more.

You'll get all of this and more in an entertaining and easy-to-reference format. Thanks to this book, you'll never again have to say, "I don't do Windows."

SYBEX. Help Yourself.

2021 Challenger Drive
Alameda, CA 94501
1-510-523-8233
1-800-227-2346

SYBEX

SYBEX

FREE CATALOG!

Complete this form today, and we'll send you a full-color catalog of Sybex Computer Books.

Please supply the name of the Sybex book purchased.

_____

How would you rate it?

_____ Excellent   _____ Very Good   _____ Average   _____ Poor

Why did you select this particular book?

_____ Recommended to me by a friend

_____ Recommended to me by store personnel

_____ Saw an advertisement in _____ _____

_____ Author's reputation

_____ Saw in Sybex catalog

_____ Required textbook

_____ Sybex reputation

_____ Read book review in _____

_____ In-store display

_____ Other _____

Where did you buy it?

_____ Bookstore

_____ Computer Store or Software Store

_____ Catalog (name: _____)

_____ Direct from Sybex

_____ Other: _____

Did you buy this book with your personal funds?

_____Yes   _____No

About how many computer books do you buy each year?

_____ 1-3   _____ 3-5   _____ 5-7   _____ 7-9   _____ 10+

About how many Sybex books do you own?

_____ 1-3   _____ 3-5   _____ 5-7   _____ 7-9   _____ 10+

Please indicate your level of experience with the software covered in this book:

_____ Beginner   _____ Intermediate   _____ Advanced

Which types of software packages do you use regularly?

_____ Accounting   _____ Databases   _____ Networks

_____ Amiga   _____ Desktop Publishing _____ Operating Systems

_____ Apple/Mac   _____ File Utilities   _____ Spreadsheets

_____ CAD   _____ Money Management   _____ Word Processing

_____ Communications   _____ Languages   _____ Other _____
                                                               (please specify)

Which of the following best describes your job title?

_____ Administrative/Secretarial _____ President/CEO

_____ Director _____ Manager/Supervisor

_____ Engineer/Technician _____ Other _____
(please specify)

Comments on the weaknesses/strengths of this book: _____

_____

_____

_____

_____

Name _____

Street _____

City/State/Zip _____

Phone _____

PLEASE FOLD, SEAL, AND MAIL TO SYBEX

SYBEX, INC.
Department M
2021 CHALLENGER DR.
ALAMEDA, CALIFORNIA USA
94501

SYBEX

SEAL

COMPUTER FOR SALE

PC IBM-Compatible

486DX2-66, 16MB (expandable to 64MB), 256KB
Cache, Dual HD Floppy Drives, 525MB Hard Drive,
CD-ROM, Modem, 17" NI SVGA Monitor

Processor	486DX2
Processor Speed	66MHz
RAM (Installed)	16MB
RAM (Maximum on Motherboard)	64MB
Cache	256 KB
Floppy Drives	$3\frac{1}{2}$" High Density
	$5\frac{1}{4}$" High Density
Hard Drive	525MB
	IDE/ SCSI/ SCSI-2
CD-ROM	Multi-Session Compliant
Modem	9600
Monitor	Super VGA
	Non-Interlaced (NI)
	17"
Video Display Card	ISA
	Local Bus
Printer	Laser (HP Compatible)
	Laser (PostScript)
	InkJet
	Dot Matrix (75DPI)
	Dot Matrix (160DPI)